Other Voices: The New Journalism in America

Everette E. Dennis
Kansas State University

William L. Rivers
Stanford University

PN
4867
.D4

Canfield Press, San Francisco
A Department of Harper & Row, Publishers, Inc.
New York, Evanston, London

International Standard Book Number: 0-06-382562-7
Library of Congress Catalog Card Number: 73-10610

74 75 76   10 9 8 7 6 5 4 3 2

Acquisition, editing, and production: *Brian Williams*
Design: *Robert Bausch*

Contents

Preface

The divergent journalistic voices that were raised in the 1960s have become such a jumble that merely identifying them is difficult. We try in this book to do much more: to define, categorize, present, and examine the voices that we believe make up the new journalism. We doubt that new journalism is a satisfactory term—and point out in the first chapter that some of the forms verge on antiquity—but we are not so audacious as to try to change a name that has caught on.

But perhaps we are audacious enough. Although no book on a subject so broad can be complete, this one is comprehensive. Whereas most of those who write and talk about the new journalism define it narrowly—as advocacy, or the underground press, or using fiction techniques in nonfiction—we believe there are *seven* types, all of which are sketched in the first chapter and developed in succeeding chapters.

Our concern for comprehensiveness is reflected in the national scope presented here, in covering developments in the major cities, on both coasts, in the Middle West and South—indeed, in every major region of the United States. Much of the research required travel and interviews, and all of it required reading almost endlessly and watching the productions of the new journalists who are building the structure of alternative television.

We have labored to offer a representative view of forms and media as well as geography, but, of course, the people who have fashioned the new journalism are central. We have tried to include all the major figures, many who are minor, and perhaps a few who are peripheral.

We do little more than mention the important growth of the black press, the Chicano press, and the American Indian press. Although such papers as *Muhammad Speaks* and the *Black Panther* are clearly journals of advocacy, they belong to a longer and richer tradition that is part of a continuing legacy. The ethnic press is best studied in its own context. Similarly, we have chosen not to include the sex press, which is tangentially related to the new journalism but is better examined in the context of attitudes toward sexual freedom.

Nor do we cover in this book two pivotal figures who were always in our minds as we wrote: the late A.J. Liebling, whose criticism of the press set a high standard, and I.F. Stone. They are not part of the new journalism, but their work has served as both example and inspiration for many who are. Significantly, when the publishers of *(More)* held the A.J. Liebling Counter-Convention in 1972 (which is described in Chapter 4), Stone was honored with an award. As we were writing this book, *I.F. Stone's Bi-Weekly* ceased publication. It did not die for lack of support—it may have been the most successful newsletter of its kind in our history—but because it was the one-man product of a man of advanced age. Stone continues to write for the *New York Review of Books*, and he continues to command the respect of a variety of new journalists who have little else in common.

Writing about any area of rapid change is a hazardous business. For this reason we have attempted to take a historical perspective, recognizing that some of the publications and the people we have discussed may not be on the scene by the time this book is published. That, however, is not important, for the well-established patterns of new journalistic styles and media that emerged in the 1960s will have progeny in the substantial changes that are sure to come by the middle and late 1970s.

We are indebted to the busy writers and editors who generously gave much time to telling us about their work. Many of our ideas were sharpened by colleagues and students in discussions and seminars. Roy Paul Nelson of the University of Oregon was especially helpful and encouraging at the beginning. Charlene Brown of Indiana University, Peter Sandman of the University of Michigan, and Don Dodson and Len Sellers, both of Stanford, were valued critics of various chapters and drafts. The manuscript was typed expertly by Jeanne Stuart at Kansas State University and by Carolyn Sellers and Ellen Wilson at Stanford. At Kansas State University, Deans William Stamey and Paige Mulhollan lent important support and encouragement.

Everette E. Dennis
William L. Rivers

1 A Coalescing of Forces

... the First Amendment presupposes that right conclusions are more likely to be gathered out of a multitude of tongues than through any kind of authoritative selection.
— Judge Learned Hand,
in *United States v. Associated Press*

In a time when old values are crumbling, when the miracle of advancing technology is suddenly seen to create as many problems as it solves, when disorder, turmoil, and violence become hallmarks of a nation—in such a time it cannot be surprising that the mass media, which are central to modern society, should feel the shock waves of change. It is not a mere coincidence that during the American upheaval of the last decade we began to hear of something called *the new journalism*. It had vague beginnings in earlier times, but the turbulence of the 1960s gave it impetus. Like that turbulence, the new journalism is complicated, a wild mixture of styles, forms, and purposes that defies simple definitions so completely that it can be summarized only in the most general way: dissatisfaction with existing standards and values.

This book is being written to push beyond this generalization, to analyze a force that has already made a place for itself, a force that may alter journalism profoundly. To do so properly, we must admit and even emphasize that the *new* journalism is a misnomer. Critics are fond of pointing out that there is nothing very new about it. And, certainly one can find antecedents. The underground press, for example, may be considered a twentieth-century recurrence of the political pamphleteering in the Colonial period. Advocacy journalism is at least similar to the personal journalism of the last century. Alternative journalism may be little more than muckraking in new dress. The pollsters have been taking surveys for decades. Wasn't Daniel Defoe writing the new nonfiction? And so on.

But to focus endless arguments on the validity of a *term* when the force it symbolizes is demonstrably real and important is semantic quibbling of an especially misleading kind. We use the term because it has caught on and become familiar. The important matter is that the several forms and practices of the new journalism, misnomer or not, have coalesced at this point in time. It is quite remarkable, after all, that practices centuries old in some cases and decades old in others should suddenly appear together today, be developed along new lines, force a place for themselves, and threaten a structure of reporting that only recently seemed strong and durable.

The chief question now is not to decide whether the new journalism has been given the right name but to define it properly and to try to judge its impact. To make that clear, it is essential to sketch conventional practices.

Until the 1930s the average reporter wrote a formula. He tried to fashion a clear, concise, straight news story, starting with the who, what, when, where, and why of an event and proceeding toward the end by placing factual details in descending order of interest and importance—a device that enabled readers to grasp the essentials immediately and editors to cut stories from the bottom up. His job was to try to hold a mirror up to an event and show its surface. Explaining why it had occurred and what should be done about it were the missions of the editorial writers and the columnists. A few reporters, primarily those overseas and in Washington, had been given license to interpret the news and explain and clarify complex events. But almost everyone else was limited to straight news reporting.

With the advent of the New Deal, the old forms suddenly seemed inadequate. Washington correspondents of the time say they can fix on the exact moment when the old journalism failed utterly—the day in 1933 when the United States went off the gold standard. They appealed to the White House for help in reporting that baffling change, and a Federal Government economist was sent over to clarify the new facts of economic life. They tried to explain what he explained, without much success. Despite the failure, the correspondents had committed themselves to explanatory journalism, an abrupt departure from the superficialities of who-what-when-where-why reporting.

The increasing complexity of public affairs made it difficult to confine reporting to the straitjacket of unelaborated fact. Relaying exactly what a government official said was often misleading: even facts didn't speak the truth. Moreover, reporters discovered that they were in effect running errands for the establishment and enshrining the status quo; the sources of news releases, press conferences, and official statements were usually men with position and power. Somewhat hesitantly, reporters like Paul Anderson and Marquis Childs of the St. Louis *Post-Dispatch* and, a bit later, James Reston of the New York *Times* began to build the interpretative reporting structure that made its way back to city rooms everywhere.

The trend was fiercely debated. In the early sixties it split the top level of the great Louisville *Courier-Journal.* Editor Barry Bingham argued: "The need for interpretative reporting becomes more insistent week by week." At the same time, executive editor James Pope attacked the interpreters, maintaining that "by definition, interpretation is subjective and means to 'translate, elucidate, construe ... in the light of individual belief or interest. ...' Interpretation is the bright dream of the saintly seers who expound and construe in the midst of the news." To Pope and others, interpretative reporters were simply abandoning objective journalism. But the *Courier-Journal* has become an excellent interpretative newspaper.

Lester Markel, the able and acid retired Sunday editor of the New York *Times,* who was the most insistent advocate of interpretation, argued several years ago in the *Saturday Review* that no form of reporting could really be defined as "objective":

> The reporter, the most objective reporter, collects fifty facts. Out of the fifty he selects twelve to include in his story (there is such a thing as space limitation). Thus he discards thirty-eight. This is Judgment Number One.
>
> Then the reporter or editor decides which of the facts shall be the first paragraph of the story, thus emphasizing one fact above the other eleven. This is Judgment Number Two.
>
> Then the editor decides whether the story shall be placed on Page One or Page Twelve; on Page One it will command many times the attention it would on Page Twelve. This is Judgment Number Three.
>
> This so-called factual presentation is thus subjected to three judgments, all of them most humanly and most ungodly made.

Such arguments and the findings of behavioral scientists seem to have persuaded nearly everyone that humans cannot be objective in the machine-like sense. Most of the proponents of objectivity now argue that it is a goal worth striving for even if it is not quite attainable.

The proponents of interpretation are right in arguing that mere facts must be placed in a context that gives them meaning. The reporter who explains facts and clarifies the meaning of events serves us well. Those who favor interpretation are also right in holding that a reporter can interpret the news—or analyze it—without becoming an advocate. One test is whether the writing is slanted in such a way that we can determine the reporter's personal views. The best example of journalistic balance is provided by Richard Strout, who writes admirable interpretative news for the *Christian Science Monitor* that does not even hint at his own leanings, and who writes equally admirable opinion pieces—suitably labeled by the *Monitor's* "Opinion and Commentary" heading—often on the same topics.

The root of the matter is made clear by James Carey of the University of Illinois, one of the most thoughtful professors of communication, who points out: "There must be greater stylistic freedom among modern journalists and a more fluid definition of news if only because the pace of social change continually presses the journalist into situations for which the conventional styles and conventional news definitions disable both perception and communication."

Proponents of objective reporting, on the other hand, are right in arguing that few reporters are capable of interpreting complex events, either because they do not know how to explain, clarify, and analyze without advocating, or because they know too little about the subjects they are reporting to do more than present the surface of an event. Even seasoned reporters can differ sharply, as the *Progressive* made clear by quoting these sentences from two of the best Washington correspondents, both published January 31, 1971:

> To be blunt about it, almost nobody believes President Nixon's budget except the high officials who put it together—and it's probable that even some of them have their doubts.—Hobart Rowen, "Credibility Is Lacking in Nixon Budget," the Washington *Post*.

> In general, then, insofar as decisions and judgments made at this stage are important, this budget appears to receive fairly high marks for credibility.—Edwin L. Dale, Jr., "The Budget Gap—Nixon Receives an A for Credibility," the New York *Times*.

How facts can be variously interpreted was also demonstrated when the Stanford University News Bureau released information on gifts to the university for the 1970-71 fiscal year.

The university-published *Campus Report* headed its story: HIGHEST NUMBER OF DONORS IN STANFORD HISTORY.

The San Francisco *Chronicle* headline said: STANFORD AGAIN RAISES $29 MILLION IN GIFTS.

The neighboring Palo Alto *Times* story was headed: DONATIONS TO STANFORD LOWEST IN FOUR YEARS.

The student-published Stanford *Daily* announced: ALUMNI DONATIONS DECLINE: BIG DROP FROM FOUNDATIONS.

These headlines accurately reflected the stories they surmounted—which were also accurate. Stanford did have more donors than ever (as the *Campus Report* said), it did raise more than $29 million for the fourth consecutive year (*Chronicle*), donations were the lowest in the past four years (*Times*), and the total was lower than in 1969-70 and it included less foundation money (*Daily*). As proponents of objective reporting contend, a positive or negative stance can make all the difference.

But to many a new journalist, all the wrangling over objective and interpretative reporting misses the main point, which is that neither is in close touch with reality. The best objective report may cover all the surfaces of an event, the best interpretative report may explain all its meanings, but both are bloodless, a world away from the *experience*. Color, flavor, atmosphere, the ultimate human meaning—all these, the new journalists contend, are far beyond the reach of conventional journalism. This is one of the central reasons for the emergence of different forms and practices, but there are others. What they are can be analyzed best in the context of the forms, practices, and media that make up the new journalism:

    —*new nonfiction*
    —*alternative journalism*
    —*journalism reviews*
    —*advocacy journalism*
    —*counterculture journalism*
    —*alternative broadcasting*
    —*precision journalism*

Reportage: The New Nonfiction

More than any other element of the new journalism, new nonfiction places its central focus on style. Tom Wolfe, who is one of the leading practitioners as well as the most dedicated promoter of the new journalism, has written: "The first time I realized there was something new going on in journalism was one day in 1962 when I picked up a copy of *Esquire* and read an article by Gay Talese entitled 'Joe Louis—The King as a Middle-Aged Man!' It wasn't like a magazine article at all. It was like a short story. It began with a scene, an intimate confrontation between Louis and his third wife:

> "Hi, sweetheart!" Joe Louis called to his wife, spotting her waiting for him at the Los Angeles airport.
> She smiled, walked toward him, and was about to stretch up on her toes and kiss him—but suddenly stopped.
> "Joe," she snapped, "where's your tie?"
> "Aw, sweetie," Joe Louis said, shrugging. "I stayed out all night in New York and didn't have time."
> "All night!" she cut in. "When you're out here with me all you do is sleep, sleep, sleep."
> "Sweetie," Joe Louis said with a tired grin, "I'm an ole man."
> "Yes," she agreed, "but when you go to New York you try to be young again."

Says Wolfe, "The story went on like that, scene after scene, building up a picture of an ex-sports hero now fifty years old.

"I couldn't believe this stuff. How did this guy Talese ever get in on all this intimate byplay in the latter-day life of Joe Louis? He piped it. That was it. He faked the quotes, goddamn it—which was precisely the cry of self-defense that many literati would sound over the next five years as New Journalism began to shake up the literary status structure.

"Talese hadn't piped it, of course. He was there all the time, and that was the simple secret of that."[1]

Talese, a former New York *Times* feature writer who now devotes most of his time to writing books, cautions those who deceptively regard the new journalism as fiction: "It is, or should be, as reliable as the most reliable reportage, although it seeks a larger truth than is possible through the mere compilation of verifiable facts, the use of direct quotations, and adherence to the rigid organizational style of the older form."

To Talese the new journalism "allows, demands in fact, a more imaginative approach to reporting, and it permits the writer to inject himself into the narrative if he wishes, as many writers do, or to assume the role of detached observer, as other writers do, including myself."

Tom Wolfe defines the new journalism as the use in "nonfiction of techniques which had been thought of as confined to the novel or the short story, to create in one form both the kind of objective reality of journalism and the subjective reality that people have always gone to the novel for."[2]

Dwight Macdonald, a *New Yorker* writer and one of Wolfe's severest critics, disagrees, calling it "parajournalism," which, he says, "seems to be journalism—the collection and dissemination of current news—but the appearance is deceptive. It is a bastard form having it both ways, exploiting the factual authority of journalism and the atmospheric license of fiction. Entertainment rather than information is the aim of its producers, and the hope of its consumers."[3]

However, Dan Wakefield, who writes articles and books, holds that writers like Wolfe and Truman Capote have "catapulted the reportorial kind of writing to a level of social interest suitable for cocktail party conversation and little-review comment."

> Such reporting [Wakefield continues] is "imaginative" not because the author has distorted the facts, but because he has presented them in a full instead of a naked manner, brought sight, sounds and feelings surrounding those facts, and connected them by comparison with other facts of history, society and literature in an artistic manner that does not diminish, but gives greater depth and dimension to the facts.[4]

As these definitions suggest, the thrust of the new nonfiction is stylistic—but not *mere* style, not style in the limited sense of choice of words, elegance of phrasing, and the like. The principal stylistic innovation of the new nonfiction springs the special quality of research that enables the writer to construct scenes of the kind quoted above from the Joe Louis story. It might be called "scenic style."

Although those who write the new nonfiction are highly individual, even idiosyncratic, they are alike in their devotion to building scenes. It is true, of course, that some conventional journalism, especially in magazines, carries scenes. Anecdotes, long a staple of feature writing in newspapers as well as magazines, are in effect little scenes. The difference is that a writer of the new nonfiction constructs a scene with the elaborate detail and life of a playwright, then constructs another, and another, and another. When the new nonfiction is pushed to the ultimate, an article reads like a short story, a book like a novel.

Alternative Journalism

Convinced that the color of the corporation is too strong on metropolitan dailies and leading magazines and that establishment ties handcuff nearly all the mass media, small as well as large, significant numbers of journalists seek to provide alternatives, publishing weeklies, monthlies, and some that must be called occasionals. The purposes of many were well expressed by the late Eugene Cervi of Denver, who wrote of his own alternative paper, *Cervi's Rocky Mountain Journal:* "We are what a newspaper is supposed to be: controversial, disagreeable, disruptive, unpleasant, unfriendly to concentrated power and suspicious of privately-owned utilities that use the power with which I endow them to beat me over the head politically.[5]

Cervi's paper, which has been published by his daughter since his death, is more successful than most of the other alternative journals, perhaps largely because it also provides mundane news of record for the Denver-area business community (mortgages, bankruptcies, and the like). In this it is unlike most of the other alternative papers. Like them, though, it exposes machinations in both business and government that businessmen and public officials try to hide. It is like the others, too, in attacking the established press for failing to probe the centers of power.

The San Francisco *Bay Guardian*, a lively, striking tabloid, may be more typical of the alternatives. For more than seven years it has shone a fierce light on the central institutions of the San Francisco Bay area, including the communications empire of the San Francisco *Chronicle*, which publisher Bruce Brugmann calls "Superchron."

Alternative journalism lends itself so easily to the personal, to highly individualized expression, that it is not surprising that the alternative journals are a heterogeneous collection. They are united and alike in one respect: the professional journalist's unhappiness that conventional journalism so seldom investigates the centers of power.

Journalism Reviews

Throughout the twentieth century, individual journalists like Will Irwin, George Seldes, and A. J. Liebling wrote notable articles and books criticizing journalistic practices. Many other journalists have long grumbled among themselves about the sad state of professional norms and the questionable practices of their employers and colleagues. Not until the late 1960s, however, did newsmen begin to establish their own publications to analyze and criticize journalistic performance.

Part of the impetus was provided by the *Columbia Journalism Review*, which began publication in 1962 and is not part of the journalism review movement as we define it. *CJR*, as it is widely known, is a bimonthly magazine of national scope published by Columbia University. We speak of the journalism reviews published—almost all of them in a newspaper or magazine format, almost all of them with a local or regional cast—by practicing journalists. Despite the distinction, there is little doubt that many of them were strongly influenced by the excellence of the *Columbia Journalism Review*.

Most were influenced, too, by the appearance of the *Chicago Journalism Review*, which was born shortly after the 1968 Democratic National Convention. It was founded by Chicago journalists who were dismayed at the way Chicago newspapers and broadcasting stations reported and commented on that explosive event.

Most of the writers and editors of journalism reviews continue to work for the established media—and prove that publishing their concerns and grievances can produce effects.

Advocacy Journalism

Advocacy journalists write with an unabashed commitment to particular points of view, casting their reporting of events along the lines of their beliefs. If the advocates could be found only among those who work for alternative papers and underground papers, they would not deserve a separate category in the new journalism. But it is quite clear that advocacy journalists are threaded through the entire fabric of journalism, in the conventional press as well as the unconventional. Clayton Kirkpatrick of the Chicago *Tribune* speaks for many of the alarmed old-timers in calling advocacy "the new propaganda" and in holding, "It threatens ... a revolution in the newsroom."[6]

Jack Newfield of the *Village Voice* recognizes the same force, but he salutes it: "Let's face it, the old journalism was blind to an important part of the truth ... it had built-in bias in its presentation: Tom Hayden *alleges*, while John Mitchell *announces*." In the old form, Newfield maintains, "authority always came first. The burden of proof was always on minorities; individuals. never get the authority that authorities get."[7]

To be involved, to be *engaged*, is central in advocacy journalism. Writers like Newfield, an avowed new leftist, participate in the events they cover.

Advocacy journalists are everywhere in the world of the underground press, of course, but it is a mistake to consider advocacy journalism and underground journalism as synonymous. The underground press is basically a communications medium for young people who are seeking different life styles because they are alienated from the conventional life style—and, of course, from the messages of the conventional media which celebrate it. In essence, most of the underground papers are published by the alienated for the alienated.

The editor of one of the first of the undergrounds, Art Kunkin of the Los Angeles *Free Press*, makes clear both the mission and the appeal in saying, "The underground press is do-it-yourself journalism. The basis for the new journalism is a new audience. People are not getting the information they desire from the existing media. The L.A. *Free Press* is aimed at the young, blacks, Mexicans and intellectuals." The underground press, Kunkin says, serves as a "mass opposition party." He urges his contributors to "write with passion, show the reader your style, your prejudice."[8]

Another perspective was offered in 1967 by David Sanford of the *New Republic*:

> There is nothing very underground about the underground press. The newspapers are hawked on street corners, sent to subscribers without incident through the U.S. mails, carefully culled and adored by the mass media. About three dozen of them belong to the Underground Press Syndicate, which is something like the AP on a small scale; through this network they spread the word about what is new in disruptive protest, drugs, sex. Their obsessive interest in things that the "straights" are embarrassed or offended by is perhaps what makes them underground. They are a place to find what is unfit to print in the New York *Times*.[9]

Most undergrounds are printed by offset. This "takes the printing out of the hands of the technicians," says Kunkin, a former tool and die maker. The undergrounds use a blend of type and free-hand art work and are a kind of collage for the artist-intellectual, some editors believe. The content is dominated by political and artistic concerns (especially an establishment versus the oppressed theme), sexual freedom, drugs, and social services. Much of the content that is not written by the staff and contributors comes from the Underground Press Syndicate and Liberation News Service.

Some critics foresee the end of the underground press, but the larger papers are now lucrative properties. This, of course, raises a basic question: Can a paper like the Los Angeles *Free Press* with a circulation of 90,000 stay underground? Will success make it conventional? These are among the many unresolved questions about the underground papers. They have been called the most exciting reading in America. Even critic Sanford pays them tribute: "At least they try—by saying what can't be said or isn't being said by the staid daily press, by staying on the cutting edge of 'In' for an audience with the shortest of attention spans."

Alternative Broadcasting

Broadcasting has long been dominated by networks and stations that are nearly all establishment by definition; with few exceptions, it has been such a closed preserve that the controversial open-microphone Pacifica radio stations and the rock stations stand out. But just as new technology enabled print journalists to create the counterculture press, technological change has opened avenues for alternatives in broadcasting. The few opportunities for diversity in broadcasting have become many with the development of cable television. The high cost of producing television programs has been reduced strikingly, primarily because of the development of portable half-inch videotape.

How all this helps provide an alternative is indicated by an hour-long program entitled "The World's Largest Television Studio," which was broadcast over many cable television systems late in the summer of 1972. It is a video scrapbook of the 1972 Democratic National Convention in Miami.

Richard Reeves, an excellent political writer, wrote in *New York* magazine in August 28, 1972:

> The documentary, put together by 26 young people calling themselves "Top Value Television" (TVTV) on a $12,000 budget, does exactly what CBS and NBC with all their millions didn't do enough of: TVTV *reports* more than it interviews; it *shows* the California delegation getting instructions on how to vote on important questions; it *shows* the confusion on the floor as delegates look for telephone and hand signals from George McGovern's manipulators; it *shows* what the networks only tried to talk about. The film, edited from 80 hours shot by a bunch of scrambling kids with hand-held cameras, is an uneven and flawed little masterpiece—the major flaw is repetitious and self-indulgent footage showing the kids themselves at work and play. But, foot-for-foot, TVTV—a group loosely built around Michael Shamberg, a drop-out *Time* correspondent, Allen Rucker and Megan Williams—has produced the best electronic coverage of the Democratic Convention that I've seen.

Precision Journalism

By the standards of the precisionists, all the other new journalists deal in mere subjective reactions. Ben Wattenberg, coauthor of *The Real Majority,* said in an interview in 1970:

I like to think that we are the new new journalism—journalism which is not subjective but which is becoming more objective than ever before. We've got the tools now—census, polls, election results—that give us precision, that tell us so much about people. Yet, at precisely the time when these tools have become so exact, the damned New Journalists have become so introspective that they're staring at their navels. The difficulty is that when you put in tables you bore people. Yet when I was in the White House [as an assistant to Lyndon Johnson], knowing what was going on, reading the New Journalists was like reading fairy tales. They wrote political impressionism.[10]

The indictment is too sweeping, but it is certainly true that the other new journalists are subjective to a degree that disturbs conventional journalists and horrifies precision journalists. In essence, all the other new journalists push reporting toward art. Precision journalists push it toward science.

How the precision journalist works is illustrated by the methods of Philip Meyer of the Washington bureau of Knight Newpapers (Miami *Herald,* Detroit *Free Press,* and others). Meyer and his survey team interviewed hundreds of Detroit residents after the 1967 Detroit race riot. Meyer's study, "The People Beyond 12th Street," was one of the few examples of race relations reporting praised by the Kerner Commission. In this and other cases, Meyer has combined survey research and depth interviewing to probe for the causes of events. An editor's note that appeared with one series in the Miami *Herald* explains the approach:

> What happens to college radicals when they leave the campus? The whole current movement of young activists who want to change American society began just five years ago at the University of California's Berkeley campus. In a landmark survey, Knight Newspapers reporters Philip Meyer and Michael Maidenberg located more than 400 of the original Berkeley rebels, and 230 of them completed detailed questionnaires. Of the respondents, 13 were selected for in-depth interviews. The results based on a computer analysis of the responses, are provided in a series beginning with this article.[11]

Meyer explains, "When we cover an election story in Ohio we can have all the usual description—autumn leaves, gentle winds—but in addition we can offer the reader a pretty accurate profile of what his neighbors are thinking." The precision journalists combine the computer with vivid description.

These thumbnail sketches draw the broad outline. The rest of this book is devoted to exploring the full dimensions, effects, and future of the new journalism.

A Schematic View of the New Journalism: Practices and Media

Form	Medium	Content	Practitioners
The new nonfiction	Magazine articles, news-paper columns, books	Social trends, celebrity pieces, the "little people," public events	Tom Wolfe, Jimmy Breslin, Gay Talese, Norman Mailer, Truman Capote
Alternative journalism	Alternative newspapers and magazines	Exposés of wrongdoing in establishment organ-izations, attacks on bigness of institutions	Editors and writers for San Francisco *Bay Guardian, Cervi's Journal, Maine Times*
Journalism reviews	Newspapers and magazines	Analyses and exposés of journalistic practices	*(More), Chicago Jour-nalism Review*
Advocacy journalism	Newspaper columns, point-of-view papers, magazines, broadcast-ing and cable television	Social change, politics, public issues	Gloria Steinem, Pete Hamill, Nicholas von Hoffman, new advocacy papers
Counterculture journalism	Counterculture papers and magazines	Radical politics, psychedelic art, the drug culture, social services, protest	Editors and writers for L.A., New York, and Washington *Free Presses;* Berkeley *Barb*
Alternative broadcasting	Television (especially cable) and radio	Novel approaches to broadcast programming and practice, mostly reflecting counterculture	Raindance Corporation, Johnny Videotape, TVTV
Precision journalism	Newspapers, magazines, books	Survey research in re-porting of social indica-ators, public concerns	Philip Meyer, Scammon and Wattenberg, news magazines

12

Notes

[1] Tom Wolfe, "The New Journalism," *Bulletin* (of the American Society of Newspaper Editors), September 1970, p. 1.

[2] L. W. Robinson, Harold Hayes, and Tom Wolfe, "The New Journalism," *Writer's Digest*, January 1970, p. 32.

[3] Dwight Macdonald, "Parajournalism, or Tom Wolfe and His Magic Writing Machine," *New York Review of Books*, August 26, 1965, p. 3.

[4] Dan Wakefield, "The Personal Voice and the Impersonal Eye," *Atlantic*, June 1966, p.86.

[5] Eugene Cervi, "The Crybaby Millionaire Publishers," *Grassroots Editor*, November-December 1967, p. 14.

[6] Clayton Kirkpatrick, "The New Propaganda," *Bulletin*, September 1970, p.28.

[7] Jack Newfield, Robert F. Kennedy Memorial Symposium, University of Missouri at Kansas City, February 27, 1970.

[8] Arthur Kunkin, Robert F. Kennedy Memorial Symposium, University of Missouri at Kansas City, Feburary 27, 1970.

[9] David Sanford, "Seedier Media: The Underground Press," *New Republic*, December 2, 1967.

[10] Cleveland Amory, "Trade Winds," *Saturday Review*, September 26, 1970, p. 8.

[11] Philip Meyer and Michael Maidenberg, "Berkeley Rebels of '64: They'd Do It Again," Miami *Herald*, February 1, 1970, p. 1.

The New Nonfiction: Brain Candy and Beyond

2

What is the difference between literature and journalism? Journalism is unreadable, and literature is not read.

—Oscar Wilde,
in "The Critic as Artist"

No form of new journalism has been more attention compelling than the new nonfiction. It has brought success at several levels: a degree of fame and fortune for individual writers, a boon to the sagging circulations of some magazines, and a wise investment for publishing houses. All this has happened in the midst of colliding values and raging controversy.

Intensely human and individualistic, the new nonfiction conjures up images: Truman Capote memorizing telephone books; Lillian Ross unobtrusively taking notes; Tom Wolfe resplendent in an ice cream suit; Norman Mailer spewing obscenities; Jimmy Breslin listening to a bookie agonize over losing his son in Vietnam; Gay Talese peering into the minds of his subjects with what seems to be x-ray vision. These and other literary entrepreneurs are the mix that critic Theodore Solotaroff called "a kind of howling forum where all manner of ideas, styles, and standards contended for attention."[1]

The new nonfiction emerged at a time—the 1960s—when, as Solotaroff puts it, there was a "shrinkage of extremes between the serious and the trivial, between hard thought and easy attitudinizing, between originality and novelty, relevance and chic, distinction and celebrity. The sixties," he observes, were "a period in which the literary consensus, like the political and social ones, broke apart and began to fly off in various directions."[2]

Curiously, magazines were the leading showplace for the stylistic experimentation that became the new form. Most nonfiction articles in magazines had for years adhered to a formula. As former *Esquire* editor Harold Hayes said, "The magazine article was a form very largely taken for granted among editors and writers. The writers knew precisely what we [magazine editors] required of the writer on any given assignment. The magazine article was a convention of writing and those who were successful at it understood the convention in the same way that a reporter understands the demands of a news story. There was an anecdotal lead opening into the general theme of the piece; then some explanation, followed by anecdotes or examples. If a single individual was important to the story, some biographical material was included. Then there would be a further rendering of the subject and the article would close with an anecdote."[3]

Hayes oversimplified, of course, but it *is* remarkable how many articles were based on this formula. Considering such rigidity, it was no wonder magazine writers were largely ignored by the literary hierarchy. "The magazine men weren't even in the game . . . they turned out brain candy," Tom Wolfe states. He continues:

> For 75 years, at least, there had been a very pat status in the literary world. Novelists, also playwrights, and poets . . . ranked first. They were the holy beasts. They represented the realm of the spirit and man's higher emotions. In the second place were the gentlemen-amateur essayists—all descendants of Hazlitt, Lamb, Carlyle, plus the Bergsons, Santayanas, Sartres, Shaws, Menckens. . . . They represented the realm of intellect and serious analysis. At the bottom were newspapermen, and the bottom was a long ways down. They were the plugs, drays whose only usefulness was the hauling up of raw data, the facts that writers of higher powers might make use of.[4]

Dan Wakefield said of nonfiction, "The term itself indicates that 'fiction' is the standard, central sort of serious writing and that anything else is basically defined by being 'not' of that genre."[5]

Magazine journalists and those who wrote occasionally for magazines had one great advantage: because they had low status, they were free to experiment. "Anything went," Wolfe wrote, "because there were no rules worth leaving unbroken."

Breaking out of their mold brought them attention, but the change did not come simply because the writers wanted to improve their standing in the hierarchy. Of all the media, magazines were hit hardest by the broadcasting revolution. Television took over much of the entertainment function of magazines, and the result was a fierce scramble for the advertising dollar. Magazines began devoting more space to nonfiction to offer something that broadcasting could not provide as profitably as it could provide situation comedies. But to offer more of the conventional kind of nonfiction was hardly good enough. Enter the writers of the new nonfiction.

The new form became a blending: the reporter's penchant for outlines of issues and events with the novelist's intense physical description, lively dialogue and inner thoughts. It was nurtured by a climate of introspection in an affluent time when Americans could afford to give pause to how one's head was put together instead of where the next meal was coming from. Solotaroff observes that for writers there "was a distinct shift . . . from a preoccupation with values as the ground of experience to a preoccupation with experience as the ground of values."[6] As they plunged into the turbulent events of the sixties, the new nonfiction writers ignored old notions of journalistic importance and carried the youthful slogan "tell it like it is" into physical and psychological perspectives.

Their work was essentially the application of fiction methods to nonfiction. As Tom Wolfe said, the new nonfiction was "technique—technique, not subject matter nor moral passion nor personal involvement." This seems hardly the stuff that might ignite a controversy, but it did, and for several important reasons. The strongest was the threat to fiction writers. Might not the new nonfiction cut into the already-reduced space magazines were allotting to fiction? How many good novels would be squeezed out by such works as Truman Capote's *In Cold Blood*? The more the "bastard form" got into print, the less room for fiction.

The new form was even more threatening to critics and essayists, many of whom hoped that the success of *The New York Review of Books* signaled the revival of the literary essay.

To traditional journalists, the new nonfiction was a challenge to objectivity and the traditional news story. Older reporters recalled another era of "new journalism," for that was the name given to the yellow journalism of Hearst and Pulitzer. Magazine writers who had been producing article after article for decades with little recognition found that Wolfe and Talese were becoming famous because of the new form.

The opposition was not "any sort of conscious policy on the part of literati or journalists," Wolfe wrote in an article that appeared in *New York* in February, 1972, "but merely a natural instinct for self-preservation."

But jealousy was far from the only reason for criticism. The debate over the role of the new nonfiction was concerned with at least five attitudes that were central to traditional journalism:

1. *The journalist's aversion to blending fact and opinion, coupled with his aversion to including himself in his article.* To move beyond surface facts, the writer of the new nonfiction immerses facts in the sights, sounds, and atmosphere that surrounds them in life, and he sometimes connects them by comparison with other facts of history, society, and literature. Even when the writer of the new nonfiction does not overtly state an opinion, his opinions are often apparent from the choices he makes about what to include beyond the surface facts. And even when the writer does not include himself as "I"—some, like Talese, never do—his presence usually looms in the mind of the reader because of the personal quality of the writing.

2. *The journalist's belief that description, especially applied to people, is subjective and thus taboo.* The tentative one- and two-word descriptions that are the norm in most journalism suggest the aversion to description. This grows from the belief that thorough description is almost automatically subjective—or may be taken to be by many readers. The extreme is indicated by a recent discussion by a group of Kansas newsmen about the advisability of including in news stories the diminutive stature of the Kansas governor. "I won't do it," one declared, "because people will think less of us and of him." The new nonfiction, with its vivid metaphors, goes so far beyond the conventional that it invites attacks.

3. *The journalist's concern with what is usually regarded as the obvious and significant trends, events, and people.* Some of the writers of the new nonfiction focus on occasion on the obvious national trends, issues, and events—political conventions, riots, space flights, and the like. But it is remarkable how many of them choose subjects that seem, to the conventional journalist, to be peripheral: Tom Wolfe treating the automobile as the central organizing force of our time, Gay Talese studying failures, Truman Capote recreating a gruesome crime in rural Kansas, Lillian Ross examining the internal dynamics of a motion picture, Jimmy Breslin giving much of his attention to Little People. The critics of the new nonfiction do not say that such matters should not be treated, but they do object to giving them significance bordering on pretension. Dwight Macdonald's criticism of Breslin is indicative: "Suitable game for the parajournalist is the Little Man (or Woman) who gets into trouble with the law; or who is interestingly poor or old or ill or, best, all three; or who has some other Little problem like delinquent children or a close relative who has been murdered for which they can count on Jimmy Breslin's hard-breathing prose."

4. *The new journalist's seeming disregard for accuracy and his penchant for spoofing.* Sometimes, the new journalists sacrifice details to create a mood. Accuracy, some new journalists believe, sometimes gets in the way of truth. Shortly after the publication of Capote's *In Cold Blood,* a writer for *Esquire* wrote "In Cold Fact," which challenged the veracity of Capote's reporting. Officials in the mayor's office in San Francisco deny that some of the conversations reported by Tom Wolfe in "Mau-Mauing the Flak-Catchers" ever took place.

Perhaps the most sustained attacks were aimed at two articles that Wolfe wrote about the *New Yorker* in 1965. Titled "Tiny Mummies! The True Story of the Ruler of 43rd Street's Land of the Walking Dead," the first article linked the personal idiosyncrasies of the editor of the *New Yorker,* William Shawn, with his magazine, which Wolfe called "an American institution which everybody knew in their heart of hearts was dead as a doornail." The second article was similarly scathing.

Responding to those articles, Dwight Macdonald compared Wolfe with Hitler and Joseph McCarthy: "The difference between Tom Wolfe and such types is that he doesn't tell lies, big or small, since lying is a conscious process, recognizing the distinction between fact and fabrication. You might call him a sincere demagogue."

There is no question that several of the writers of the new nonfiction are careless with facts. Once when Breslin visited Kansas State University, he became caught up in the nostalgia of returning to the scene where Bobby Kennedy had triumphed the year before his death and wrote a column about it that was heavy with significant inaccuracies. He misunderstood names and mistakenly reported that a Negro was in jail for burning a campus building. Breslin reported that the building, which had actually housed a music department and a radio station, was an ROTC headquarters.

Finding such errors is easy, but it is sometimes difficult to distinguish errors from parody and spoofing. When is the writer producing effects that might be justified? Macdonald recognized this problem even as he attacked Wolfe:

A parodist is licensed to invent and Tom Wolfe is not the man to turn down any poetic licentiousness that is going. He takes the middle course, shifting gears between fact and fantasy, spoof and reportage, until nobody knows which end is, at the moment, up.

5. *The journalist's fear that stylistic devices will confuse and mislead the reader.* Sometimes the use of fiction techniques in journalism can mislead, however unintentionally. Gail Sheehy wrote a tragic, absorbing story about "Redpants," a New York City prostitute for *New York* in August, 1971. A few weeks later the *Wall Street Journal* blew the whistle:

Redpants is what's known as a composite character. Miss Sheehy spent weeks interviewing real hustlers and pimps, and then she combined the salient details of their lives into the characters of Redpants and Sugarman [a pimp]. So the story was true, sort of, but then again, it wasn't. The reader, however, was not told any of this.

Earlier, *New York* serialized part of David Freeman's *U.S. Grant in the City and Other True Stories of Jugglers and Pluggers, Swatters and Whores*, which included portraits that were probably composite characters, although the author wouldn't talk about it. In a guarded statement to the *Wall Street Journal* he said, "I set out to create a work of art. *I believe* Hector and Louise [two teen-age muggers] to be real." Composite characters have long been a useful but little-used literary and journalistic device. Few critics unequivocally oppose using the device, but most insist that the reader be told that he is reading about a composite character, not a real person.

Another form is the time composite. In "Tonight at the Blue Angel: Lenny Bruce," an article in *New York*, authors Albert Goldman and Lawrence Schiller presented a "day in the death of Lenny Bruce . . . based on a three-year period in Lenny's life and six years of the authors' research."

Hundreds of writers employ the techniques of the new nonfiction. Several stand out, some because of their inventiveness as writers, others because of their articulate defense of the new journalism. Here we pay special attention to six practitioners of the new nonfiction.

Singling out a few writers to illustrate the mechanics, viewpoint, and importance of the new nonfiction does not denigrate the contributions of their forerunners. A comprehensive history might include Addison, Boswell, Stephen Crane, DeFoe, and Mark Twain. It would also examine the nonfiction writing of George Orwell, Ernest Hemingway, John Hersey, Damon Runyon, John Steinbeck, Edmund Wilson, James Agee, and others. It might also pay homage to the lively, humanistic prose of Murray Kempton, long a durable fixture in New York City journalism. But this book is about recent trends and developments.

Tom Wolfe and Pop Culture

Tom Wolfe has become the high priest, a leading practitioner and chief promoter and defender of the new nonfiction. He has his own distinctive view of what is important for the writer to treat: "As a writer I'm concerned with the liberation of thinking. At the moment a sort of nineteenth century pattern of thinking has a grip on the country . . . we are all oriented to think about the war on poverty, civil rights, housing problems; but the changes are occurring on a different level of thinking." Perhaps, he says, "the automobile is the unifying symbol in society." With such convictions, Wolfe seeks out what have been called "psychic changes on the social landscape."

Wolfe's attempt to break the stranglehold of the old mind-set has caused his detractors to accuse him of everything from lack of compassion to intellectual weakness. But none of this seems to faze Wolfe, who has been controversial since he "burst spectacularly upon the American literary horizon in the mid-1960s with his *outre* articles on pop culture for *New York*."[7]

Wolfe's route to the new journalism was improbable. Born in 1931 in Richmond, Virginia, to a middle-class family (his father was an agronomy professor and agricultural editor), he attended Washington and Lee University, where he majored in English and played baseball. Hoping for a career in the major leagues, he tried out as a pitcher for the old New York Giants, failed, and went on to Yale, where five years later he earned a Ph.D. in American studies. Tired of academic life, he worked for a time moving furniture, then turned to newspapering, first for the Springfield, Massachusetts, *Union*, later for the Washington *Post*. He had a dual assignment at the *Post*—Latin American news and humor—and won awards for both from the Washington Newspaper Guild. Traditional feature writing did not satisfy Wolfe's inner urgings. "I got tired of it," he once said, "of covering the poet of the week, or the month, or the decade." Newspaper reporting was, after a time, little more than "shaking hands with old assignments," he said.

He began to write free-lance articles for magazines when he joined the New York *Herald Tribune*. During the 1963 New York newspaper strike he was sent by *Esquire* to California to write an article on customized cars —automobiles with lowered chassis, souped-up engines, and added fins and chrome—and their young aficionados. Then, as *Current Biography* described it:

> After months in California, Wolfe returned to New York with plenty of notes but no story. Byron Dobell, the managing editor of *Esquire*, anxious because a two-page illustration for the story was already locked into the printing presses, badgered him for the article, to no avail. "Finally I told Byron Dobell . . . that I couldn't pull the thing together," Wolfe later recounted. "O.K., he tells me, just type out my notes and send them over." Wolfe did and Dobell ran the rough memorandum just as it was.[8]

The story, "The Kandy-Kolored Tangerine-Flake Streamline Baby," a first-person narrative, used sources and subject matter that Wolfe later said would have been unsuited for the "totem newspapers," which would have regarded it as "a sideshow, a panoption, for creeps and kooks; not even wealthy, eccentric creeps and kooks, which would be all right, but lower class creeps and nutballs with dermatitic skin and ratty hair.[9] Here is a nontotemistic paragraph from the piece:

> He never took his eyes off that car. It's what is called semi-custom. Nothing has been done to it to give it a really sculptural quality, but a lot of streamlining details have been added. The main thing you notice is the color—tangerine flake. This paint—one of Barris' [George, custom car celebrity] Kandy Kolor concoctions—makes the car look like it has been encrusted with a half-inch of clear lacquer. There used to be very scholarly and abstruse studies of color and color symbolism around the turn of the century, and theorists concluded that preferences for certain colors were closely associated with rebelliousness, and these are the very same colors many of the kids go for—purple, carnal yellow, various violets and lavenders and fuchsias and many other of these Kandy Kolors.[10]

After this successful piece—which he says marked the "liberation" of his style and which was widely quoted and reprinted—Wolfe prowled the land applying the form to pop cult stories. One about Las Vegas began with the word "hernia" repeated over fifty times (what a drugged, boozy patron hears as the croupier's patter). Others introduced new typographic devices, with type dribbling down the page, as in this question about media philosopher Marshall McLuhan:

What if he's right. What . . . if . . . he . . . is . . . right
W-h-a-t i-f h-e i-s r-i-g-h-t

```
            R
   W        I
   H  IF    G    ?
   A  HE    H
   T  IS    T
```

And there were strange, mind-massaging words like "infarcted." Above all, Wolfe offered a kind of machine-gun staccato description of his characters, piling adjective on adjective, to achieve effects.

In researching one story, Wolfe discovered that "fitting in" isn't important for the reporter. It had always been a journalistic article of faith that reporters should be gray and innocuous. Says Wolfe, "when I first started out in 1963, I used to worry about how I ought to act, what I ought to wear and so forth." But when he tried to "fit in" while working on the "Last American Hero," the folks in the hollows of North Carolina thought him a "strange, little green man." He decided then to "come on wide open and interested."[11] Wolfe began to wear ice-cream suits, wide ties, colored shirts, and electric zig-zag socks long before they became popular.

The liberation of Tom Wolfe's dress and writing styles came at about the same time. His wardrobe expanded as he produced dozens of articles for *Esquire* and *New York*. He interviewed disc jockeys, underground film queens, strippers, English teen-agers, and others. The stories made social statements. Consider this passage about a San Francisco dancer's body image:

> Even Carol Doda has started thinking of them as them. There they were secured to her pectoralis major like acquisitions. When a man asks me out, I never know if he is interested in me or them. That is the way she thinks about it. Them! Carol Doda has had injections of a silicone emulsion put into her breasts in regular installments over the past three years. They have grown, grown, grown, enlarging like . . . dirigibles, almost as if right in front of the eyes of the crowds—they line up out there—who come every night of the week to see Carol Doda's "topless" act.[12]

Wolfe tries to humanize even those whose work requires abstract analysis, as in this description of Marshall McLuhan:

> The first thing I noticed about him was that he wore some kind of a trick snap-on necktie with hidden plastic cheaters on it. He was a tall man, 53 years old, handsome, with a long strong face, but terribly pallid. He had gray hair, which he combed straight back. It was a little

thin on top, but he could comb it into nice sloops over the ears. Distinguished-looking, you might say. On the other hand there were the plastic cheaters. A little of the plastic was showing between his collar and the knot of the tie. I couldn't keep my eye off it. It's the kind of tie you buy off a revolving rack in the Rexall for about 89¢. You just slip the plastic cheaters—they're a couple of little stays sticking out of the knot like wings—you slip them under your collar and there the tie is, hanging down and ready to go, Pree-Tide.[13]

After compiling two collections of his magazine articles (in *The Kandy-Kolored Tangerine-Flake Streamline Baby* and *The Pump House Gang*), Wolfe turned to book-length reportage with *The Electric Kool-Aid Acid Test*. In this massive job of subjective-reality reporting, Wolfe followed hip novelist Ken Kesey, author of *One Flew over the Cuckoo's Nest,* and his Merry Pranksters around the country, conducted endless interviews, and observed, observed, observed:

The cops now know the whole scene, even the costumes, the jesuschrist strung-out hair, Indian beads, Indian headbands, donkey beads, temple bells, amulets, mandalas, god's-eyes, flourescent vests, unicorn horns, Errol Flynn dueling shirts—but they still don't know about the shoes. The worst are shiny black shoes with shoelaces in them. The hierarchy ascends from there although practically all low-cut shoes are unhip, from there on up to the boots the heads like, light, fanciful boots, English boots of the mod variety, if that is all they can get, but better something like hand-tooled Mexican boots with Caliente Dude Triple A toes on them. So see the FBI—black—shiny—laced up—FBI shoes—when the FBI finally grabbed Kesey.[14]

Most critics were delighted, and the book sold well. A razzle-dazzle insight into the hippie counterculture, the book was especially popular with high school and college students. To some it seemed to be the glorification of the new life style of drugs and communal living. Others like Malcolm Bauer of the Portland *Oregonian* said, "No writer is better at this impertinent needling than is Tom Wolfe, who exposed the idiocies and excesses of Ken Kesey and his Merry Pranksters." Wolfe seemed to have achieved a kind of new objectivity in which the vastness of detail allowed the reader to make his own judgments, unobstructed by condescending advice from the author.

In 1970, when Wolfe had achieved considerable celebrity—a *Newsweek* assessment called him "some kind of great writer"—he might have coasted on his reputation by repeating his earlier themes. But his preoccupation with style—in writing, dress, and thought—lured him into reporting a party given by conductor and liberal Leonard Bernstein for the Black Panthers which was largely attended by wealthy New Yorkers. The mixture of black rage and upper class inspired Wolfe to write "Radical Chic: That Party at Lenny's," which appeared in *New York* in June 1970:

... and now, in the season of Radical Chic, the Black Panthers. That huge Panther there, the one Felicia Bernstein is smiling her tango smile at, is Robert Bay, who just forty-one hours ago was arrested in an altercation with the police, supposedly over a .38 caliber revolver that someone had, in a parked car in Queens at Northern Boulevard and 104th Street or some such unbelievable place, had been taken to jail on a most unusual charge called "criminal facilitation." And now he is out on bail and walking into Leonard and Felicia Bernstein's thirteen-room penthouse duplex on Park Avenue.[15]

Wolfe needled the "beautiful people" flirting with radical politics: "After awhile, it all comes down to servants. They are the cutting edge of Radical Chic. Obviously if you are giving a party for the Black Panthers . . . you can't have a Negro butler and maid." There was, Wolfe saw, "a collision course . . . between absolute need for servants—and the fact that the servant was the absolute symbol of what the new movements, black or brown, were struggling against."

The article provoked a turbulent response, and many of Wolfe's former admirers denounced him as uncommitted, malicious, and racist. Critic Irving Howe spoke of Wolfe's "snobbism," which, he said, "fixates on marginal details of manner and appearance in order to pass sentences of dismissal for inadequacies of style." Even the fact that Wolfe had admittedly hit upon an important subject "must lead to a chastening of verbal mannerisms," Howe felt, "through a chastening not yet complete." A *Commonweal* review tried to parody Wolfe's style: "Apolitical Tom has got himself into the midst of a wing-ding poly feud. The ultimate issue: Do you blast out that the emperor's not wearing any clothes or, as in Lenny's case, that he's overdressed, when it kills fund-raising for civil rights causes?" Critic Jason Epstein probably came down on Wolfe the hardest when he said that he "represents and envies the rich and talented, is scared silly of the alienated poor, and suffers from a middle-brow hang-up that allies him emotionally with [Spiro] Agnew & Co."[16]

But Wolfe picked up some support from new friends, many of them conservatives. William Buckley wrote, "Tom Wolfe is an unfortunate victim of ideological ire. His wit attracts the witless among the critics. . . . Tom Wolfe will survive the humorless of this world—that or else the world will not, should not, survive." Columnist Stewart Alsop hailed the article as "brilliantly funny," then declared: "What has happened is that Radical Chic suddenly isn't chic any more. Instead it has become a bore and because it has become a bore, it is dying."

"Radical Chic" was published in 1970 in book form along with "Mau-mauing the Flak Catchers," a story about black youths who badger a terrified Office of Economic Opportunity bureaucrat. Here is how Wolfe introduces the so-called "flak catcher" (described as a "Number 2 bureaucrat"):

This man comes out, and he has that sloppy Irish look like Ed McMahon on TV, only with a longer nose. . . . But he doesn't have to open his mouth. All you have to do is look at him and you get the picture. The man's a lifer. He's stone civil service. He has it all down from the wheatcolor Hush Puppies to the wash 'n dry semi-tab-collar short-sleeves white shirt.[17]

Also vividly described are the mau-mauers: "The monsters have tight curly hair, but it grows in long strands, with a Duke pomade job. They've got huge feet, and they're wearing sandals. The straps on those sandals look like they were made from the reins on the Budweiser draft horses."[18]

As these passages indicate, when Tom Wolfe sets out to construct the scenes that are the heart of the new nonfiction, he is not content with the large overview; he tries to make his scenes alive through memorable metaphor.

Nor is he content to write only new nonfiction; he may, in fact, have written as much *about* it. He is by all odds its most passionate promoter and defender. He speaks about it in public lectures and on radio and television programs—good-humoredly when he is challenged, but never leaving a doubt that he believes it to be the salvation of journalism.

Lillian Ross: Unobtrusive Observer

Twenty years ago, Lillian Ross's nonfiction novel *Picture*, a behind-the-scenes look at film-making, was hailed as a landmark in the history of journalism. In an arena with flamboyant contemporaries like Tom Wolfe and Norman Mailer, Ross, a quiet, unobtrusive woman, is often overlooked. Even when her writing has been the center of controversy, she herself, like a one-dimensional stick figure, has blended into the background, perhaps because she has made it clear that her personal life is not open to public scrutiny. Photographs of her are rare, and she has been said to "regret having made the mistake of publicly admitting as much as the place of her birth."[19] (It is Syracuse, New York, 1926.)

The very qualities that make reading about Lillian Ross quite dull—"She becomes just any 37-year-old woman, as inconspicuous as her chair"[20]—become the strength of her writing. Her forte is the interview. "You try not to get in the way of the person you're trying to show," she has been quoted as saying. "You are trying to follow along the person you're interviewing, to respond to him instead of coming along with a lot of prepared questions, you just get him going. And don't bother him. And listen. It's just a question of listening."[21]

A staff writer of profiles for the *New Yorker* since 1946, her subjects range from Ernest Hemingway to the Miss America pageant. Her reportorial technique, one critic writes, "is sound camera, neutrally and exhaustively recording the scene." According to *Newsweek*: "In the long history of the sport called reading between the lines, few writers have topped her at demonstrating just how loaded that white space can be. Some admirers claim the space is simply blank, to be filled in with whatever mental doodles the reader wishes to supply. Some, including both admirers and critics, claim it is a channel flowing with pure acid." *Time* observed:

> Lillian Ross declines assignments that do not interest her; she avoids subjects who show the least resistance to holding still. And even where the landscape is expansive, she applies a curious restrictive principle. "In my work I don't make judgments of people," she says, "I think you should let them be the way they are." Whether they are what they are is what brings on the argument. For what they are is how they were observed, and therefore judged, by Lillian Ross.

One such argument involved the Ross profile of Hemingway, which brought her both praise and invective. Of the article, she wrote, "It was a sympathetic piece, covering two days Hemingway spent in New York, in which I tried to describe as precisely as possible how Hemingway, who had the nerve to be like nobody else on earth, looked and sounded when he was in action, talking, between work periods—to give a picture of the man as he was, in his uniqueness and with his vitality and enormous spirit of fun intact."[22] The trouble was that any true picture of Hemingway made him seem a caricature of himself. Here's how the *New Yorker* article described him:

> Hemingway had on a red plaid wool shirt, a figured wool necktie, a tan wool sweater-vest, a brown tweed jacket tight across the back with sleeves too short for his arms, gray flannel slacks, Argyle socks and loafers, and he looked bearish, cordial, and constricted. His hair, which was very long in back, was grey, except at the temples, where it was white; his mustache was white, and he had a ragged half-inch white beard. There was a bump about the size of a walnut over his left eye. He had on steelrimmed spectacles, with a piece of paper under the nosepiece.[23]

It also featured dialogue:

> Mrs. Hemingway looked up. "Any girl who marries Papa has to learn how to carry a gun," she said, and returned to her letter writing. . . .
> "Hunting is sort of a good life," Hemingway said. "Better than Westport or Bronxville, I think."[24]

Before the article was published, a galley proof was sent to Hemingway, who, according to Miss Ross, found it "funny and good" and suggested only one deletion. Later Ross was to write that "Nothing like it ever happened to me in my writing experience, or has happened since. To the complete surprise of Hemingway and the editors of the *New Yorker* and myself . . . what I had written was extremely controversial." Some readers who disliked Hemingway thought Ross did too, thus admiring the profile for the wrong reasons; some, in fact, thought she had written a "devastating" attack. However, a gentle note from Hemingway assured her that occasionally people simply got things mixed up.

Ross always stays out of the action, letting the description and dialogue speak. With simple honesty, her story of a group of rural Indiana high school students experiencing New York became a case study of "future shock" ten years before Alvin Toffler popularized the term:

> The next morning, a meeting of the class was held in the hotel lobby to take a vote on when to leave New York. . . . The class voted for the extra day in New York and Niagara Falls.
>
> "I'm glad," Becky Kiser said, with a large, friendly smile, to Dennis Smith. Several of her classmates overheard her and regarded her with a uniformly deadpan look. "I like it here," she went on. "I'd like to live here. There's so much to see. There's so much to do."
>
> Her classmates continued to study her impassively until Dennis took their eyes away from her by saying, "You get a feelin' here of goin' wherever you want to. Seems the city never closes. I'd like to live here, I believe. People from everyplace are here."
>
> "Limousines all over the joint," Albert Warthan said.
>
> "Seems like you can walk and walk and walk," Dennis went on dreamily. "I like the way the big buildin's crowd you in. You want to walk and walk and never go to sleep."
>
> "I hate it," Connie Williams said, with passion. . . .
>
> "There's no place like home," Mike said. "Home's good enough for me."
>
> "I believe the reason of this is we've lived all our lives around Stinesville," Dennis said. "If you took Stinesville out of the country, you wouldn't be hurt. But if you took New York out of the country, you'd be hurt. The way the guide said, all our clothes and everything comes from New York."[25]

Through the years Ross has maintained a crisp, unpretentious style. In an admiring view of her craftsmanship, a *Time* writer said, "Miss Lillian Ross names names, and at the same time she uses all the selectivity of a good novelist. Hers, indeed, is what might be called the technique of the candid typewriter, which is no more truly candid camera, since neither clicks unless and until the operator chooses." She is very much the neutral observer, once the subjectivity of topic selection is over. Or at least she says she tries to be. The following passage from *Picture* illustrates why her self-styled pursuit of truth sparks bitter controversy:

The door of [movie producer John] Huston's suite was opened by a conservatively-attired young man with a round face and pink cheeks. He introduced himself as Arthur Fellows. "John is in the next room getting dressed," he said. "Imagine getting a layout like this all to yourself! That's the way the big studios do things." He nodded with approval at the Waldorf's trappings. "Not that I care for the big studios," he said. "I believe in being independent. I work for David Selznick. I've worked for David for fifteen years. David is independent. I look at the picture business as a career. Same as banking, or medicine or law. You've got to learn it from the ground up. I learned it from the ground up with David. I was an assistant director on 'Duel in the Sun.' I directed the scene of the fight between two horses. Right now, I'm here temporarily on publicity and promotion. David—" He broke off as Huston strode into the room. Huston made his appearance in the manner of an actor who is determined to win the immediate attention of his audience.[26]

Ross does not offer an empathetic view of Arthur Fellows. Are his stuffy words softened by his manner? Is he simply nervous? Is he trying to rationalize his feelings about his job? Such questions go unanswered as Ross turns to focus on Huston.

Are people simply pawns in Ross's zeal to tell a story? Again, her work seems uncomplicated by any motive other than to tell a story while keeping herself out of view. In a bittersweet assessment, Tom Wolfe says: "The *New Yorker*'s insistence on a uniform, flat style for its readers tended to keep her from ever creating the novel-like sense of immediacy and subjective reality that *Esquire* was shooting for."[27] Nonetheless, Ross did depart significantly from the traditional magazine article and tested many of the novelist's tools ten years before the blossoming of the new journalism.

Gay Talese and the Interior Monologue

There is a fairly common belief that writing for newspapers erodes creativity. However, one of the most creative practitioners of the new nonfiction, Gay Talese, was a reporter and feature writer for the New York *Times* for twelve years. Born into the Italian-American culture of New Jersey in 1932, he attended the University of Alabama and was a journalism major, a fraternity man, and an ROTC cadet—unlikely preparation for a new journalist. He served briefly in the Army, then joined the *Times* staff in 1953. Here, at this "fundamental old school of journalism," as he put it, at "the citadel of old-fashioned reporting . . . I found I was leaving the assignment each day, unable with the techniques available to me or permissible to the New York *Times* to really tell, to report, all that I saw; to communicate through the techniques that were permitted by the archaic copy desk."[28]

Talese found a receptive outlet for his creative energies in *Esquire*. Taking cues from the writing of his heroes John O'Hara and Irwin Shaw, Talese began to apply the techniques of the short story writer to his magazine pieces. An early attempt was the celebrated Joe Louis story quoted in Chapter 1, which Talese says was only partly successful. After initial scene-setting Talese fell back on "straighter reportage, indicating my own uncertainty with the form at that point . . . and still later the form is scene setting and dialog and away from rigid reporting."[29]

In a later article, "The Soft Psyche of Joshua Logan," Talese said he was more successful at using "fictional techniques for factual situations." As he explains:

I happened to be in the theatre one afternoon watching Logan rehearse his play when, suddenly, he and his star, Claudia McNeil, got into an argument that not only was more dramatic than the play itself, but revealed something of the character of Logan and Miss McNeil in ways that I could never have done had I approached the subject from the more conventional form of reporting.[30]

In a symposium at Columbia University, Talese recalled the Logan story:

I was just trying to write a piece for Harold [Hayes, former editor of *Esquire*] about this once-famous and now somewhat obscure theatrical director who was trying to make a new success of an old play on Broadway, and his failure to do so. I was writing really about failure. It is a subject that intrigues me much more than success.

The explosive scene between Logan and Miss McNeil represents Talese's vivid reportage at its best:

"Don't raise your voice, Claudia," Logan repeated.
She again ignored him.
"CLAUDIA!" Logan yelled, "don't you give me that actor's vengeance, Claudia!"
"Yes, Mr. Logan."
"And stop Yes-Mr.-Logan-ing me."
"Yes, Mr. Logan."
"You're a shockingly rude woman!"
"Yes, Mr. Logan."
"You're being a beast."
"Yes, Mr. Logan."
"Yes, Miss Beast."
"Yes, Mr. Logan."
"Yes, Miss Beast."
Suddenly, Claudia McNeil stopped. It dawned on her that he was calling her a beast; now her face was grey and her eyes were cold, and her voice almost solemn as she said, "You . . . called . . . me . . . out . . . of . . . my . . . name!"
"Oh, God!" Logan smacked his forehead with his hand.

"You . . . called . . . me . . . out . . . of . . . my . . . name."

She stood there, rocklike, big and angry, waiting for him to do something.

"Oliver!" Logan said, turning toward the coproducer, who had lowered his wiry, long body into his chair as if he were in a foxhole. He did not want to be cornered into saying something that might offend Logan, his old friend, but neither did he want Claudia McNeil to come barreling down the aisle and possibly snap his thin frame in half. . . .[31]

Talese's principal contribution to the new nonfiction has been the interior monologue, a demanding device that automatically raises questions. Many critics questioned his practice of writing at length about the inner thoughts of his subjects. Whether an obscure old bridge tender was being displaced by a modern bridge in Brooklyn or the uncommunicative Joe DiMaggio was refusing to grant an interview, Talese tried to report what they were thinking. Talese explained that in interviewing a subject he would "ask him what he thought in every situation where I might have asked him in the past what he said. I'm not so interested in what he did and said . . . as in what he thought. And I would quote him in the way I was writing that he thought something."[32]

In *The Kingdom and the Power*, the human history of the New York *Times*, Talese made effective use of the interior monologue. This and a rich descriptive narrative based on his perceptions during his years as a *Times*-man enabled him to capture the interpersonal drama of the great establishment newspaper. Instead of the usual dull press-history approach, Talese wrote about the pettiness, bickering, and self-doubts of *Times* executives. He showed how management wielded power and controlled the lives of some of America's most talented journalists. The book offended some of his subjects, but it was the frequent use of interior monologue that brought the most intense criticism. Here, for instance, Talese probes the psyche of Clifton Daniel, who had become managing editor when Turner Catledge was promoted to executive editor:

There were times when Daniel felt that Catledge was sufficiently satisfied with the way things were going, or was sufficiently uninterested, to allow Daniel free rein. During such periods Daniel felt a pleasant identity with the photographs of the men on the wall—Van Anda and Birchall, James and Catledge. He felt confidence in himself as an executive, satisfaction in the reporters or critics whom he had hired, reassurance in the style in which the *Times* was covering the world. While Daniel often gave the impression of vaingloriousness and was unquestionably proud of his title, he also saw himself as an instrument of the institution, a good soldier, a loyal subject, and there was not a man in the building less likely to betray a corporate secret than Clifton Daniel.[33]

Talese's method is not limited to the interior monologue, of course. Like the other writers of the new nonfiction, he works to picture his subjects with vivid description, as in this sketch of Daniel:

> He is a most interesting-looking man but difficult to describe because the words that quickly catch him best, initially seem entirely inappropriate for any man who is a man. But the impression persists. Clifton Daniel is almost lovely. It is his face, which is long and pale and soft and dominated by large dark eyes and very long lashes, and his exquisitely groomed, wavy hair that makes him seem almost lovely. His suits are very Savile Row, his hands and nails immaculate, his voice a soft, smooth blend of North Carolina, where he was born in a tiny tobacco town, and England, where he came of age as a journalist and squire of fashionable women and was sometimes referred to as the Sheik of Fleet Street.[34]

The style is readable and natural, as in this description of *Times* reporter John Corry:

> The next morning, as the telephone rang in Corry's apartment on West End Avenue in Manhattan, Corry decided not to answer it. He was tired. His wife and children had chicken pox. He was disillusioned—this whole experience [working at the *Times*] was distorting so many wonderful illusions he had once had about fame and power, and he had stayed up drinking the night before, hoping it would calm his nerves and allow him to sleep. It had not. Now the phone was ringing and he was sure it was the office. It was probably [*Times* editor Claude] Sitton calling, Corry thought, and he let it ring four, five times. Then he picked it up. It was Sitton.[35]

The book stirred a controversy. Some writers said Talese could not possibly know what was going on inside the mind of another person, that he was presumptuous to attempt it. Others charged that he had violated the confidences of many whom he had observed in his years at the *Times*. He had broken the paper's unwritten rule that "What you do here and see here stays here when you leave here." Few before him had written of the dynamics of the story behind the story.

Talese seems always to search for powerful, graphic imagery. He does it with dialogue, scenes, flashbacks, and other devices. His early pieces were, as one writer pointed out, a prototype of "the half-reverent, half-arch tone that characterized the *Esquire* treatment."[36] During the sixties Talese experimented, varying his formula, using a little more dialogue in one story, reducing it in another. By the seventies he would attempt a book using "almost entirely interior monologue. No quotes, scenes . . ."[37]

Talese does research almost endlessly, but his humanistic treatment of massive detail makes his writing flow smoothly and knowledgeably. In a story about actor Peter O'Toole, Talese seems to have thoroughly immersed himself in the history and folklore of film-making. Writing about the *Paris Review*, he not only records the action but seems to know what editor George Plimpton and his cronies were up to and why. A piece about Floyd Patterson is a knowing look at boxing and the feelings of the former champion. At times, Talese relies on his understanding of the Italian family structure, as in a sensitive article about Frank Sinatra: ". . . Frank Sinatra is *Il Padrone*. Or better still, he is what in traditional Sicily have long been called *uomini rispettati*—men of respect: men who are both majestic and humble, men who are loved by all and are very generous by nature, men whose hands are kissed as they walk from village to village, men who would personally go out of their way to redress a wrong."[38]

In his first *Esquire* article in 1960, Talese did an essay on "obscurity in New York City," as he called it, "a series of vignettes on the unnoticed people, the odd facts and bizarre events that had caught my fancy during my travels around town as a newspaperman." Later, what began as an article became a book, *New York: A Serendipiter's Journey*, which reveals Talese's fascination with the old and mundane. In this respect Talese differs significantly from other new journalists who stay on the cutting edge of "in." Above all, he is a craftsman, and as even one of his critics has said, "Talese's use of the new journalism makes both the famous and the obscure come alive, even when the ring of truth is muted."[39]

Talese's professed goal of writing nonfiction with all of the impact of fiction is demonstrated with remarkable finesse in his 1971 best seller, *Honor Thy Father*. In this extraordinary account, Talese takes the reader into the daily life of a Mafia family—the Bonannos. Written from the viewpoint of Mafia don Joseph (Joe Bananas) Bonanno's son Bill, the book is a revealing analysis of the human side, with sensitive portraits of the wives and children. More than a contemporary account, the book traces the roots of organized crime back hundreds of years into Sicilian history and sociology. The story is the tragedy of Bill Bonanno, a handsome, college-educated Mafioso son, who must cope with the interface of ancient tradition and modern society. As he "honors his father" in the ways of the past, he nearly destroys himself.

Honor Thy Father offers a rich expansion of the interior monologue. Talese reports the thoughts of Bill Bonanno without fictionalizing but by focusing on what Bonanno says he thought. The writer was thus able to fashion intimate scenes because he "became a source of communication within a family that had been long repressed by a tradition of silence."

Jimmy Breslin and the Little People

Tom Wolfe once wrote that Jimmy Breslin looks like an "industrial fire hydrant." Breslin then included Wolfe on his list of "People I'm Not Speaking To This Year," which appeared annually for several years in *New*

York magazine. Breslin is like that. He comes on as a rough-and-tumble, tough-talking New Yorker but is basically a romantic. He has become a conduit for the hopes and aspirations of the "little people," the politically invisible, common-folk mass. Through his books and magazine articles Breslin orchestrates a symphony of run-of-the-mill people whose concerns he elevates to significance.

Characteristically, Breslin still lives in Queens, where he was born in 1930. He became a newspaper reporter as a teen-ager, then enrolled in Long Island University, which, according to *Who's Who in America*, he attended from 1947 to 1950. But, as *Newsweek* put it, "facts on his education are hazy because he lies so much about it. He has claimed he has a doctorate from Cambridge. He also has said he attended Elmira Reformatory [and] there is a valid question as to whether he graduated from high school, which he attended for five years."[40]

Settling on a career as a reporter, Breslin worked successively for the Newhouse, Scripps-Howard, and Hearst newspaper chains, which he calls the "Folsom, Sing Sing and Leavenworth of American journalism." In 1945 he married Rosemary Dattalico (who is frequently mentioned in his columns and stories) and continued his career as an underpaid sportswriter. Breslin struggled until 1960 when he got away from daily newspapers long enough to write a book about the New York Mets, *Can't Anybody Here Play This Game?* The book came to the attention of John Hay Whitney, publisher of the New York *Herald Tribune*, who bought serial rights and later hired Breslin as a sports columnist.

Breslin eventually made it to the front page with a column that has been called a daily short story. He created a world of Irish blarney from the streets and bars of New York. Most New York writers center on midtown Manhattan, but Breslin wrote with equal vigor about Queens, Brooklyn, and the Bronx. In interviews with cops, barmaids, and street vendors, Breslin introduced characters the likes of which New York had not seen since the heyday of Damon Runyon:

> Fat Thomas, the bookmaker, his 415 pounds encased in a plaid jacket, stood in the doorway of the bedroom. He would not come any closer.[41]

> Marvin the Torch never could keep his hands off somebody else's business, particularly if the business was losing money. Now this is accepted behavior in Marvin's profession, which is arson. But he has a bad habit of getting into places where he shouldn't be and promising too many favors.[42]

The *Herald Tribune* was a symbol of well-heeled pedigree, a voice of the Eastern Republican establishment, but it was there that Breslin punctured pompous balloons and poked fun at pretentiousness, treating the alma mater of Marvin the Torch, Attica State Prison, with as much awe as if it were Harvard. Breslin did this in a unified prose style, much like a short story, unlike the blunter satiric style of such columnists as Art Buchwald or Mike Royko, who seldom use fiction devices.

Breslin wrote with passion about the deprived, about Southern blacks on freedom marches, and soldiers dying in Indochina jungles. When the *Herald Tribune* editors sent him to cover a story in Alabama or Vietnam, Breslin could be counted on to bring back a uniquely human impression, usually about people on the periphery of the main event. In one such story, "A Death in Emergency Room One," Breslin wrote about a surgeon at Parkland Memorial Hospital in Dallas, called to try to save the dying President Kennedy: "Now, Malcolm Perry's long fingers ran over the chest under him and tried to get a heart beat, and even the suggestion of breathing, and there was nothing. There was only the still body, pale white in the light, and it kept bleeding, and now Malcolm Perry started to call for things and move his hands quickly because it was all running out."[43]

In writing about Kennedy's death Breslin was up against fierce competition with many other first-rate newsmen. Breslin did what came naturally—write about a little-known figure, the doctor. His widely praised effort was honored with Sigma Delta Chi's National Award for Reporting in 1964. Another unique Breslin story was an interview with the man who dug the President's grave in Arlington National Cemetery, humanizing an aspect of a monumental crisis.

When the *Herald Tribune* folded in 1966, Breslin wrote for the *World-Journal-Tribune*, then for the New York *Post*. His column was syndicated, but only to a few papers, and the restless Breslin then joined *New York* magazine as a contributing editor and vice president, writing frequently on topics ranging from local political issues to Marvin the Torch.

In 1968 Breslin was attracted to the political campaign of Robert Kennedy. He wrote many dispatches along the campaign trail and was in Los Angeles when Kennedy was shot. Again, Breslin wrote a moving account of the pandemonium and horror as another Kennedy lay dying. Covering Kennedy's campaign was a natural for Breslin because the late Senator was widely admired by many of Breslin's people—blacks, hardhats, the poor and the young:

> Bobby Kennedy began his campaign . . . with his right leg shaking and his hands trembling and his voice flat with nervousness. He began it this way and then his people came to help him. His people were the 14,000 young who were in the building. They were not Eastern young, with long hair and shades. These were Kansas young with scrubbed faces and haircuts and ties. But they were young and their faces told Bobby Kennedy, yes, we do not want to live in what they were trying to give us, and they shouted to him and his leg calmed and his hand began waving and his voice became very strong.[44]

In 1969 Breslin seemed to be switching to novelist. But his novel *The*

Gang That Couldn't Shoot Straight grew from his reporting and is built on a favorite Breslin notion that most of organized crime is highly unorganized, run by a sleazy band of incompetents. This passage about a Mafia chieftain and his wife reflects Breslin's view: "Mrs. Baccala slid behind the wheel of a black Cadillac. Baccala sat down on the kitchen floor and closed his eyes and folded his arms over his face. Mrs. Baccala started the car. When the car did not blow up from a bomb, Baccala got up from the kitchen floor and walked out into the driveway, patted Mrs. Baccala on the head as she came out of the car, got in, and backed down the driveway."[45]

Breslin left *New York* and turned to writing a novel about Ireland. Seymour Krim, a co-worker on the *Herald Tribune,* doubtless spoke for many readers in suggesting that writers like Breslin should stay with reportage instead of writing indifferent novels. Krim is not uncritical of Breslin's reporting, pointing out that he himself covered stories on a follow-up basis after Breslin had cut a swath through them and found that Breslin's work was marred by mistakes in names, embellished quotations, emotional sidings with one party to a dispute, and highly colored versions of events. Nonetheless, Krim credited Breslin with writing stories that were, as he put it, "doubly important to the life of our time because not only did they entertain, engross, make you laugh, even bring on an embarrassing snuffle to the nose and that damned fluid to the eye—do everything that fiction was traditionally supposed to do—they also put you in touch with a whole section of society that fate had heretofore crossed off your list."[46]

Capote and Mailer: From Fiction to Nonfiction

Their images as novelists fading, Truman Capote and Norman Mailer joined the experiment. In the sixties, first Capote, then Mailer produced book-length new nonfiction. Their reputations and craftsmanship quickly placed them in the front ranks of those who practiced the new form. Different in temperament, upbringing, and method, Capote and Mailer have little in common except talent.

Capote had long wanted to explore reportage as a literary method, even though "most good writers, good literary craftsmen, seldom use this metier," he told Roy Newquist, a Chicago newsman, in a radio interview. Capote said he considered John Hersey a first-rate journalist and an excellent writer, but not an artist. Even the remarkable Rebecca West, he said, "doesn't do what I'm talking about." Capote reasoned that "a factual piece of work could explore whole new dimensions in writing." In his quest for a subject that would help him develop a new method, Capote decided to choose a topic "truly banal." Asking himself what was the most banal thing in journalism, he decided it was "an interview with a film star, the kind of thing you would see in *Photoplay* magazine." After interviewing Marlon Brando, Capote spent a full year writing and polishing his product. The result was a sensitive article that appeared in the *New Yorker*. Capote said of himself: "I worked on other things, now feeling in complete control of myself within this form, becoming technically adept, just like one becomes technically adept at drawing skeletons to become a doctor. What I wanted to do, of course, was a great deal more ambitious than sketching skeletons. I was going to fill it in, flesh it out."[47]

Several years passed before Capote found his subject—and then it happened at an unlikely moment as he scanned the business section of the New York *Times*. A small item, EISENHOWER APPOINTEE MURDERED, told of the mysterious murder of a Western Kansas wheat grower, his wife, and two children. Capote says he "suddenly realized that perhaps a crime . . . would be the ideal subject for the massive job of reportage I wanted to do. I would have a wide range of characters, and most importantly, it would be timeless," an event that would stir "permanent emotions in people."[40] The result was *In Cold Blood*.

Born in New Orleans in 1924, Capote had been a writer since his early years, but his experience was in the South and the East, not the Middle West. The mentality of the midlands intrigued him, and he embarked on his experimental venture determined to create "a new art form." One of the tools that would help him create it was an aural memory technique he had developed in interviewing Brando which enabled him to remember a conversation an hour later. Believing that a tape recorder would inhibit his subjects, he trained himself to remember conversations almost verbatim. (The extent to which Capote mastered this technique has been challenged by a knowledgeable Kansas newspaper editor who says Capote relied on his cousin, author Harper Lee, to take shorthand notes during some interviews.) Capote spent six years researching and writing the book about the Clutter family murder. His fetish for absolute accuracy was commended by author and critic Granville Hicks in *Saturday Review*: "Although the testimony of eye-witnesses, as anyone knows who has ever sat on a jury, is never quite dependable, Capote, by an elaborate process of checking and cross-checking, has probably come as close to the facts of his case as is humanly possible."

The installments of *In Cold Blood* began appearing in the *New Yorker* as "Annals of Crime" in September 1965. The articles satisfied Capote's conviction that journalism could yield a serious art form. But by the time the book version appeared, Capote's work had become the center of controversy. Some writers disputed that it was a new art form. Others questioned the accuracy of the scenes Capote had reconstructed. One critic suggested that earlier publication might have aided the case of the two convicted murderers, who had been executed by the time the articles appeared. But there was almost universal agreement that the book was written with extraordinary skill. The real-life dialogue, the images, even the point of view won high praise. The New York *Times* found the book "remarkable, tensely exciting, superbly written," and other reviewers agreed. Capote captured the gentle, quiescent mood of the town where the murder occurred:

> The village of Holcomb stands on the high wheat plains of Western Kansas, a lonesome area that other Kansans call "out there." Some seventy miles east of the Colorado border, the countryside, with its hard blue skies and desert-clear air, has an atmosphere that is rather more Far Western than Middle West. The local accent is barbed with a prairie twang, a ranch-hand nasalness, and the men, many of them, wear narrow frontier trousers, Stetsons, and high-heeled boots with pointed toes. The land is flat, and the views are awesomely extensive; horses, herds of cattle, a white cluster of grain elevators rising as gracefully as Greek temples are visible long before a traveler reaches them.[49]

And the horror of a witness who identified the bodies of the Clutter family:

> The sheriff was wearing a hip pistol, and when we started up the stairs, going to Nancy's room, I noticed he kept his hand on it, ready to draw.
>
> Well, it was pretty bad. That wonderful girl—but you would never have known her. She'd been shot in the back of the head with a shotgun held maybe two inches away. She was lying on her side, facing the wall, and the wall was covered with blood. The bedcovers were drawn up to her shoulders. Sheriff Robinson, he pulled them back, and we saw she was wearing a bathrobe, pajamas, socks, and slippers—like, whenever it happened, she hadn't gone to bed yet. Her hands were tied behind her, and her ankles were roped together with the kind of cord you see on Venetian blinds. Sheriff said, "Is this Nancy Clutter?"—he'd never seen the child before. And I said, "Yes. Yes, that's Nancy."[50]

In portraying the two men who were convicted of the murder, Richard Hickock and Perry Smith, Capote relied less on the piling-up of detail than on impressionism and atmosphere, building slowly to a vivid image, as in this passage:

> . . . The young man breakfasting in a cafe called the Little Jewel never drank coffee. He preferred root beer. Three aspirin, cold root beer, and a chain of Pall Mall cigarettes—that was his notion of a proper "chow-down." Sipping and smoking, he studies a map spread on the counter before him—a Phillips 66 map of Mexico—but it was difficult to concentrate, for he was expecting a friend, and the friend was late.[51]

With dramatic force Capote describes one of the executions:

The hangman coughed—impatiently lifted his cowboy hat and settled it again, a gesture somehow reminiscent of a turkey buzzard huffing, then smoothing its neck feathers—and Hickock, nudged by an attendant, mounted the scaffold steps. "The Lord giveth, the Lord taketh away. Blessed is the name of the Lord," the chaplain intoned, as the rain sound accelerated, as the noose was fitted, and as a delicate black mask was tied around the prisoner's eyes. "May the Lord have mercy on your soul." The trap door opened, and Hickock hung for all to see a full twenty minutes before the prison doctor at last said, "I pronounce this man dead."[52]

By 1971 more than three million copies of In Cold Blood had been sold in the United States alone. Encouraged by this response, Capote said he would continue to use such reportage, announcing that he planned to write a book that would follow a cleaning woman by night, gaining her view of the people who employ her, interviewing her employers by day, thus contrasting two markedly different outlooks. Still fascinated with capital punishment, Capote also was researching a multiple murder case in Nebraska.

Norman Mailer is as noisy as Capote is quiet. While Capote almost never injects himself into his writing, Mailer usually makes himself the central figure. In Armies of the Night, his third-person-but-autobiographical contribution to the new journalism, Mailer described himself as a "warrior, presumptive general, ex-political candidate, embattled aging enfant terrible of the literary world, wise father of six children, radical intellectual, existential philosopher, hard working author, champion of obscenity, husband of four battling sweet wives, amiable bar drinker, and much exaggerated street fighter, party giver and hostess insulter."

Like Capote, Mailer was an established writer long before undertaking to develop his own method of writing the new nonfiction. When, shortly after World War II, he wrote the best-selling war novel, The Naked and the Dead, he was only twenty-five. In 1965, William Buckley called him the "single best-known living American writer." Born in 1923 in New Jersey and raised in Brooklyn, Mailer took an engineering degree at Harvard in 1943, then studied at the Sorbonne and entered the military service. After his first novel, his next novels, Barbary Shore and The Deer Park, sold briskly, though they were not strong successes. He contributed to many literary magazines and was a founder of the radical journal Dissent, helped establish the New York Village Voice, and in 1962 became a monthly columnist for Esquire.

Advertisements for Myself, a 1959 collection of essays and reportage, began to venture farther into nonfiction, but it was a 1960 Esquire article, "Existential Hero: Superman Comes to the Supermarket," on the presidential nomination of John Kennedy, that, as critic Theodore Solotaroff put it, was a harbinger "initiating the vogue of personal journalism or reportage, that was to burgeon in the ensuing years, as it always has in times of strife when literary men are drawn toward the drama of events and issues and to the human burden of their meaning."[53] Thus Mailer viewed John Kennedy: "His personal quality had a subtle, not quite describable intensity, a suggestion of dry pent heat perhaps, his eyes large, the pupils gray, the whites prominent, almost shocking, his most forceful feature: he had the eyes of a mountaineer. His appearance changed with his mood, strikingly so, and this made him always more interesting than what he was saying."[54]

The complete contemporary man, Mailer avoids the periphery to burrow into the critical center. This is demonstrated by *Armies of the Night*, his first book-length example of the new nonfiction. Mailer begins it by throwing down the gauntlet to the old journalism, quoting an item from *Time* which described Mailer's antics at a 1967 antiwar forum in Washington, then declaring, "Now we may leave *Time* in order to find out what happened." Then for more than 300 pages the reader is situated inside Mailer's mind to get his view of what happened. Initially, the third-person references seem a little strange: "the phone rang one morning and Norman Mailer, operating on his own principle of war games and random play, picked it up. That was not characteristic of Mailer." But like Talese, Mailer was offering an interior monologue—his own. Consider this scene between Mailer and poet Robert Lowell:

> "You know, Norman," said Lowell in his fondest voice, "Elizabeth and I really think you're the finest journalist in America."
> Mailer knew Lowell thought this—Lowell had even sent him a postcard once to state the enthusiasm. But the novelist had been shrewd enough to judge that Lowell sent many postcards to many people—it did not matter that Lowell was by overwhelming consensus judged to be the best, most talented, and most distinguished poet in America—it was still necessary to keep the defense lines in good working order. A good word on a card could keep many a dangerous recalcitrant in the ranks. Therefore, this practice annoyed Mailer.[55]

Chronicling the antiwar protest march on Washington, D.C., in 1967, the book takes the reader both to the inner counsels of the planners and to the front ranks of those who put their bodies on the line at the Pentagon against the U.S. Government. Here Mailer describes a scene from the demonstration:

> On the Mall, since the oncoming night was cold, bonfires were lit. On the stairs, a peace pipe was passed. It was filled with hashish. Soon the demonstrators were breaking out marijuana, handing it back and forth, offering it even to the soldiers here and there. The Army after all had been smoking marijuana since Korea, and in Vietnam—by all the reports—were gorging on it. The smell of the drug, sweet as the

sweetest leaves of burning tea, floated down to the Mall where its sharp bite of sugar and smoldering grass pinched the nose, relaxed the neck. Soon most of the young on the Mall were smoking as well. Can this be one of the moments when the Secretary of Defense looks out from his window in the Pentagon at the crowd on the Mall and studies their fires below? They cannot be unreminiscent of other campfires in Washington and Virginia little more than a century ago. The Secretary of Defense is by all reports a complex man, a reader of poetry—does he have a secret admiration for the works of Robert Lowell as he stands by the window?

But what has happened to Lowell, to MacDonald and Lowell, to Dellinger, to Dr. Spock, and Father Rise, and Lens, and all? We must move on.[56]

A feeling for the country and its internal conflict over the war is on Mailer's mind throughout the book. "Brood," he says, "on that country who expresses our will. She is America, once a beauty of magnificence unparalleled, now a beauty with a leprous skin. . . . Deliver us from our curse, for we must end on the road to that mystery where courage, death, and the dream of love give promise of sleep."

Armies of the Night won wide critical acclaim, the National Book Award, and the Pulitzer Prize. That same year, 1968, Mailer wrote *Miami and the Siege of Chicago*, an informal history of the 1968 Republican and Democratic conventions. Again he came face to face with a great public issue and again used a third-person autobiographical technique:

> And had no second thoughts about anything all the while he was writing the piece—except for Spiro Agnew. The Greek was conducting himself like a Turk. There was a day when he accused Hubert Humphrey of being soft on Communism. Everyone knew that Communism was the only belief Hubert Humphrey had ever been hard on. Nixon had obviously gotten himself an ignoramus or a liar. So while the writer thought that the Republic might survive a little longer with old Tricky Dick and New Nixon than Triple Hips, Norman Mailer would probably not vote unless it was for Eldridge Cleaver.[57]

A stream-of-consciousness book about the space program, *Of a Fire on the Moon*, also stirred controversy when it was published in 1970, but Mailer's most provocative effort may be *The Prisoner of Sex*, which was printed in its entirety in *Harper's* magazine in 1971. Los Angeles *Times* critic Digby Diehl wrote of the book: "And so Norman Mailer, having been crowned chief male chauvinist pig by Kate Millett and Co., determined to do a job on women's liberation that would be a credit to even Marvin the Torch. . . . The result is an explosive, witty, thoughtful and surely outrageous . . . book . . . a massive amalgam of polemic, literary criticism, biography, philosophy and biological musings."

This brand of nonfiction is so intensely personal that most of those who dislike Mailer automatically dislike his writing. From the vantage point of Mailer's mind the reader gets a voyeur's-eye view of social turbulence and interpersonal bickering. Above all, though, there is what Diehl calls his "freight-train rush of ideas." Not all are valuable, of course, and the wild mingling of the valuable and the artificial often makes it seem that Mailer's ups and downs are total. But ideas are his greatest strength—and a pit for his imitators. Because they do not have the ideas that inform Mailer's work, those who imitate him are able to match only his self-indulgence. One young writer who cured himself of trying to be Mailer, a graduate assistant in journalism at the University of Illinois named Daniel J. Balz, observed in the September/October 1971 issue of *Columbia Journalism Review*:

> Norman Mailer's *Armies of the Night*, as most now recognize, pushed us even further because hundreds of us had gone to the Pentagon, either as participants or reporters, and had failed to come to grips with it in any way comparable to Mailer. Of course we blamed that on form, not on ourselves. We didn't relate Mailer's earlier political pieces, his reports on the 1960 and 1964 conventions, to the Pentagon book. We simply related the book to what we had written—form against form—and believed Mailerian thoughts rested in all of us, waiting to be sprung.

And Others

We have described Lillian Ross, Gay Talese, Jimmy Breslin, Truman Capote, Norman Mailer, and Tom Wolfe at some length—first, because they are chiefly responsible for developing the new nonfiction and, second, because most of their reportage quite clearly applies the techniques of fiction writing to the writing of nonfiction.

There are others, of course, no doubt hundreds, considering the appeal of the new nonfiction. A few widely known writers should be considered on the periphery of the new nonfiction because they use the techniques at least intermittently.

Joan Didion is a novelist and critic whose brilliantly witty pieces on the Haight-Ashbury and new life styles have appeared in the *New York Times Magazine*, *Saturday Evening Post*, and *Holiday*. Her graceful style, writer Dan Wakefield said, "deserves a wide audience among readers who may still be turned on by such qualities as grace, sophistication, nuance, irony." In a collection of her essays and reportage titled *Slouching Towards Bethlehem*, she wrote, "My only advantage as a reporter is that I am so physically small, so temperamentally unobtrusive, and so neurotically inarticulate that people tend to forget that my presence runs counter to their best interests. And it always does. That is the one last thing to remember: *writers are always selling somebody out*."[58]

George Plimpton, journalistic activist, has been both the subject and practitioner of new nonfiction techniques. Building his reputation as editor of the *Paris Review,* whose "Writers at Work" pieces made important observations about some of the century's greatest writers, Plimpton practices a kind of participatory journalism which results in autobiographical accounts like *Paper Lion,* Plimpton's story of himself as a novice football player for the Detroit Lions. Probably because Plimpton writes primarily about sports, he is not usually included among the new journalists, but *Paper Lion* and several of his articles are models of participatory reportage that yield unusually graphic scenes.

Studs Terkel, who is known primarily as a Chicago radio and television interviewer, gained some national attention in the late sixties with his *Division Street, America,* interviews with ordinary people which explain the human fabric of the city. The book was so successful that Terkel wrote another, *Hard Times: An Oral History of the Depression,* which mixes the views of the famous and the little-known to create a sensitive portrait of the monumental period that Terkel considers a major gap between generations.

Others who often use fiction methods in writing nonfiction include:

☐ Michael J. Arlen, a frequent contributor to magazines and author of *Living Room War;*

☐ Stanley Booth, who often writes for *Playboy* and wrote the inventive *The True Adventures of the Rolling Stones Outlaw Band;*

☐ David Halberstam, a forceful writer who won a Pulitzer Prize for his Vietnam reporting for the New York *Times,* also author of *The Unfinished Odyssey of Robert Kennedy* and *The Best and the Brightest;*

☐ Larry L. King, author of the award-winning *Confessions of a White Racist;*

☐ Calvin Trillin, who collected his articles for the *New Yorker* in the readable and perceptive book, *U.S. Journal;*

☐ Nat Hentoff, who writes for the *Village Voice* and many magazines;

☐ Hunter S. Thompson, author of *Hell's Angels* and *Fear and Loathing in Las Vegas,* who has enlivened *Rolling Stone* with exciting, first-person political pieces, assembled as *Fear and Loathing on the Campaign Trail.*

The staff of *New York,* which Wolfe has called "the red-hot center of the New Journalism," has several first-rate practitioners of the new nonfiction, among them Peter Blake, Jane O'Reilly, Fred Powledge, Edwin Diamond, Nicholas Pileggi, and Gail Sheehy.

The Editors

As always, those who orchestrate the action are obscure to the reading public. It is not possible to identify all of the editors who helped develop the new nonfiction, but three should be mentioned.

During his four years (1967-71) as editor of *Harper's*, Willie Morris, himself an excellent writer, became widely known as a writer's editor, one who encouraged writers to experiment with new forms and approaches. Halberstam, King, and John Corry are among the writers who pay tribute to Morris for allowing them to treat experience unconventionally, and it was Morris's *Harper's* that gave Norman Mailer the chance to display his unique form of participatory journalism.

Harold Hayes, editor of *Esquire* from 1956 to 1973, played a pivotal role in developing the work of Tom Wolfe and Gay Talese, primarily by opening the pages of *Esquire* to imaginative reportage. He says, "If there's any great change to accelerate the possibility of writers dealing more flexibly with language and with form, it's not because of the birth of a new journalistic form, but because there is a commercial disposition among magazines to see the more imaginative writing now is more appealing to their readers." The magazines, Hayes says, "express themselves better because writers are expressing themselves better."

Esquire's influence in the development of the new nonfiction was the result of a happy coincidence. The magazine's fortunes sagged in the late 1950s and "it was obvious that we needed to once again establish ourselves as a unique magazine," said Hayes. "We decided to go to very good writers." There were at the same time such writers as Mailer, Gore Vidal, William Styron, and James Baldwin who "wanted to express themselves in nonfiction on the issues of the day." Said Hayes, "We suited each other's purposes. For these writers the move to *Esquire* was a step down critically; but a step up in terms of national exposure."

While the big-name fiction artists were displaying their wares in *Esquire*, the magazine functioned in an eclectec, unconstricted manner and offered encouragement to young writers like Wolfe and Talese.

Unlike *Harper's* under Morris, *Esquire* under Hayes attempted to maintain a balance between writing and editing. "Often the idea for a story has started with the magazine, not the writer," said Hayes. "The idea is central to what is done: for example, many of Mailer's pieces were done on direct assignment." It is the job of the editor to "keep writers stylistically oriented to the center of the magazine."

Clay Felker, the editor of *New York* since it began as an independent magazine in 1967, certainly belongs in the front rank of editors who have been midwives to the new nonfiction. Like Morris and Hayes, he is a writer's editor. "I can't tell intelligent and accomplished writers how to think," he says. Rather than prescribing subjects and guiding the writing, he encourages his writers to "pinpoint important trends before they become universal" and challenges his writers' ideas. Gloria Steinem has said of Felker, "Clay is a walking test area for ideas. He grasps them, makes them grow—and doesn't care where they come from."

The task of the editor is complex, especially when the magazine of general appeal must find a place for itself among a growing multiplicity of media. In such a time, the development of a new form requires an editor with courage and vision. Although his influence is difficult to measure, it is impossible to disregard.

The New Nonfiction: An Example

THE LAST AMERICAN HERO

by Tom Wolfe

This example of the new nonfiction shows Tom Wolfe at his best. Although it is doubtful that any example can illustrate the wide range of new nonfiction—Gay Talese's writing is much quieter, and so is Lillian Ross's, and even Truman Capote's—almost everything Wolfe writes illustrates the freedom of the form. In fact, as the following passage indicates, the new nonfiction has no "form," especially if one compares its many styles to the formulas of conventional journalism.

Sunday! Racing day! There is the Coca-Cola sign out where the road leads in from the highway, and hills and trees, but here are long concrete grandstands for about 17,000 and a paved five-eighths-mile oval. Practically all the drivers are out there with their cars and their crews, a lot of guys in white coveralls. The cars look huge . . . and curiously nude and blind. All the chrome is stripped off, except for the grilles. The headlights are blanked out. Most of the cars are in the pits. The so-called "pit" is a paved cutoff on the edge of the infield. It cuts off from the track itself like a service road off an expressway at the shopping center. Every now and then a car splutters, hacks, coughs, hocks a lunga, rumbles out onto the track for a practice run. There is a lot of esoteric conversation going on, speculation, worries, memoirs:

"What happened?"

"Mother—condensed on me. Al brought it up here with him. Water in the line."

"Better keep Al away from a stable, he'll fill you up with horse manure."

". . . they told me to give him one, a creampuff, so I give him one, a creampuff. One goddam race and the son of a bitch, he *melted* it. . . ."

". . . he's down there right now pettin' and rubbin' and huggin' that car just like those guys do a horse at the Kentucky Derby. . . ."

". . . They'll blow you right out of the tub. . . ."

". . . No, the quarter inch, and go on over and see if you can get Ned's blowtorch. . . ."

". . . Rear end's loose. . . ."

"... I don't reckon this right here's got nothing to do with it, do you? ..."

"... Aw, I don't know, about yea big. ..."

"... Who the hell stacked them gumballs on the bottom? ..."

"... th'owing rocks. ..."

"... won't turn seven thousand. ..."

"... strokin' it. ..."

"... blistered. ..."

"... spun out. ..."

"... muvva. ..."

Then, finally, here comes Junior Johnson. How he does come on. He comes tooling across the infield in a big white dreamboat, a brand-new white Pontiac Catalina four-door hard-top sedan. He pulls up and as he gets out he seems to get more and more huge. First his crew-cut head and then a big jaw and then a bigger neck and then a huge torso, like a wrestler's, all done up rather modish and California modern, with a red-and-white candy-striped sport shirt, white ducks and loafers.

"How you doing?" says Junior Johnson, shaking hands, and then he says, "Hot enough for ye'uns?"

Junior is in an amiable mood. Like most up-hollow people, it turns out, Junior is reserved. His face seldom shows an emotion. He has three basic looks: amiable, amiable and a little shy, and dead serious. To a lot of people, apparently, Junior's dead-serious look seems menacing. There are no cowards left in stock car racing, but a couple of drivers tell me that one of the things that can shake you up is to look into your rear-view mirror going around a curve and see Junior Johnson's car on your tail trying to "root you out of the groove," and then get a glimpse of Junior's dead-serious look. I think some of the sportswriters are afraid of him. One of them tells me Junior is strong, silent—and explosive. Junior will only give you three answers, "Uh-huh," "Uh-unh," and "I don' know," and so forth and so on. Actually, I found he handles questions easily. He has a great technical knowledge of automobiles and the physics of speed, including things he never fools with, such as Offenhauser engines. What he never does offer, however, is small talk. This gives him a built-in poise, since it deprives him of the chance to say anything asinine. "Ye'uns," "we'uns," "H'it" for "it," "Growed" for "grew" and a lot of other unusual past participles—Junior uses certain older forms of English, not exactly "Elizabethan," as they are sometimes called, but older forms of English preserved up-country in his territory, Ingle Hollow.

Kids keep coming up for Junior's autograph and others are just hanging around and one little old boy comes up, he is about thirteen, and Junior says: "This boy here goes coon hunting with me."

One of the sportswriters is standing around, saying: "What do you shoot a coon with?"

"Don't shoot 'em. The dogs tree 'em and then you flush 'em out and the dogs fight 'em."

"Flush 'em out?"

"Yeah. This boy right here can flush 'em out better than anybody you ever did see. You go out at night with the dogs, and soon as they get the scent, they start barking. They go on out ahead of you and when they tree a coon, you can tell it, by the way they sound. They all start baying up at that coon—h'it sounds like, I don't know, you hear it once and you not likely to forget it. Then you send a little old boy up to flush him out and he jumps down and the dogs fight him."

"How does a boy flush him out?"

"Aw, he just climbs up there to the limb he's on and starts shaking h'it and the coon'll jump."

"What happens if the coon decides he'd rather come back after the boy instead of jumping down to a bunch of dogs?"

"He won't do that. A coon's afraid of a person, but he can kill a dog. A coon can take any dog you set against him if they's just the two of them fighting. The coon jumps down on the ground and he rolls right over on his back with his feet up, and he's *got* claws about like this. All he has to do is get a dog once in the throat or in the belly, and he can kill him, cut him wide open just like you took a knife and did it. Won't any dog even fight a coon except a coon dog."

"What kind of dogs are they?"

"*Coon* dogs, I guess. Black and tans they call 'em sometimes. They's bred for it. If his mammy and pappy wasn't coon dogs, he ain't likely to be one either. After you got one, you got to train him. You trap a coon, live, and then you put him in a pen and tie him to a post with a rope on him and then you put your dog in there and he has to fight him. Sometimes you get a dog just don't have any fight in him and he ain't no good to you."

Junior is in the pit area, standing around with his brother Fred, who is part of his crew, and Ray Fox and some other good old boys, in a general atmosphere of big stock car money, a big ramp truck for his car, a white Dodge, number 3, a big crew in white coveralls, huge stacks of racing tires, a Dodge P.R. man, big portable cans of gasoline, compressed air hoses, compressed water hoses, the whole business. Herb Nab, Freddie Lorenzen's chief mechanic, comes over and sits down on his haunches and Junior sits down on his haunches and Nab says:

"So Junior Johnson's going to drive a Ford."

Junior is switching from Dodge to Ford mainly because he hasn't been winning with the Dodge. Lorenzen drives a Ford, too, and the last year, when Junior was driving the Chevrolet, their duels were the biggest excitement in stock car racing.

"Well," says Nab, "I'll tell you, Junior. My ambition is going to be to outrun your ass every goddamned time we go out."

"That was your ambition last year," says Junior.

"I know it was," says Nab, "and you took all the money, didn't you? You know what my strategy was. I was going to outrun everybody else and outlast Junior, that was my strategy."

Setting off his California modern sport shirt and white ducks Junior has on a pair of twenty-dollar rimless sunglasses and a big gold Timex watch, and Flossie, his fiancée, is out there in the infield somewhere with the white Pontiac, and the white Dodge that Dodge gave Junior is parked up near the pit area—and then a little thing happens that brings the whole thing right back there to Wilkes County, North Carolina, to Ingle Hollow and to hard muscle in the clay gulches. A couple of good old boys come down to the front of the stands with the screen and the width of the track between them and Junior, and one of the good old boys comes down and yells out in the age-old baritone raw-curtle yell of the Southern hills:

"Hey! Hog jaw!"

Everybody gets quiet. They know he's yelling at Junior, but nobody says a thing. Junior doesn't even turn around.

"Hey, hog jaw! . . ."

Junior, he does nothing.

"Hey, hog jaw, I'm gonna get me one of them fastback roosters, too, and come down there and get you!"

Fastback rooster refers to the Ford—it has a "fastback" design—Junior is switching to.

"Hey, hog jaw, I'm gonna get me one of them fastback roosters and run you right out of here, you hear me, hog jaw!"

One of the good old boys alongside Junior says, "Junior, go on up there and clear out those stands."

Then everybody stares at Junior to see what he's gonna do. Junior, he don't even look around. He just looks a bit dead serious.

"Hey, hog jaw, you got six cases of whiskey in the back of that car you want to let me have?"

"What you hauling in that car, hog jaw!"

"Tell him you're out of that business, Junior," one of the good old boys says.

"Go on up there and clean house, Junior," says another good old boy.

Then Junior looks up, without looking at the stands, and smiles a little and says, "You flush him down here out of that tree—and I'll take keer of him."

Such a howl goes up from the good old boys! It is almost a blood curdle—

"Goddam, he *will*, too!"

"Lord, he better know how to do an *about-face* hissef if he comes down here!"

"Goddam, get him, Junior!"

"Whooeeee!"

"Mother dog!"

—a kind of orgy of reminiscence of the old Junior before the Detroit money started flowing, wild *combats d'honneur* up-hollow—and, suddenly, when he heard that unearthly baying coming up from the good old boys in the pits, the good old boy retreated from the edge of the stands and never came back.

Later on Junior told me, sort of apologetically, "H'it used to be, if a fellow crowded me just a little bit, I was ready to crawl him. I reckon that was one good thing about Chillicothe.

"I don't want to pull any more time," Junior tells me, "but I wouldn't take anything in the world for the experience I had in prison. If a man needed to change, that was the place to change. H'it's not a waste of time there, h'it's good experience.

"H'it's that they's so many people in the world that feel that nobody is going to tell them what to do. I had quite a temper, I reckon. I always had the idea that I had as much sense as the other person and I didn't want him to tell me what to do. In the penitentiary there I found out that I could listen to another fellow and be told what to do and h'it wouldn't kill me."

Starting time! Linda Vaughn, with the big blonde hair and blossomy breasts, puts down her Coca-Cola and the potato chips and slips off her red stretch pants and her white blouse and walks out of the officials' booth in her Rake-a-cheek red show-girl's costume with her long honeydew legs in net stockings and climbs up on the red Firebird float. The Life Symbol of stock car racing! Yes! Linda, every luscious morsel of Linda, is a good old girl from Atlanta who was made Miss Atlanta International Raceway one year and was paraded around the track on a float and she liked it so much and all the good old boys liked it so much, Linda's flowing hair and blossomy breasts and honeydew legs, that she became the permanent glamor symbol of stock car racing, and never mind this other modeling she was doing . . . this, she liked it. Right before practically every race on the Grand National circuit Linda Vaughn puts down her Coca-Cola and potato chips. Her momma is there, she generally comes around to see Linda go around the track on the float, it's such a nice spectacle seeing Linda looking so lovely, and the applause and all. "Linda, I'm thirstin', would you bring me a Coca-Cola?" "A lot of them think I'm Freddie Lorenzen's girl friend, but I'm not any of 'em's girl friend, I'm real good friends with 'em all, even Wendell," he being Wendell Scott, the only Negro in big-league stock car racing. Linda gets up on the Firebird float. This is an extraordinary object, made of wood, about twenty feet tall, in the shape of a huge bird, an eagle or something, blazing red, and Linda, with her red showgirl's suit on, gets up on the seat, which is up between the wings, like a saddle, high enough so her long honeydew legs stretch down, and a new car pulls her—Miss Firebird!—slowly once around the track just before the race. It is more of a ceremony by now than the national anthem. Miss Firebird sails slowly in front of the stands and the good old boys let out some real curdle Rebel yells, "Yaaaaaaaaaaa-aaghhhhooooooo! Let me at that car!" "Honey, you sure do start my motor, I swear to God!" 'Great God and Poonadingdong, I mean!"

And suddenly there's a big roar from behind, down in the infield, and then I see one of the great sights in stock car racing. That infield! The cars have been piling into the infield by the hundreds, parking in there on the clay and the grass, every which way, angled down and angled up, this way and that, where the ground is uneven, these beautiful blazing brand-new cars with the sun exploding off the windshields and the baked enamel and the glassy lacquer, hundreds, thousands of cars stacked this way and that in the infield with the sun bolting down and no shade, none at all, just a couple of Coca-Cola stands out there. And already the good old boys and girls are out beside the cars, with all these beautiful little buds in short shorts already spread-eagled out on top of the car roofs, pressing down on good hard slick automobile sheet metal, their little cupcake bottoms aimed up at the sun. The good old boys are lollygagging around with their shirts off and straw hats on that have miniature beer cans on the brims and buttons that read "Girls Wanted—No Experience Required." And everybody, good old boys and girls of all ages, are out there with portable charcoal barbecue ovens set up, and folding tubular steel terrace furniture, deck chairs and things, and Thermos jugs and coolers full of beer—and suddenly it is not the up-country South at all but a concentration of the modern suburbs, all jammed into that one space, from all over America, with blazing cars and instant goodies, all cooking under the bare blaze—inside a strange bowl. The infield is like the bottom of a bowl. The track around it is banked so steeply at the corners and even on the straightaways, it is like the steep sides of a bowl. The wall around the track, and the stands and the bleachers are like the rim of a bowl. And from the infield, in this great incredible press of blazing new cars, there is no horizon but the bowl, up above only that cobalt-blue North Carolina sky. And then suddenly, on a signal, thirty stock car engines start up where they are lined up in front of the stands. The roar of these engines is impossible to describe. They have a simultaneous rasp, thunder and rumble that goes right through a body and fills the whole bowl with a noise of internal combustion. Then they start around on two build-up runs, just to build up speed, and then they come around the fourth turn and onto the straightaway in front of the stands at—here, 130 miles an hour, in Atlanta, 160 miles an hour, at Daytona, 180 miles an hour—and the flag goes down and everybody in the infield and in the stands is up on their feet going mad, and suddenly here is a bowl that is one great orgy of everything in the way of excitement and liberation the automobile has meant to Americans. An orgy!

The first lap of a stock car race is a horrendous, a wildly horrendous spectacle such as no other sport approaches. Twenty, thirty, forty automobiles, each of them weighing almost two tons, 3700 pounds, with 427-cubic-inch engines, 600 horsepower, are practically locked together, side to side and tail to nose, on a narrow bank of asphalt at 130, 160, 180 miles an hour, hitting the curves so hard the rubber burns off the tires in front of your eyes. To the driver, it is like being inside a car going down the West Side Highway in New York City at rush hour, only with everybody going literally three to four times as fast, at speeds a man who has gone eighty-five miles an hour down a highway cannot conceive of, and with every other driver an enemy who is willing to cut inside of you, around you or in front of you, or ricochet off your side in the battle to get into a curve first.

The speeds are faster than those in the Indianapolis 500 race, the cars are more powerful and much heavier. The prize money in Southern stock car racing is far greater than that in Indianapolis-style or European Grand Prix racing, but few Indianapolis or Grand Prix drivers have the raw nerve required to succeed at it.

Although they will deny it, it is still true that stock car drivers will put each other "up against the wall"—cut inside on the left of another car and ram it into a spin—if they get mad enough. Crashes are not the only danger, however. The cars are now literally too fast for their own parts, especially the tires. Firestone and Goodyear have poured millions into stock car racing, but neither they nor anybody so far have been able to come up with a tire for this kind of racing at the current speeds. Three well-known stock car drivers were killed last year, two of them champion drivers, Joe Weatherly and Fireball Roberts, and another, one of the best new drivers, Jimmy Pardue, from Junior Johnson's own home territory, Wilkes County, North Carolina. Roberts was the only one killed in a crash. Junior Johnson was in the crash but was not injured. Weatherly and Pardue both lost control on curves. Pardue's death came during a tire test. In a tire test, engineers from Firestone or Goodyear try out various tires on a car, and the driver, always one of the top competitors, tests them at top speed, usually on the Atlanta track. The drivers are paid three dollars a mile and may drive as much as five or six hundred miles in a single day. At 145 miles an hour average that does not take very long. Anyway, these drivers are going at speeds that, on curves, can tear tires off their casings or break axles. They practically run off from over their own wheels.

Notes

[1] Theodore Solotaroff, *The Red Hot Vacuum and Other Pieces on the Writing of the Sixties* (New York: Atheneum, 1970), ix.

[2] *Ibid.*, p. 151.

[3] L. W. Robinson, Harold Hayes, Gay Talese, Tom Wolfe, "The New Journalism," *Writer's Digest*, January 1970, p. 32.

[4] Tom Wolfe, "The New Journalism," *Bulletin* (of the American Society of Newspaper Editors), September 1970, pp. 19-20.

[5] Dan Wakefield, "The Personal Voice and the Impersonal Eye," *Atlantic*, June 1966, p. 86.

[6] Solotaroff, iv.

[7] "Wolfe, Tom," *Current Biography*, January 1971, p. 42.

[8] *Ibid.*, p. 43.

[9] Tom Wolfe, *The Kandy-Kolored Tangerine-Flake Streamline Baby* (New York: Farrar, Straus & Giroux, 1965), xii.

[10] *Ibid.*, p. 96.

[11]Wolfe, "The New Journalism," p. 22.

[12]Tom Wolfe, *The Pump House Gang* (New York: Farrar, Straus & Giroux, 1968).

[13]*Ibid.*, p. 107.

[14]Tom Wolfe, *The Electric Kool-Aid Acid Test* (New York: Farrar, Straus & Giroux, 1968).

[15]Tom Wolfe, *Radical Chic and Mau-mauing the Flak-Catchers* (New York: Farrar, Straus & Giroux, 1970), p. 6.

[16]Linda Keuhl, "Dazzle-Dust: A Wolfe in Chic Clothing," *Commonweal*, May 7, 1971, p. 14.

[17]Wolfe, *Radical Chic*, p. 108.

[18]*Ibid.*, p. 113.

[19]"Invisible Observer," *Time*, May 1, 1964, p. 67.

[20]*Ibid.*

[21]"I Take a Lot of Notes," *Newsweek*, December 18, 1961, p. 102.

[22]Lillian Ross, *Reporting* (New York: Simon and Schuster, 1964), p. 189.

[23]*Ibid.*, p. 195.

[24]*Ibid.*, p. 221.

[25]*Ibid.*, pp. 25-26.

[26]*Ibid.*, p. 224.

[27]Wolfe, "The New Journalism," p. 18.

[28]Robinson, "The New Journalism," p. 33.

[29]Gay Talese, *Fame and Obscurity* (New York: World, 1970), ix.

[30]*Ibid.*, p. ix.

[31]*Ibid.*, p. 69.

[32]Robinson, p. 34.

[33]Gay Talese, *The Kingdom and the Power* (New York: World, 1969), p. 443.

[34]*Ibid.*, p. 2.

[35]*Ibid.*, p. 401.

[36]Solotaroff, p. 149.

[37]Robinson, p. 34.

[38]Talese, *Fame and Obscurity*, p. 8.

[39]"Portraits by Gay Talese: Fame and Obscurity," *Quill*, September 1970, p. 32.

[40]Jimmy Breslin, *The World of Jimmy Breslin* (New York: Ballantine, 1967).

[41]*Ibid.*, p. 3.

[42]*Ibid.*, p. 37.

[43]*Ibid.*, p. 188.

[44]*New York*, June 9, 1969.

[45]Jimmy Breslin, *The Gang That Couldn't Shoot Straight* (New York: Viking, 1969).

[46]Seymour Krim, "Won't You Come Home, Jim Breslin?" *New York Times Book Review*, March 1, 1970, p. 2.

[47]"Truman Capote," in *Counterpoint*, Roy Newquist, ed. (Chicago: Rand-McNally, 1964), p. 78.

[48]*Ibid.*

[49]Truman Capote, *In Cold Blood* (New York: Random House, 1965), p. 13.

[50]*Ibid.*, p. 78.

[51]*Ibid.*, p. 24.

[52]*Ibid.*, p. 380.

[53]Solotaroff, p. 285.

[54]Norman Mailer, "The Existential Hero: Superman Comes to the Supermarket," *Esquire*, November 1960, p. 119.

[55]Norman Mailer, *The Armies of the Night* (New York: New American Library, 1968), p. 32.

[56]*Ibid.*, p. 293.

[57]Norman Mailer, *Miami and the Siege of Chicago* (New York: New American Library, 1968), p. 223.

[58]Joan Didion, *Slouching Towards Bethlehem* (New York: Farrar, Straus & Giroux, 1969), xiv.

[59]Susan Sontag, *Against Interpretation* (New York: Dell, 1969), p. 5.

[60]Robinson, "The New Journalism," p. 33.

3

The Modern Muckrakers: Alternatives in Traditional Markets

The harpooner is seldom cherished by the whales . . . and so Gene Cervi was not universally loved.

—Tom Gavin, *Denver Post*

By almost any standard it seems to be no more than a small and unimpressive newspaper, struggling to maintain a tiny circulation. But the appearance of the feisty San Francisco *Bay Guardian* is deceptive. Its battles with the defense industry, media monopolies, and city planners as well as its efforts on behalf of consumers, the poor, and draftees have brought it national attention. Rare is the press critic who does not mention the *Guardian* as a first-rate alternative journal.

In the December 23, 1970, issue, which appeared a month after *Time* had published an appreciation of the paper, the *Guardian* asked:

> Why did *Time* mention several of the Guardian's major stories? PG & E's [Pacific Gas & Electric] illegal power monopoly in San Francisco? The cracking of the supermarket codes? The *Guardian's* suit against Superchron [the San Francisco *Chronicle*] and the Newspaper Preservation Act? Unrepresentative SF grand juries? The scramble for war bodies from Vietnam among local undertakers? The banning of the *Guardian* from the Press Club's Pulitzer of the West contest? U.S. Steel, the Ford Foundation, Chase Manhattan Bank, Mayor Alioto seeking to, as *Time* put it, "destroy the beauty of the city with high rises"? Why did *Time* say *Guardian* stories get "results," as well as praise and rewards? . . .

Obviously, *Time* respects the *Guardian*. So do other journalists who value investigative reporting. Many believe that some of the best investigative journalism is the work of *Guardian* editor Bruce Brugmann, San Francisco's modern muckraker.

Some discount Brugmann's work on the ground that his paper screams—and often—like the boy who cried wolf. But the *Guardian's* credibility was long enhanced by "Pulitzer of the West" awards from the San Francisco Press Club, an organization not likely to praise irresponsible sensationalism. Then, in 1969, as *Time* reported, "the club reworked the entry rules for the 'Pulitzer of the West' competition, effectively excluding the *Guardian* from entry. Brugmann claimed that the committee had too many *Guardian* victims on its board." An alternative editor in Denver agreed:

> Unbelievable tho it sounds, the *San Francisco Bay Guardian*, a crusading newspaper that tried to remain a weekly publication but was forced by fierce forces to reduce itself to a monthly was denied the right to enter a San Francisco Press Club annual awards contest even tho it had previously won the award. Disclosure of the membership of the Committee to conduct the "Pulitzer of the West" competition showed the Guardian was blackballed by non-newspaper members who were mainly public relations agents for giant California monopolies.[1]

The alternative journalism of the *Guardian* and similar papers elsewhere is part of the reformist surge identified with the new journalism of the sixties, although *Cervi's Rocky Mountain Journal* and New York's *Village Voice* are of earlier vintage. The alternative journals were founded to present news and information not available in the conventional press. Usually edited by veteran newsmen, the papers were also a reaction to "policy" in the conventional press, a term that sociologist Warren Breed, in his widely known study, "Social Control in the News Room," examined thus: "Every newspaper has a policy, admitted or not. One paper's policy may be pro Republican, cool to labor, antagonistic to the school board, etc. The principal areas of policy are politics, business, and labor; much of it stems from considerations of class. Policy is manifested in slanting."[2] Most alternative journalists quit conventional newspapers and magazines to start their own journals at least partly because they were unhappy with news room policies that were more often than not of a conservative, business-oriented persuasion.

To the late Eugene Cervi, alternative journalism was "personal journalism returned in the dress and format of the age." It strikes out at the impersonal, dehumanizing effect of corporate journalism, but seldom is it fullfledged advocacy. As an alternative editor in New Hampshire expressed it: "[We] were restive about the kind of journalism that advocates solutions or alternatives without presenting the facts." Alternative journalists are fact-finders, doggedly determined investigators. Brugmann adopted Civil War journalist William L. Storey's motto: "It is a newspaper's duty to print the news and raise hell." *Guardian* stories, he says, are "subjective journalism thoroughly checked for accuracy. I have no patience with objective reporting. . . . I aim my derringer at every reporter and tell him, 'By God, I don't want to see any objective pieces.' This is point-of-view journalism. We don't run a story until we feel we can prove it or make it stick."[3]

A theme of personal responsibility is strong in the alternative press. Cervi said, "I use my name with the name of my newspaper, not out of vanity, but as a self-imposed police force so anything which brings dishonor to my newspaper also brings dishonor to me and my family." One can hardly imagine such sentiments from corporate giants like Newhouse or Hearst.

Alternative journalism is a response not only to metropolitan dailies' sins of exclusion but also a reaction to their dehumanizing influence. To Cervi this was a prime consideration:

> I am against chain-owned newspapers. They fail to fix individual responsibility. They discourage the natural inclinations of man for self-expression. They are dedicated largely to the enrichment of absentee owners and only incidentally to public service as intended, in my opinion, by the men who included that precious right in the first amendment. . . . I am against any kind of distant, foreign, disinterested, obscure and/or otherwise irresponsible ownership of an instrument as powerful as the free press of the country.[4]

The alternative journalist attempts to point up the failings of even the largest and most impersonal of institutions—big business, big labor, and big government. Most alternative journalism is both issue and event oriented. In this sense it is unlike the traditional press, which is usually on an event-oriented threadmill with little regard for long-range trends, and unlike the underground press, which is almost entirely issue oriented. The alternative journalist takes a middle ground, covering compelling major events and at the same time digging for underlying causes and long-term consequences.

Most of the alternative journals considered here are edited by journalists who range in age from mid-twenties to late middle-age. Many are old reformers in the New Deal tradition, progressives, and latter-day populists. Most are liberals. Few are identified with the counterculture or the youth cult. The following examples suggest the range, but they do not make up a definitive inventory.

The Parochial Alternatives

Although they are located in far-flung corners of our national landscape, papers like the San Francisco *Bay Guardian, Cervi's Rocky Mountain Journal, Maine Times,* and the *Village Voice* are similar in many ways. All are blatantly parochial, intensely focused on local activities. They are not alternatives to vague constituencies of interest but instead to readers of specific newspapers like the San Francisco *Chronicle,* the Denver *Post,* and the New York *Times.* Much of their content, though vividly written and attractively displayed, has little meaning or interest for one who is not intimately acquainted with the political and economic forces in the area where each paper is published. The editors' eagerness to dig out stories neglected by the local press accounts for the success of the alternatives—that and the fact that they fight against the bland sameness which afflicts the traditional media, a sameness brought about by overreliance on wire services and stodgy reporting of the news of record. Dramatic proof of this sameness is demonstrated when one cuts out all the AP and UPI wire stories from the pages of almost any metropolitan daily. What remains is a confetti-like string of newsprint, little of it challenging.

Cervi's Rocky Mountain Journal

Few Denver residents actively urged a critical journal when Eugene Cervi, then a young reporter for Scripps-Howard's *Rocky Mountain News*, began his paper in 1949. This probably accounts for Cervi's initial caution. His paper was largely a service which provided Denver businessmen with news about real estate transactions, building permits, new businesses, bankruptcies, car sales, and construction projects. But Cervi's dream of an alternative newspaper had earlier origins. As he told it:

> We were standing at the press club bar in Denver one night during the latter part of the depression years. I was a red-hot Roosevelt man in those days. I was discussing the New Deal with a wholesale druggist—one of the fat cats of the community that we were delighted to have as an associate member of the press club to keep the doors open in those pre-Guild days.
>
> "Do you mean to tell me," I remember saying to my friend, "that a young man has a chance in this day and age to go out and start a newspaper for himself in the midst of all of these entrenched, monopolistic and greedy giants?" My friend, an older and wiser man, but still a fat cat, smiled and calmly said, "I certainly do, if you have the courage and are willing to work."[5]

As his performance over the years demonstrated, Cervi had both. Cervi became one of the most outspoken voices in American journalism, a fact acknowledged even by the lofty New York *Times*. The Denver *Post*, often a target of Cervi's gibes, called him "a lively, provocative, intelligent, colorful and tempestuous man who brought vitality and excitement to Denver journalism."

Denver *Post* columnist Tom Gavin has written that Cervi was often wrong, "but seven times in 10, he was right, searingly, piercingly, abrasively right. And listen, it's good for a community and for a community's so-called leaders—yes, and for its newspapers, too—to know that out there somewhere is somebody ready to shout and point and jump up and down in outrage when bum decisions are made."[6]

Cervi's paper, which has continued to grow in circulation despite the founder's death, is an unlikely combination of mundane business listings and hard-hitting investigative reporting. An example of the latter was a story in 1967 that took on some of Denver's most influential citizens: TAX-EXEMPT FOUNDATIONS ALLOW CUSTODIANS TO THROW WEIGHT AROUND. This was a four-part series that applied congressional studies of tax-exempt foundations to activities in the Denver area. A detailed analysis of "where money went" reinforced the impressionistic comments of the story.

Some of the other stories that helped build the reputation of *Cervi's Rocky Mountain Journal* are as follows:

> This newspaper does not trust City Hall on the mass transportation issue. This newspaper does not accept Mayor William H. McNichols' explanation—and here's why. (November 11, 1970)

> Leveling a withering denunciation of waste, inefficiency and secrecy at Denver's Model Cities program as it is currently operated, mayoral candidate Dale Tooley says taxpayers were nipped nearly $1,000 per tree and more than $1,000 per child to support two ineffective programs last year. (March 15, 1971)

> Multimillion dollar losses and non-payment of dividends assured a roily annual meeting of Frontier Airlines stockholders . . . last week. (April 29, 1970)

> When a person becomes editor and publisher of the *Denver Post* that person automatically becomes a significantly powerful factor in the public opinion making in these mountain states. He also becomes the hired, well-paid non-owning custodian of the policies, trade practices, functionary purposes and subtle blackmailing techniques and other vested privileges rooted in illegality and immorality that systematically go with monopolies in which great effort must be made to conceal evils. (September 9, 1970)

Asked what it was his readers were buying, Cervi responded, "a solid, useful, profitable reporting service made interesting and entertaining with some of the guffaws and reportorial gymnastics I picked up as a police and political reporter in Denver—and there isn't necessarily a connection between the two."[7]

Writing in *The Unsatisfied Man: A Review of Colorado Journalism,* William Gallo called the content of *Cervi's Rocky Mountain Journal* "the sort of humanitarian service impulse . . . propelled by an uneven lyricism. . . . Gene Cervi always viewed the paper as an intensely personal undertaking, and he has been a strong crusader and somewhat of a liberal philosopher."

Regular features in *Cervi's* newspaper are columns entitled "Of Politics and Power and Poker and Things," "Journal Joustings," "Cervi's Journalism Review," "Mile High Observations," and "People." Until 1969 when he went into semiretirement, Cervi wrote all the columns himself. After that his only regular contribution to the paper was "Mile High Observations," a testy column usually related to national or international issues with frequent local references. For example, a September 1970 column on dissent, protest, and national upheaval asserted: "The old Democratic leadership has brought nothing new to these telescoped crises. That's why there is revolt in the young and opposition to unchanging tenets to those long in power. A man like George Meany, made by Democrats, is hard to distinguish from a conservative Republican leader at the Denver Club."

In December 1970, a few days after an automobile accident, Eugene Cervi suffered a heart attack and died. "Damn!, damn, damn, damn!, Gene Cervi's dead," wrote Tom Gavin. Always a man to have the last word, Cervi had written his own obituary for the *Journal*. Of himself, he said, "Mr. Cervi had a basic personal tenet that editors should own and that owners should edit."[8] About one thing there was no doubt: the *Journal* would continue; the founder's daughter, Mary Claire (Cle) Cervi continues as editor and publisher (although editors of the *Unsatisfied Man*, the journalism review, lamented in 1972, "Since Gene Cervi's gone, nobody hunts big game"). In March 1971, *Cervi's Rocky Mountain Journal*, for twenty-seven years a weekly, began publishing twice weekly.

The San Francisco Bay Guardian

The San Francisco *Bay Guardian* comes on with force and style. Unlike the quieter typography of *Cervi's Rocky Mountain Journal*, the *Guardian* is alive with large striking headlines and dramatic line drawings. Visually reflecting both the moral indignation and mordant humor of the paper, the drama of design leads the reader into equally exciting stories. It is both a magazine and newspaper, an intriguing package of almost incredible information, nearly all of it unavailable in the conventional newspapers of the San Francisco Bay area.

While many of the *Guardian's* targets are natural adversaries for a liberal, iconoclastic newspaper, some are not, which makes the paper unpredictable. One unexpected target was the radical-liberal *Ramparts* magazine, which was roasted in the March 27, 1969, *Guardian* under the headline, RAMPARTS—REVOLUTION WITH LIMOUSINE SERVICE. Beneath the inch-high head was an editorial cartoon showing Warren Hinckle, *Ramparts'* publisher, standing atop a castle turret with a machine gun in one hand, a martini in the other. A second headline added: RAMPARTS IN CHICAGO—[editor Robert] SCHEER GASSED IN THE STREETS, HINCKLE PARTIES 15 FLOORS UP. The story began on a meandering note:

Frederick C. Mitchell, 29-year-old publisher of *Ramparts* is somberly reflecting on the expenses run up by the magazine's former president and editorial director Warren Hinckle. "Big, big," he says softly. His handsome boyish face has the look of a betrayed child. He leans back slowly, fingers drumming on his creaking chair, which suddenly sounds loud in his tiny, cluttered office. The window is fiercely bright with sunlight and the murmur of cars and tourists from nearby Fisherman's Wharf floats through clearly.

Then he looks up and a light smile instantly wipes aside the pensive look. "Are those what I think they are?," he asks eagerly. He glances happily at the green slip handed to him by a casually-dressed employee who has walked in. It is a payroll check for $318.55. The publisher is like a small boy who has just been given a raise in his pocket money.

Mitchell, unassuming, likable university professor who has sunk an inheritance from his grandfather of nearly half a million dollars into *Ramparts*, was getting his first salary check in four months.

The story went on to document the excesses of Hinckle and the poor judgment of Edward Keating, once the magazine's financial angel. The same issue also carried these headlines: HOW PG & E [Pacific Gas & Electric] SWINDLES SAN FRANCISCO, THE MESS AT THE YOUTH GUIDANCE CENTER, CONSERVATION POWER—THE BATTLE OVER THE SIERRA CLUB'S DAVE BROWER, and others. The conservation story was a detailed analysis of Brower's performance as leader of the Sierra Club. A headline asked: WAS THE SIERRA CLUB A POLITICAL FORCE OR A HIKING CLUB? A boxed sidebar story analyzed the charges against Brower under the headings of FINANCIAL IRRESPONSIBILITY and GENERAL ARROGANCE. Each of nine charges made against Brower was followed by a defense, so the reader could make his own decision.

A typical issue of the *Guardian* carries stories about the style of the city, reviews of the arts, and occasional poetry. A 1967 story about draft boards asked, "Do you know anybody on your local San Francisco draft board? Almost nobody else does either." The article attacked with hard facts the notion that draft boards are "little groups of neighbors." A box listed board members' occupations (mostly business and the professions), and a map showed the location of board offices, demonstrating that the boards were unrepresentative both geographically and socioeconomically. The story itself documented specific abuses as well as considered more general concerns such as the amount of time spent on each case (thirty seconds) and draft quotas.

San Francisco newspapers are a favorite *Guardian* target. In February 1968 a *Guardian* story screamed SECRET MERGER DEAL—"now, proof that the booming *Chronicle* went into equal partnership with the ailing *Examiner* and the touchy 1965 deal." The article stated: "The *Chronicle* . . . was willing to give up its dominant position, its traditional independence and all that was meant by its long-time slogan, 'the city's only home-owned newspaper' in exchange for higher profits promised by a joint operation that would destroy the need for expensive competition." The story even began with a teaser—"There's an obscure 23-page document in Nevada's State Capitol that lays to rest all the speculation over who really controls San Francisco's merged newspapers"—and a headline inside declared that the joint operation "began with a bogus name, fake directors and a Reno address." A photograph of a photostat copy of the merger document leaped out of the page.

Publisher Brugmann relishes his attacks on San Francisco's establishment papers. In 1969 he began covering the efforts of two former "Superchron" employees to challenge the license of KRON-TV, a station owned by the San Francisco Chronicle Company. The reader was given the intrigue behind the story, as headlined in the May 22 issue: "Witnesses Shadowed . . . Friends and Relatives Were Asked Personal, Intimidating Questions in Pending Government License Renewal Hearings for KRON-TV."

Under a larger headline, THE DICKS FROM SUPERCHRON, Brugmann quotes Al Kihn, one of the complainants, who was tailed by private detectives. Inside the same issue, the paper carried a story headlined AL KIHN'S DIARY—A CASE STUDY OF TV'S WEALTHY WASTELAND.

Kihn, a KRON photographer for eight years, kept a diary of KRON news and corporate transgressions for the past six years. He has complained to the FCC and provoked a nationally important license renewal hearing. Kihn's three major issues: (1) KRON has slanted the news to protect its corporate parent, the *Chronicle*; (2) produced programs to promote the *Chronicle*'s CATV interests and (3) managed and distorted the news. We are running Kihn's major complaints because his story, though covered nationally in *Newsweek* and on PBL educational television, has been virtually blacked out in San Francisco. The major FCC documents are on file in KRON's offices . . . and can be inspected upon request.

On July 23 the San Francisco *Chronicle* reported: "A law firm retained by the Chronicle Broadcasting Co. of San Francisco has acknowledged to the Federal Communications Commission that it hired a firm of private detectives to investigate two former employees who asked the FCC not to renew the licenses held by the company for KRON-TV and KRON-FM."

Brugmann wrote in the *Guardian* on August 18:

When General Motors was caught red-handed trying to harass and intimidate Ralph Nader with private dicks, the president of GM . . . publicly apologized twice to the young auto critic. His apology got nationwide publicity. Three years later when the *Guardian* caught

Superchron using private dicks in the Ralph Nader case of communications, the *Chronicle* publisher, Charles de Young Thieriot, admitted retaining the private dicks and said it was "entirely reasonable and proper to do so." This admission got four inches in his paper. This, ladies and gentlemen, is in microcosm the state of monopoly journalism in the summer of 1969.

When the Federal Communications Commission was preparing to hold hearings in the spring of 1970 to determine whether to renew the license of KRON-TV, Brugmann printed the names of all the witnesses who would appear and summarized the testimony they would give. Numerous spectators at the hearings carried the *Guardian* with them like a program for a sporting event. The *Guardian* summaries were quite accurate. How did the *Guardian* do it? By calling the witnesses and asking them what they would say.

Brugmann says his paper has built its reputation by:

1. Incisive, carefully researched investigations.
2. Articulating major political and cultural trends.
3. Making news and getting results by printing stories nobody else will print.
4. Injecting stories and ideas into the political and intellectual bloodstream.

Some sort of competitive press must be established, Brugmann feels, to challenge the monopolies in news coverage and editorial commentary. He worries that people are getting their news through an "ever more restricted pipeline" which is restricted at its very source—the gathering and sending of news by the two major wire services. AP and UPI, he says, "are not much interested in passing along news that is not published by client papers. My newspaper has broken several major stories, many of which were picked up by radio and television." In support, Brugmann tells of his appearance on a radio program with San Francisco bureau chiefs of AP and UPI:

Throughout the program, I made several critical remarks about the monopoly *Examiner-Chronicle*, citing specific stories the papers had not covered. I described in detail how each paper had refused to dig into the major story of the mayor's election (a story we had published in considerable detail)—how a secret deal was put together to lure the mayor out and thrust a pro-Johnson businessman into the race.

Afterward both men came up to me and said in effect, "I hope the radio listeners could tell it was you who made those remarks and not us."

"Why?" I replied. "Why didn't you take me on?"

Both seemed startled by my question.

"Because they're our clients, that's why," one said. "We don't want to get into anything."[9]

An activist editor who loves to be on the firing line, Brugmann is testing the Newspaper Preservation Act with a suit against the San Francisco newspapers. His extensive journalistic career includes work while a teenager on an Iowa weekly, editor of the University of Nebraska student newspaper, and stints with *Stars & Stripes,* the Milwaukee *Journal,* and the Redwood City (California) *Tribune.* He has a remarkable store of energy—besides publishing his paper he often teaches journalism part time—and constructs an editorial content that almost overwhelms the reader. Every page of the *Guardian* is so bold and striking that it is sometimes difficult to differentiate among various categories and levels of injustice. The paper seems always to shout at full volume, an editorial formula that over time may promote the "cry wolf" feeling of sameness—the very weakness of the more conventional papers Brugmann is trying to counter.

But Brugmann's activism is calculated. "I feel we must more than print the news, since disclosure itself may not be enough to bring change." Brugmann's antidote is legal action, and he has filed suits on a variety of issues. His guidelines for legal action, as revealed in an interview, are:

> First, I insist that a suit flow naturally from news and editorials. Secondly, we do it as a last resort, after we are certain that there is nobody else around to do it. Thirdly, it is done openly, and, finally, it is not allowed to interfere with our editorial operation.

How does Brugmann, now in his mid-thirties, maintain the momentum? The tall, serious editor points to success. "We have made KRON a better TV station and we have made the public aware of a whole range of things that the *Chronicle* and the *Examiner* would not report."

Perhaps the *Bay Guardian's* greatest achievement is the publication of a book, *The Ultimate High Rise,* which has been praised by urban affairs authorities as "solid evidence of the real costs of skyscrapers." The book, like the *Bay Guardian's* articles, is a detailed investigative report.

The *Guardian* is a severe test of the viability of the no-holds-barred alternative paper. It has long been in financial trouble. By fearlessly taking on so many targets, Brugmann may have sacrificed much of his advertising potential, even in a sophisticated, liberal city like San Francisco. Brugmann raised enough money in 1972 to publish the *Guardian* every other week, thus giving it the stability to attract advertisers—if they can be lured to a paper that never seems to side-step any issue.

The Oregon Times

The struggle to survive is constant in alternative journalism. When Phillip Stanford founded the *Oregon Times* in the winter of 1971, he was strongly influenced by I. F. Stone, editor and publisher of the famous *I. F. Stone's Bi-Weekly* (mentioned earlier), for whom he had once worked as a research assistant. Because of what he regarded as incompetence in the local press—"I don't know of any place in the country which has such poor newspapers"—Stanford decided another spokesman was needed.

Stone's influence on him was considerable, Stanford feels. "He taught me the importance of researching and reporting. Working with him was an inspiration in many ways, but mainly because he regards journalism as an honorable calling, something worthy of respect. I noticed that Stone was proud to call himself a newspaperman and after awhile I was too. I also learned that style isn't all that important. What you say is more important than how you say it. Sincerity comes through even if the style isn't highly polished."

Stanford began producing a handsomely designed news magazine to take on Oregon's business leaders, politicians, and public programs, as well as Portland's Newhouse-owned newspapers, the *Oregonian* and the *Oregon Journal*. "We will try to be a watchdog of Oregon's press and politics," Stanford told his readers, "an advocate of the traditional liberal values of toleration, equality and personal freedom."

Working with a volunteer staff, Stanford originally thought he could organize support for the paper by drawing on contributors who helped liberal political candidates such as Senator Eugene McCarthy in his 1968 presidential campaign. But in a state where McCarthy had won the Democratic presidential nomination, Stanford had only 1000 mail subscribers a year after he started. Can I. F. Stone's formula for financial success be transplanted to another locale, another situation? "No," says Stanford. "You have to remember that Stone was already famous when he started. He had 5000 subscribers right away." (Stone had previously been a popular Washington correspondent for the experimental newspaper *PM* before beginning his *Bi-Weekly* in 1953.)

Stanford often published twenty or more 8½ x 11-inch pages, including three major interpretive stories, editorial comments, and art work, usually line drawings of local politicians. He concerned himself from the beginning with sniping at conventional media. An article evaluating the performance of Oregon newspaper editorial pages in their coverage of the transgressions of the GOP state chairman charged: "Many editorial writers for Oregon dailies secretly long to be members of the Republican state central committee."

Later, the *Times* shamed Portland's two dailies into printing a story about alleged election-law violations of a city commissioner. The story resulted in a grand jury investigation, and when the Portland dailies started carrying the story, they attributed the original investigation to the staff of the *Oregon Times*. Using good humor as a weapon, Stanford and his staff have taken on such local media leaders as the managing editor of the *Oregonian*: "The only times he writes a story is when President Nixon invites him to breakfast."

Not long after he launched the *Times*, a local television station invited Stanford to join the editors of several major papers in an "Oregon Week in Review" program. This gave him a chance to "take them on in front of a lot of viewers," as Stanford put it, but despite this exposure, he found the paper's circulation growing too slowly for financial strength. Long articles, art work, and many pages are costly. "I've found," Stanford says, "that an increased number of pages means a quantum leap in research and business needs."

Another major problem is finding enough writers who really believe in journalism and are willing to dig for stories. "Everyone wants to write a movie review," Stanford says, "but they learn very fast that investigative journalism is damned hard work." The result is an increasing burden on the editor, with less and less time for fund raising.

Stanford learned that journalism of the sort practiced by I. F. Stone requires dedication and unbelievably hard work. Finding others to make the commitment is sometimes as difficult as finding money for survival. Still, when Stanford left Portland for a job with Ralph Nader in 1972, he was able to pass the paper on to a new management.

The Village Voice

Certainly the most widely known alternative paper in America is the *Village Voice*, founded in 1955, which is also an exceptional commercial success. It began as an alternative to the *Villager*, a bland weekly offering superficial coverage of the exiciting bohemian section of New York City. From the beginning, the *Voice* covered reform politics, the arts, and the public affairs of the neighborhood, largely ignored by the city's other papers. Robert Glessing has written: "The *Voice* was the first newspaper in the history of modern American journalism to consistently report news with no restriction on language. . . . The *Voice* was also the first paper to give unsung and unpublished authors from the Village's substantial bank of creative talent a chance to be heard. Over the years, the *Voice's* list of contributors is a *Who's Who* of topical American journalism."[10]

Once considered radical, the *Voice* has been outdistanced by the many new advocacy and underground papers that have emerged in the last ten years. In fact, a recent appraisal declares: "The *Village Voice* stood well to the left of regular New York newspapers. . . . [But] once in the vanguard, the *Voice* now finds itself written off by much of the underground press as hopelessly square. A writer in *Evergreen Review* calls it a 'middle-age matron in [a] miniskirt.' "[11]

Unlike its counterparts, the *Voice* no longer focuses exclusively on local matters. Many articles originate outside of New York. A December 1970 article, "A Montage of Two Vermonters," offered comparative interviews with Ray Mungo (formerly of the Liberation News Service) and Harvard professor John Kenneth Galbraith, both of whom have farms in Vermont.

The *Voice* has a number of regular columns, including one called "Personal Testament," which is open to contributions from readers, who may write on anything in any style, but with the editors selecting manuscripts for publication "on the basis of literacy and interest." A personal testament of December 17, 1970, for instance, was "the unmaking of a fattie": "Twenty-nine years ago I emerged from my mother's womb weighing 13 pounds, unusually heavy for a newborn infant, and for 27 years after that there was rarely a time when I was not grotesquely overweight in relation to my peers."

Although the *Voice* now reflects academic liberalism rather than the contemporary counterculture, the underground papers have not hesitated to use copy from it when it suits their purposes. The Berkeley *Barb* issue of February 5, 1971, for instance, reprinted an article by Michael Zwerin, European editor of the *Voice*, about a dispute between Black Panther leader Eldridge Cleaver and Timothy Leary.

The financial success of the *Voice* is evident from its eighty to 100 pages, which are heavy with advertising. Although it has been called the granddaddy of the underground newspapers, the forces that shaped the early undergrounds bear little resemblance to those that shaped the *Voice*.

The Maine Times

Far north of the urban rumblings that provide fodder for the *Voice* is a more recent entry in the field of alternative journalism. In a tiny village a few miles from Portland, Maine, is the *Maine Times*, described by *Time* magazine as "a plucky weekly newspaper . . . with punchy headlines and a tabloid format."[12]

The paper was established in 1968 by two Yale graduates, John N. Cole, 46, the editor, and Peter W. Cox, 32, the publisher. Cole had been an advertising man in New York who later took up commercial fishing and eventually served as editor of several Maine newspapers. Cox is the son of a well-known international lawyer. They raised $100,000, rented a building, and hired two full-time reporters. Their paper came to national attention via *Time* magazine in 1969 for its forthright coverage of Maine environmental issues:

> The paper unflaggingly alerts its 10,000 readers to each week's environmental toll—an oil spill off Casco Bay, a fish kill at Mystery Lake, a historic barn razed at the University of Maine. Much vitriol is aimed at the paper industry, a major source of water pollution in the

state. The *Times* recently flayed a new wave of fly-by-night operators who reopened abandoned paper mills for short term profit and long term pollution. Happily the muckraking pays off. Largely because of the *Times* one of those reopened mills closed. . . . One article detailed how mills in the Pacific Northwest took the smell out of making brown paper, with the implication that Maine's mills should do the same. Another story started a cleanup of the Saco River by pinpointing 39 specific sources of pollution along its 125 mile length. . . . the paper has single-handedly fought to ban snowmobiles from the virgin wilderness of Baxter State Park—successfully.[13]

Although it is published on newsprint, it resembles a magazine more than a newspaper. The front page always features a striking photograph surrounded by a rectangular block of color, and vivid pictures of Maine's natural beauty dot each issue. Unlike most alternative papers, the *Times* is more than a muckraker. The range of interest is suggested by these recent cover stories:

MAINE'S OLD FARMS BROUGHT BACK TO LIFE BY A NEW LIFE STYLE

MAINE BAPTISTS—THE YANKEE CHURCHES

AT THIS MAINE SCHOOL IF THEY TALK THEY WALK

HOW TO LIVE HAPPILY IN MAINE ON $80 A WEEK WITH SIX CHILDREN

THE MAINE WAGE EARNER'S FRIEND

THE TIDE TURNS FOR THE MAINE LOBSTERMAN

A regular feature of the *Times* is "John's Column," written by Cox, a personal perspective of his reaction to Maine life. His column on March 13, 1970, ran:

In those days [1945] I could extract five days and about three full nights of riotous living from those [Christmas] holidays, and my adrenalin began flowing when the plane crossed Bangor. I [had] never looked down at Maine; and when I did I can remember being impressed by the vast stretches of trees and the relative absence of humanity. For a boy in his early 20's who had grown up in New York City, the Maine landscape was wild and remote. Besides in 1945 I had absolutely no notion whatsoever that Maine would become the state of my life.

The paper has a liberal stance, but politics seems less important than that Cox and Cole are loving critics of Maine. They have a passion to preserve the state's natural beauty and to keep out the industrial polluters. As Cole has said: "If enough people are concerned about the state, we can do something with it."

Tailoring its often barbed message to the political and social climate of the Lone Star state, the *Texas Observer*, published biweekly in Austin, appears in an unpretentious letter-size format with quiet typography and graceful line drawings. Inside, however, are impassioned investigations of corruption and questionable ethics among politicians, business leaders, and others in the Texas power structure.

Sometimes called the "political conscience of Texas," the *Observer* always offers a liberal evaluation and seems never to be intimidated by oil or banking interests. Among the oldest and steadiest of the alternative papers, the *Observer* has offered inspiration for other venturesome journalistic entrepreneurs. Like other alternatives, it has struggled for survival since its beginnings in 1954 making a profit for the first time in 1969.

Founded by Ronnie Dugger, a University of Texas graduate, the paper has had on its staff such journalistic luminaries as Willie Morris (later editor of *Harper's*), Robert Sherrill, and Larry King. The *Observer* has always been the personal enterprise of a few staffers working feverishly to turn out the necessary 40,000 words an issue. Morris described to *Time* magazine how he and Dugger edited the paper: "Every Friday afternoon we'd have a full-fledged conference at Scholz's beer hall. Then, one of us would go out of town, and the other would stay behind and put out the paper. The guy who remained had to do everything: editing, copy reading, makeup. He would even set up a desk next to the linotype operator and read over his shoulder."[14]

During this time, Morris says, "Only the *Observer* ever bothered to show any interest in the last words of a 17-year-old rapist on death row, or in the terror of a 17-year-old Negro child in the adult ward for the mentally ill, or in what Norman Mailer said or did not say to college students in Austin."[15]

At times over the years, readers have accused the paper of slipping below Morris's high standards. Although there may have been uneven periods, the *Observer* now has two dynamic young women at the helm— Moll Ivins and Kaye Northcott—and seems as lively as ever.

Says co-editor Ivins, "We try to use the *Observer* as a vehicle to make people aware of the peculiarities of [Texas]. We even try to reflect the special oral tradition of the state and show how Texans use the language inventively and with great affection."

Moll Ivins is tall, red-haired, and irreverent—even about the *Observer*. Asked, "Just what does the *Observer* stand for?", she opened the most recent issue, located the masthead, and read it off in a sing-song Texas twang that is somehow melodious: "We will serve no group or party but will hew hard to the truth as we find it and the right as we see it. We are dedicated to the whole truth, to human values above all interests, to the rights of man as the foundation of democracy; we will take orders from none but our own conscience, and never will we overlook or misrepresent the truth to serve the interests of the powerful or cater to the ignoble in human spirit."

She agreed that this noble statement of principle was somewhat out of keeping with the tone of the *Observer,* making it clear that one of the editor's purposes is to capture the spirit and style of Texas politics. "Somehow the big dailies covering Austin send writers who go out of their way to make the legislature dull," she said. The *Observer* is seldom dull, in part because the editors are not restricted by the conventions of journalism that require dispassionate reports. An example of the *Observer's* free-swinging style appeared on page 6 of the April 14, 1972, issue under a headline announcing THE LOBBY WINS AGAIN: "the Texas House of Representatives, that great elephant of reform, did labor and labor mightily, bellowing great gales of rhetoric, moaning under the lash of public opinion and heaving under the necessity for change, and the elephant did at last produce—a mouse, in the unprepossessing form of Rayford Price of Palestine."

Aware of the counterculture and new life styles, the *Observer* still sees itself as a medium for social change as it pursues the culture and politics of the state with vigor. As the paper has aged, its tone has become less strident and more mature, more given to humor and satire rather than invective. The editorial formula is better paced and offers readers a mix of muckraking exposés and quieter and more measured prose.

The Intermountain Observer

Published in Boise, Idaho, the *Intermountain Observer* fulfills much the same function as the *Texas Observer* but serves the northern mountain states. As *Newsweek* reported, the paper has championed such causes as:

... immediate withdrawal from Vietnam, the right of servicemen at local military bases to oppose the war and the extension of full membership in the human race to women, blacks and long-haired youths. Despite such heretical stands, the *Observer* has won influence out of all proportion to its small size (twelve pages) and paltry circulation (about 3,000). Among its regular readers are Gov. Cecil Andrus, more than half the members of the state legislature, the Idaho Congressional delegation and almost anyone else who wields any power in the state.

The paper's content is often explosive. In Feburary 1972, editor Sam Day wrote "Intensive Treatment in Name Only," his story about accompanying an unannounced investigating group to a state mental hospital. The report was knowledgeable and detailed and also contained recommendations for immediate change, much like other articles that have explored public education, industry, courts, and the legislature. The mental health story brought a swift response. The hospital director resigned and the state took a hard look at its overall health program.

Another example of the paper's consistency is a February 24, 1973, article which called the state legislature "sanctimonious and uptight." As columnist Bill Hall put it:

> Earlier legislatures were populated with outrageous hams who could provoke even a tired observer to everything from anger to mirth. . . . Some of the giants remain or have returned. And there is a handful of promising freshmen. But I worry about them, because they are discouraged. That means they might not return. They may step aside and make room for still more mediocrity. It has nothing to do with philosophy or political differences. What is lacking is a matter of color and tolerance. This is a sanctimonious, uptight, humorless legislature which takes itself too seriously and contains too many closed minds for compromise and creativity to flourish.

It is always difficult to chart the impact of individual stories or even of the collective thrust of the paper's strongly worded editorials, stories, and exposés. But John Stevens and Bert Cross, two journalism professors who have watched the paper for years, concluded in an article in the Summer 1968 *Columbia Journalism Review*: "The *Intermountain Observer* claims to be written by opinion makers for opinion makers. Even its critics agree that it comforts the afflicted and afflicts the comfortable."

The paper is the result of the 1967 merger of two struggling opinion weeklies, the *Intermountain* of Pocatello and the *Observer* of Boise. The *Intermountain*, begun in 1951 under another name, was edited by Perry Swisher, former state legislator, teacher, and writer. The *Observer* traces its origins to a neighborhood weekly founded in 1952 but did not really become an opinion journal until 1964 when editor Day took over. Day is a Swarthmore graduate who had worked for the Associated Press and several Idaho newspapers. When the papers merged, Day continued as editor and Swisher became an associate editor and columnist.

Until 1972 the *Intermountain Observer* was owned by KBOI radio and television, which allowed it to exist as a counterweight to Boise's conservative *Idaho Statesman*. To some, the ownership pattern was "stranger than its political stance." Station manager Wes Whillock saw the paper as helping the station meet its obligation to serve the "public interest, convenience, and necessity." This was a curious view for a broadcast station, but Whillock was apparently the paper's protector and benefactor for a time. As Stevens and Cross wrote: "When the conservative directors of the broadcasting company have made noises about discontinuing the paper, the station manager . . . has kept them in line by threatening to move his CBS affiliation (his personal property) to nearby Caldwell."

In 1972 after a dispute with the broadcast management, Day came up with a scheme to convert the *Observer* to a reader-owned paper. After selling stock to more than 200 *Observer* readers, Day and his circulation director, Methodist minister Milton Jordan, bought the paper.

Point of View

Former *Wall Street Journal* and Cleveland *Plain Dealer* reporter Roldo Bartimole founded the one-man biweekly *Point of View* in Cleveland, Ohio, in the belief that "the future of relevant journalism will be based on personal, subjective reporting, evolving from participation in the events that shape our society." *Point of View* was started, he said in an interview, "to offer a different perspective—backed by fact—to the insipid Cleveland media. It was started in the belief that the mass media is incapable of honest reporting. They will not report with honesty because they are so much a part of the system producing the worst in today's society. *Point of View* is not a newspaper but a *views*paper."

Point of View is printed, Bartimole says, for "the news nobody else sees fit to print." It is modest in appearance—tiny, book-sized pages published biweekly on light-brown stock. Although not graphically impressive, each issue carries a detailed report that must make Cleveland media executives shudder. Bartimole says much of his information comes from reporters who were "unable to use it in their media because of stiff internal censorship." He hopes that presenting this embarrassing information will enable other reporters to use it as leverage to wring some freedom from editors.

Many of Bartimole's stories eventually do surface in the establishment press. For example, in the June 26, 1969, paper he wrote: "Cleveland business leaders last summer bought peace ... by paying some black activists about $40,000 in a 10-week period to do what they had decided to do already—keep it cool ... Ralph Besse headed it up." A month later the Cleveland *Press* reported: "last summer when $40,000 reportedly was raised in the business community for a Peace in Cleveland project ... Ralph Besse, illuminating company board chairman, headed the fund-raising, according to reports. Today he said he had no comment on it."

Bartimole describes his investigative stories as having "scathing language with a verbal twist of the knife." Though he covers only northern Ohio, some of his stories have gained national attention. Writing in the *Village Voice*, Howard Smith called attention to a *Point of View* story about a shootout between police and black militants that "lucidly detailed the discrepancies between the official mayor's report and the accounts of the witnesses and media."

Bartimole has taken on what he calls "self-dealing, double dealing" activities of the Cleveland powerful who served on the board of a local foundation. He attacked the local United Appeal as an "art of extortion" and accused the *Plain Dealer* of engineering a vendetta against a develop-

68

ment corporation to "protect white elites." Analyzing local television news, he wrote: "The state of journalism in Cleveland is at such a low level that one can best describe the reporting here as the production of poor fiction. Nowhere is the world of Make Believe more evident than on the television screen at news time." After analyzing specific programs offered by local stations, he wrote: "Frontal attacks on Cleveland television stations must be made. Their record demands the attacks. Some organizations are already interested in compiling the failures of local television stations." The stations should "get relevant," he said, or "face challenges to their licenses."

A September 1970 *Point of View* story examined a running battle between two Cleveland reporters writing about the supersonic transport aircraft. A *Plain Dealer* reporter's critical story of the SST was attacked, Bartimole said, by a *Press* aviation reporter who "loves the SST and thinks everybody else should too." Bartimole suggested that the aviation writer's enthusiasm "may have something to do with the fact his son works for Boeing on the SST."

Persistent surveillance of the Cleveland media has given Bartimole a national reputation. Carey McWilliams, editor of the *Nation*, wrote that Bartimole exemplifies the resurgence of reform journalism. A sociologist said, "All cities are entitled to a Bartimole, but the supply is terribly scarce."

Other Alternatives: The Shoppers

Although economic pressures threaten several alternative journals, their numbers and their circulations have increased, making them an expanding new journalistic force. Some were the brainchildren of energetic journalistic entrepreneurs who wanted a new paper to challenge the status quo. Others sprang from traditional media which were given a facelifting and became alternatives.

Another avenue for developing alternative media may be the shoppers, those free-distribution, throw-away advertising sheets which spread across the land during the 1960s. Many shoppers are searching for respectability, and some are beginning to offer their readers editorial matter not otherwise available. The *Weekender* in Traverse City, Michigan, for example, has engaged in critical investigative reporting. One muckraking story in 1970 in which *Weekender* editors revealed a discrepancy in death reports at a local hospital brought considerable pressure from advertisers, who reduced their advertising in the paper by 40 percent.

The shoppers may have some difficulty attracting a serious reading audience among consumers, who have until recently used them to line garbage cans. But the potential for molding shoppers into critical alternatives may provide a middle ground for financial solvency somewhere between the prosperity of the *Village Voice* and the economic instability of the *Bay Guardian*.

In presenting their papers as alternatives to the conventional media, which are better financed and better staffed, one would expect these feisty journalists to suffer continued embarrassment. Few do. In the main, their work is highly respected by other journalists.

Although the very existence of the alternative papers seems anachronistic in an age of mass production, the leading alternative journalists make it clear with nearly every new issue that their work is needed.

Alternative Journalism: An Example

THE DEATH PENALTY INITIATIVE

by   Project Director: Bruce B. Brugmann
     Writer: Peter Petrakis
     Research Coordinator: Madeline Nelson
     Legal Research: Dan Segal
     Researchers: Dorothy Ehrlich, Debbie Boyce, Gary Sowards

"The Exclusive Story of How the Governor, the Prosecutors, Police, and Jailers Took the Law into Their Own Hands to Bring Back Capital Punishment," the second headline read. This story is typical of many of the Guardian's *major articles. Note that this is an exposé, a probing for hidden facts, and that much of it is written in an outraged tone. Most alternative journals justify their existence on the ground that conventional newspapers accept official explanations without attempting to dig for the truth. Most alternative journalists are contemptuous of the bland style of conventional journalism.*

The voters' initiative was conceived as a citizen's weapon against the misdeeds and abuse of government.

That's how the populist farmers saw it in 1898 when they originated the idea back where I come from in South Dakota. That's how Robert LaFollette saw it when he fought for it in Wisconsin in 1900, and that's how Hiram Johnson saw it when he fought for it in California in 1911. The very name "initiative" implies initiation of legislation by the citizens—not by their government officials.

An exhaustive Guardian investigation of the campaign to qualify the Death Penalty Initiative for the November [1972 California] ballot (Proposition 17) has uncovered a wealth of evidence that proves that this was, not a citizen's initiative, but an official act of the executive branch of state government, acting through its police forces.

Death penalty advocates in the police/prosecution/penal establishment in California, led by Gov. Reagan, Atty. Gen. Evelle Younger and State Sen. George Deukmejian, lost the fight to retain capital punishment.

Reprinted by permission from the San Francisco *Bay Guardian*, October 4, 1972.

They lost in the State Supreme Court. They lost in the U.S. Supreme Court. They lost in the California legislature.

Then they decided to take the law into their own hands. The chief law enforcement officers of the state, most notably Younger, founded, led and organized the campaign to secure signatures. ⟋

They put together a county-by-county campaign structure using as leaders the local district attorneys, sheriffs and police chiefs and using as circulators the local policemen, sheriffs' deputies and bailiffs, deputy DA's, California Highway Patrol officers, correctional officers and their wives.

The result of this use of police power to gather signatures was phenomenally successful: the troops collected more than 1 million signatures in 60 days (75% in the last 14-day blitz) at a piddling cost of between $25,000 and $30,000, about 3¢ per signature (professionals figure $1 per signature). Younger and his men set records in terms of speed, cost and ease in gathering signatures in a statewide campaign.

Thus, the campaign as a whole demonstrated how statewide police power could be almost instantly transformed and mobilized into a political machine. Not only did the campaign subvert the initiative process and the democratic process, but its leaders and men, law enforcement in California, openly stretched and broke the law. For example, our investigation showed that:

☐ Research and drafting of the petition and other legal services were provided for a private organization of correctional officers by the attorney general, chief law officer of the state, in violation of law. (Cal. Govt. Code 12504, which directs the attorney general to spend his entire time on state work.)

☐ The attorney general pledged and used the official power and influence of his public office in the service of an initiative in which he had a personal and political interest, to the exclusion of other initiatives, in violation of law. (Article V, sec. 13 of the Cal. Constitution which provides for equal enforcement of the laws.)

☐ District attorneys and other officials in the state converted their tax-supported offices into political headquarters to organize and conduct the initiative campaign, in violation of law. (Article XIII, sec. 21 of the Cal. Constitution which prohibits the use of state funds for any non-state institutions or associations.)

☐ Police stations, sheriffs' offices, fire stations, correctional facilities, even some city halls, were also converted into headquarters and subheadquarters for the petition drive, in violation of law. (Art. XIII, sec. 21 of the Cal. Constitution, see above.)

☐ Public employees were recruited into working on the initiative by their superiors, in violation of law. (Govt. Code 19730, 19734, which prohibit recruiting subordinates for political work.)

☐ Public employees worked on the initiative on public time, in violation of law. (Gov. Code 3204.5, which says "no officer or employee . . . shall participate in political activities of any kind while he is in uniform." Also, Article XIII, sec. 21 prohibits use of state funds to pay employes for anything but official business.)

As State Sen. George Moscone, chairman of No on 17, put it, "We have seen a most shocking perversion of and usurpation of the public trust by several of our leading public officials.

"The question goes well beyond the merits of the proposition. It goes directly to the possible misuse of public funds and personnel in an effort designed to create a political machine within the administration in order to circumvent the California State Supreme Court, the U.S. Supreme Court, the California Legislature and, most importantly, the petition process itself."

ITEM: On May 4, 1972, Officer Donald Menzmer entered a classroom of the California Highway Patrol Academy in Sacramento and held up a batch of Death Penalty Initiative petitions. Menzmer, a staff services officer, explained the petitions and told the cadets he had petitions for several counties in the state.

Cadets, he said, raise your hands as I call out the names of your counties. As they did, he gave each the appropriate petition to sign. He did not ask if the cadets were registered to vote in their counties.

A cadet from the senior class entered the room and Menzmer asked him if the petitions had been circulated in his class. They had, the senior cadet said. The next day, the cadet found the petitions in the junior class mailbox, apparently destined for another circulator. The petitions covered 11 counties: L.A., Sacramento, Butte, Yuba, Inyo, Alameda, San Bernadino, Fresno, San Luis Obispo, Riverside, Orange.

"Officer Menzmer was in full uniform (except for hat), he was on state-owned facilities, on state time and interrupting a scheduled training class," the cadet wrote. "Officer Menzmer did not appear to be doing this out of deep personal feelings but more as a matter of paper work which someone else told (or asked) to see that it was done. I do not believe it was his idea but [one of] a person of higher authority."

ITEM: In early April, Police Inspector Douglas Stevenson entered the Alameda County District Attorney's office and circulated the Death Penalty Initiative petition among workers on public time. When workers became upset, he explained that Lt. Warren Hanson wanted the signatures and that he was doing what he was told. Later, a worker spotted another inspector at the corner of 16th and Telegraph in Oakland also soliciting signatures on county time.

ITEM: Early in the campaign, a four-page memorandum went out to personnel of the Los Angeles County Sheriff's Department, outlining the county campaign structure (DA, sheriff, police departments), setting up the sheriff's end along the department's lines of authority, establishing quotas. The L.A. sheriff's quota: "150,000 valid signatures." The L.A. sheriff/DA/police quota: "438,000 valid signatures."

Responsibility was delegated according to rank, specific public facilities were designated as headquarters and command posts, specific rooms were set aside for, as the memo put it, "24-hour operation if necessary." Result: 447,248 signatures, about half the total collected throughout the state, a remarkable performance in the county where Younger was once the DA.

ITEM: District Atty. C. Robert Jameson of Yolo County told Gary Sowards, a researcher, that he and his six deputies worked overtime in the office precincting petitions and all got compensatory time off in payment.

ITEM: On June 1, another researcher entered the Sausalito Police Department and saw the Death Penalty Initiative petition on the counter. The secretary explained that "someone" (whatever police officer happened to be at the desk, she explained) would witness the signatures. Researchers also found petitions put out for signing and distribution in police stations in Mill Valley and San Anselmo and in the Marin County District Attorney's office.

ITEM: The petitions were in SF fire and police stations until Sup. Terry Francois kicked up a big fuss.

Several law violations are involved in this handful of incidents: Policemen in uniform circulating petitions. Solicitors carrying petitions for more than one county. Public employes circulating petitions on public time. Public employes even getting overtime compensation to work on a petition. Circulators failing to maintain personal supervision of their petitions. And all of them using public administrative facilities for political activities.

They are but the tip of an iceberg of lawbreaking on a massive scale by law enforcement agencies in California. In virtually every one of California's 58 counties, public facilities were openly misused in the signature drive for the Death Penalty Initiative.

In at least 23 counties, police stations, sheriffs' stations, district attorneys' offices or fire stations (or all four) were openly designated in newspaper stories as headquarters or distribution points for the petition. . . .

On May 18, State Sen. Deukmejian (R-Long Beach) announced to the press that petitions were available "at most police and sheriffs' offices in the state." Deukmejian was the statewide chairman of the petition drive. He mentioned only one other specific place in his press release, the California Correctional Officers Association in Sacramento.

In late May, Dorothy Ehrlich, a Guardian researcher, called every DA, sheriff's office and police department in the Bay Area and, with the notable exception of the SF Sheriff's Department, was able to get information on the petition on the telephone, where to sign it, etc. All publicly employed office workers who responded to telephone inquiries, it was obvious from their replies, had been coached on what to say and, on public time and using public facilities, would direct inquiries to the proper place. Our researchers found the same situation prevailed in city after city, county after county.

No suggestion is intended here that law enforcement officials are not entitled to the same rights of citizenship as anyone else, including advocacy and the right of petition.

But this campaign went far beyond that and, for the first time in California and perhaps American history, the law enforcement power of the badge was used openly to put together an organized government machine to power a political campaign that would, among other things, (1) pervert the initiative process reserved for citizens to combat abuses of their government; (2) simultaneously subvert both the judicial process (both the State and U.S. Supreme Court ruled against the Death Penalty) and the legislative process (the State Senate refused to approve the Death Penalty referendum); (3) abuse their public trust as law enforcement officers and promote lawbreaking on a wide scale; (4) open up the potential for police power to be used again and again for such issues as wire-tapping, arrest powers, criminal and penal procedures and perhaps judicial recall designed to install "hanging judges" throughout the state.

The Guardian interviewed several political science and criminal law experts at the University of California, Stanford and elsewhere and could come up with only one comparable situation where police power was put together as an organized political machine.

That was in New York City in 1966 when the law enforcement agencies rammed through an initiative petition to repeal the city's civilian police review board. But as Prof. Anthony Amsterdam of Stanford University Law School pointed out, "The lines of organization and command structure were themselves not used as a political apparatus" in New York and the campaign was through the police union, the Patrolman's Benevolent Association.

Amsterdam emphasized that organization "is the difference between success and failure" in an initiative drive. "Virtually any measure can be put there if the organization is there to do so. If the regular machinery of a preexisting organization of police is used, then the police have disproportionate political clout.

"We are coming perilously close to accepting a political police who both make the laws and enforce them, something alien to our tradition."

Dan Segal, our legal researcher, said in his memorandum, "Apparently, no U.S. court has ever been faced with an attempt by police officials to take over state political processes after being disappointed by a court's ruling."

The death penalty advocates hardly went to the trouble of hiding the public involvement of law enforcement officials, Ken Brown, PR man for the California Correctional Officers Association, admitted this to me in September. "Naturally," he said, "we worked through law enforcement people, but we also did some grass roots organizing through Republican organizations like the United Republicans of California. (UROC, let us recall, is so rightwing it refused even to endorse Richard Nixon at its state convention in June. But then Brown described himself as a "right-wing conservative.")

It didn't take much more probing to discover how sparse were the grass roots.

Brown and Moe Camacho, the CCOA president, notified Atty. Gen. Younger on March 9 that they were "in the process of developing a 58-county organizational structure to provide the necessary mechanics to secure the required 520,806 valid signatures."

(I asked Brown how the organizing was done. He told me it was from his office in Sacramento, mostly by telephone, and that his channels of communication were the directors of the associations of law enforcement officers. They then endorsed the initiative and proceeded to organize their rank and file within the law enforcement agencies, he continued.)

Brown and Camacho asked Younger—as private citizens representing a private organization—to draft the initiative. Younger didn't have to oblige them. He wasn't even supposed to; Sec. 12504 of the Government Code requires him to devote his time to official business.

Nevertheless, Younger assigned his staff to work on it. One deputy who worked on the draft, Herbert L. Ashby, told the Guardian that "a lot of people worked on it, peace officers, DA's," as well as Ashby, Ronald George and other AG staffers. "We had a staff meeting on it," he said, before the draft was given to Deukmejian who then submitted it formally to the AG office.

Ashby and George were also attorneys of record on the AG's appeal to the State Supreme Court. Gov. Reagan has since rewarded both with judgeships—George with a municipal judgeship in Los Angeles and Ashby with an appellate judgeship in Los Angeles. There is speculation in Sacramento that Reagan is now considering a reward for Younger in 1974: Reagan's support for governor.

Younger's role didn't end with providing free legal services (at taxpayers' expense) to a private organization. On March 28, he vowed in an AG press release that he would use the "power and prestige" of his office to insure the success of the Death Penalty Initiative. He was true to his word.

The attorney general's power and influence are considerable, and he applied them enthusiastically, in press conferences, meetings with DA's, speechmaking around the state and press releases. He even used his weekly statewide "Attorney General Reports" radio broadcasts to plug the death penalty, which were aired by many radio stations as public service announcements. Concluded the one on April 9, Black and Mexican-American leaders (he didn't identify any) who voice opposition to the death penalty, are merely "self-proclaimed spokesmen." They do not represent the views of their communities, most of whom favor the death penalty, he said. Younger didn't reveal who had appointed him to speak for those communities.

Early in the campaign, it became apparent that a large batch of petitions had been printed incorrectly and Younger, as legal counsel for the Death Penalty Initiative, recommended they be recalled, lest the signatures be invalidated.

Younger even took his politicking on the death penalty into the State Supreme Court itself. While the court was considering his petition for a rehearing on the death penalty decision, Younger wrote a letter to Justice Marshall McComb, the lone dissenter on that decision.

He wanted McComb to incorporate into his dissent some of the language from Younger's petition. McComb disappointed him: he never wrote a dissenting opinion when the petition for rehearing was denied. Several lawyers expressed dismay over Younger's attempt to tell a judge how to write his opinion and his statement in his petition that the court showed "lack of respect" for the separation of powers under the constitution when it ruled against the death penalty.

On May 9, four of five candidates for judgeships told the Barristers Club of San Mateo County they thought Younger's involvement in the initiative campaign and his attacks on the Supreme Court were improper. Here are quotes, reported in the San Mateo Times:

Municipal Court Judge Charles Becker: "I think it is wrong," adding, "there's lots of work the Attorney General can do in his office without taking on the Supreme Court."

William Doherty: "I don't think he should try to break down the authority or respect of the Supreme Court."

John Roake: "I don't think it's proper."

Edward Plishka: "I'm against that."

However, Younger had one group of lawyers almost solidly behind him on the Death Penalty Initiative. These were the district attorneys. Ken Brown told me that 60% of the county campaign chairmen were DA's or were DA-appointed.

Only three DA's in all of California refused to cooperate on the initiative, he told me. Brown declined to reveal their names, but I later found out two of the three were William Ferrogiaro of Humboldt County and Bernard McCullough of San Benito County.

Police Inspector Ken Samuels, SF chairman of the drive, told interviewer Debbie Boyce that Younger called a meeting of Bay Area law enforcement officials, including DA's, to organize the Bay Area campaign, and at that meeting he appointed SF DA John J. Ferdon as the San Francisco coordinator.

The choice of DA's as county coordinators or chairmen for this political drive was natural and logical, once it was decided that police forces and other law enforcement agencies were to run and man the show. Just as the attorney general is the chief law officer of the state, with extensive work relationships with the DA's, so is the district attorney the "chief law officer of the county," with extensive work relationships and daily contacts with police departments in his county.

The Los Angeles County Sheriff's Department memo provides a striking example of the misuse of public administrative facilities for political purposes, and the almost military table of organization superimposed on pre-existing lines of authority.

The memo sets up the internal organization of the Sheriff's Department itself for the petition drive, revealing explicitly the heavy, exclusive use of public facilities and the use of the law enforcement chain of command for purely political ends.

Captain E.H. Swanson is to be "Department Coordinator," with the duty "to develop overall program and coordinate Departmental effort." Unnamed captains are to "coordinate division activity." Unnamed lieutenants are to "coordinate station or unit activity, schedule volunteers, brief individual solicitors, solicit volunteers from civic groups and wives, solicit donations from employes and citizens' groups, review petitions for completeness, and forward completed petitions to Regional Headquarters."

Regional Headquarters are to be "West Hollywood" and "Temple Station" facilities. They are to have a "volunteer staff" consisting of "Deputies, Wives and Citizens." A "Central Headquarters" is to be situated in "Main Central Jail, Room 1004." Its job is to process petitions submitted by "Civic Center units" and to "Forward completed petitions to Hall of Justice Jail, 13th floor, daily."

Like the "Regional Headquarters," the "Central Headquarters" is to have a "volunteer staff" consisting of "Deputies, Wives and Citizens," and both are to have "24-hour operation if necessary."

Sheriff's deputies are to be "encouraged" to devote at least eight hours of off-duty time to the petition work. Their wives are to be similarly "encouraged" to work alongside their husbands on the petition.

And all of them, of course, used public buildings, burned public lights ("24 hours a day if necessary"), used public telephones, desks, chairs, tables, pencils and paper, all supplied by the taxpayers for the performance of official duty.

In San Francisco, Inspector Samuels promptly distributed petitions to police and fire stations throughout the city. He released this information to the press, giving a Police Department phone number for the public to call for information.

And so it went, in county after county, city after city, all over the state. In Marin County, researchers checked petitions and law agency personnel rosters and found that more than half the valid signatures in Marin County were obtained by law enforcement personnel: 3,590 out of 7,040 signatures. However, this is a minimum figure because the investigators were unable to get a complete list of all law enforcement personnel in the county to check against the signatures of petition circulators.

There were isolated, but significant, incidents that show law enforcement people were not sure of their ground in blatantly using public facilities for their politicking: where challenges were made, as in San Francisco, Chico, Marin County and Santa Cruz, officers removed their petitions.

Like Younger's, Gov. Reagan's power and influence were hard at work. Yolo County District Attorney C. Robert Jameson told Sowards that, during the closing weeks of the campaign, he received "a call a day" from

Reagan's office. He hinted that the governor's phone bill must be quite large, meaning that Yolo was not the only county getting frequent contact from the Capitol. Presumably, this was done with public funds appropriated to run the governor's office.

Ken Brown, on the other hand, insisted to Sowards that Reagan was involved only to the extent that "he let us know where he stands." Says Sowards, "It could very well be that Mr. Brown is not on Reagan's mailing list."

Indeed it could. Reagan knew where the action was: not in Ken Brown's office, but in law enforcement agencies all over California, where the actual drive was going on, and he had his official pipelines to all of them.

When the campaign lagged in early May, Jameson said, Reagan began applying pressure on the California Highway Patrol, which is directly under his office. Said Jameson, "The governor felt very strongly about the matter, and memos were coming down from on high." According to Jameson, two weeks before the filing date, more CHP officers were called upon to work on the petition and pressure was brought on officers who had not turned in petitions.

Jameson and Brown agreed the CHP was particularly effective in gathering signatures, though Brown acknowledged "tremendous help" from the CHP only in San Diego County. Jameson offered two reasons: (1) a statewide camaraderie exists among CHP officers, which does not exist between local police departments, and (2) more important, the CHP has a single chain of command that lends itself well to political organizing. That chain of command ends in the governor's office.

Consider the advantages a statewide initiative campaign has if it is run out of government offices and managed by government officials. No legal fees to pay, no offices to rent, no telephone bills to pay, no need to take time off one's job to work on the petition, an excellent distribution of neighborhood campaign headquarters (the outlying police and sheriffs' stations).

San Francisco provides an excellent case study. According to Ken Samuels, only $60 was spent here to collect 18,000 signatures. This is a fantastically low figure. Samuels raised all the money he needed from a banker, whom he refused to name, who kicked in a mere $100.

Samuels used $60 of it for the sole purpose of mailing out some petitions, then returned the remaining $40. Result: 18,000 signatures at ⅓¢ per name, no doubt a record in the annals of signature-gathering for initiatives.

Contrast this with Alvin Duskin's dirt cheap initiative campaign for a highrise control charter amendment [in San Francisco] last year. Telephone bills: $100 a month. Newspaper ads: $20,000. Salaries for three staff members, including an attorney: $2000 a month. Thousands more for informational printing—handbills, posters, letters to volunteers. It took all this to get 35,000 signatures.

The Death Penalty Initiative was one of the cheapest statewide initiative campaigns in California history. The official figures are not yet available from the Secretary of State's office in Sacramento, but Ken Brown told me the entire campaign, statewide, cost only $25–$30,000, of which $12,000 was spent in his office. That leaves $13,000 to $18,000 as the sum spent in all the rest of California, to gather nearly a million signatures. Brown himself contrasted this with the Marijuana Initiative: $80,000.

Brown talked proudly of his accomplishment, freely giving the breakdown on how it was done: "We spent no money on rental of offices. Oh, there might have been a few here and there, but they were insignificant."

Of course there was no need to rent offices. The taxpayers provided those—fully equipped—with lots of public employes to man them.

Another major factor: "We didn't do any advertising. The press was just great. They really cooperated."

I have examined countless newspaper clippings from all over the state, and they bear Brown's point out fully.... The newspapers gave fulsome news and editorial promotion to the proponents of the death penalty. Story after story provided specific information on where to sign petitions, where to get petitions, where and when to turn them in, along with exhortations from campaign leaders to the troops.

I outlined some features of this campaign, including the heavy involvement of law enforcement officers and the heavy use of public facilities, to Deputy Fred Whisman in the SF DA's office. He was not surprised. "Well," he said, "the man in the street doesn't have nearly the interest in the death penalty that the newspapers say he does. People do have opinions pro and con on it, but the average person wouldn't give much help in a campaign like this."

Whisman himself had no interest in working on the petition, he said, and added that interest in the local DA's office generally was "low level," which helps explain why San Francisco made the poorest showing by percentage of any county.

Would a legitimate citizen's initiative for the Death Penalty have sprung up without Younger & Co.? Younger maintains that's why he decided to draft one. "We hoped to avoid duplication of effort and the circulation of competing or poorly conceived petitions," he said in his March 13 press release.

In September, I called Younger's office and talked to his public relations aide, Al Gordon. Could other citizens, I asked, get the free legal services of the Attorney General to avoid duplication of effort and the circulation of competing or poorly conceived petitions?

"Well," said Gordon, "the attorney general has an official interest in this one."

"What do you mean 'official interest?' " I asked. "Is he laying the groundwork for further legal action in the courts? Is this part of some legal strategy?"

"Oh, no," replied Gordon. "Nothing like that. It's for the two reasons he cited in his press release of March 13." (Younger's reasons: to restore the legislature's "right to legislate on the matter of the death penalty" and to "reinstate the law regarding the death penalty as it was prior to the state court's ill-advised decision.")

"But what's his authority to use his power to aid one petition and not others?"

Gordon then read me the words from Article 5, Section 13, of the State Constitution: "The attorney general shall be the chief law officer of the state."

"That means," Gordon said, that "he is the head cop, the chief fuzz, if you want to put it that way. He has broad powers."

I guess so. But I interviewed several attorneys and academic specialists in this field who argued that:

(1) The AG is required by state law to spend full-time on official duties;

(2) it's none of his business if competing or poorly conceived petitions are circulated;

(3) in any case, to provide official services to a petition in which he has a personal interest and deny them to others violates the equal protection clause of the U.S. Constitution; and

(4) the AG, as a member of the executive branch, violates the constitutional separation of powers clause when he leads and organizes an initiative petition, a legislative process, because he wants to subvert decisions of the State and U.S. Supreme Courts.

In this chapter of the great Death Penalty fight, I've cited lots of moral, ethical and legal offenses. The rub is: Who is going to investigate? (The AG?) Who will order the arrests? (The DA?) Who will make the arrests? (The police?) Who will prosecute? (The DA's?)

This is the ultimate irony in this fight to the death, perhaps best symbolized by the CCOA slogan that appears at the bottom of its Death Penalty press releases: "Ethical procedure is the first step toward progress."

Notes

[1] "The Crusader's Reward," *Grassroots Editor*, September-October 1970, p. 3.

[2] Warren Breed, "Social Control in the Newsroom," *Social Forces*, May 1955, pp. 326-335.

[3] "Raising Hell on the Bay," *Time*, November 23, 1970, pp. 90-91.

[4] "Forward Look Is Encouraging, Says Cervi," *Oregon Publisher*, July 1956, p. 8.

[5] *Ibid.*

[6] Anthony Ripley, "Denver's Papers Lose 3 Leaders," New York *Times*, January 17, 1971, p. 47.

[7] *Op. cit.*, "Forward Look Is Encouraging."

[8] "Eugene Cervi," *Cervi's Rocky Mountain Journal*, December 16, 1970, p. 1.

[9] Bruce B. Brugmann, "Toward a Two-Newspaper Town" (Dean A.L. Stone Address, University of Montana), *Montana Journalism Review*, No. 11, 1968, p. 11.

[10] Robert J. Glessing, *The Underground Press in America* (Bloomington, Ind.: Indiana University Press, 1970), p. 14.

[11]John L. Hulteng and Roy Paul Nelson, *The Fourth Estate* (New York: Harper & Row, 1971), p. 204.

[12]"Trying to Save Maine," *Time*, October 31, 1969, pp. 72-74.

[13]*Ibid.*

[14]"Newspapers—The Lone Ranger Rides Again," *Time*, September 27, 1968, pp. 49-50.

[15]*Ibid.*

Guarding the Guardians: The Journalism Reviews

4

A crisis of confidence exists today between the American people and their news media.
—National Commission on the Causes and Prevention of Violence, 1970

The American news media have an identity problem.

It springs from their curious dual role: On the one hand they are expected to be detached observers of society, serving as its watchdog and conscience; on the other hand they are expected to be participants in that society, in which they are among the leading institutions. Newspapers and broadcast stations are social critics, but they are also employers and members of chambers of commerce. The result of these two roles is a collision of values and a conflict of interest. As critics have suggested, it is like asking one attorney to prepare arguments for both the prosecution and defense.

Although the alternative journalists spiritedly admonish the media for not living up to their public responsibilities, they usually restrict their criticism to community concerns not covered (or covered ineptly) by the conventional media. In recent years, however, growing numbers of dissatisfied journalists have directed their energies toward *improving* the news media. Like their colleagues at the San Francisco *Bay Guardian,* the *Texas Observer,* and the *Maine Times,* they have a fundamental regard for the present system. They are not radicals who hope to annihilate the traditions of American journalism. They simply want the press to function in a more ethical, responsible manner.

Of course, press criticism has been at work for years, in both the academic and trade press. Academic press criticism is best represented by the *Columbia Journalism Review*, established in 1961 by Columbia University's Graduate School of Journalism, which carries some articles written by professional journalists, some by academicians. What differentiates the *Review* from such scholarly publications as *Journalism Quarterly* is its impressionistic analysis and engaging style. Trade press criticism is characterized by mild, sometimes banal, evaluations in the *Masthead*, published by the National Conference of Editorial Writers, and in the *Bulletin of the American Society of Newspaper Editors*. *Editor & Publisher*, the trade magazine of the newspaper industry, and *Broadcasting*, the trade magazine of the electronic media, are usually content to report briefly on major criticisms published elsewhere. The *Quill*, the official organ of Sigma Delta Chi, the society of professional journalists, occasionally publishes sharply critical pieces.

There has been press criticism in America as long as there have been newspapers, but only in recent years have working journalists banded together to produce continuing critiques.

The Chicago Journalism Review

The press was there in the street and in the convention hall. Mixed with the crowds, reporters were often mistaken for demonstrators, and were also subjected to physical injury and verbal insult. Some police attacks on newsmen were deliberate, others accidental, but whatever the case, newsmen were deeply involved, many unwillingly.

Such brutal treatment outraged the nation's press, and for days after the "police riot" at the 1968 Democratic presidential convention, Chicago and Mayor Richard Daley became symbols of force. Chicago newspapers and broadcast stations joined in deploring the shoddy treatment of reporters. But after the convention, the media resumed what many thought was an overly cozy arrangement with the city's establishment: their criticism of the police and Daley proved to be short-lived.

Out of this was formed the Association of Working Reporters, a group of disgruntled Chicago newsmen which began to publish the *Chicago Journalism Review*, a searingly critical assessment of the city's journalism. In, its first issue the *Review* stated that "news management, news manipulation and assaults on the integrity of the working press are commonplace in this tight little city," and that they could be countered only by "a professional consciousness among our fellow newsmen—to let them know that their battle to stay pure is not a lonely, hopeless fight." The *Review* was unique. For perhaps the first time in America, working reporters were criticizing their own newspapers' shortcomings—in print in their own publication.

The *Chicago Journalism Review* got a mixed reception. An assessment in *Saturday Review* termed it "a strident, controversial compendium of political sniping, gutter language, encomiums to local favorites and cronies in press and government, Chicago chauvinism, rasping hostility toward 'the boss, seamy exposés, and, occasionally, incisive reports." But radical journalist James Aronson evaluated it as a "revolt of the slaves—not only against the Mayor and the police but against the editors and publishers of the Chicago press, and the radio and television stations." *Time* argued that there was "something distinctly disturbing about newspaper employees in effect snitching on their own bosses in public," but added, "the *Review* can clearly serve a useful purpose in Chicago. Besides, its kind of self-criticism might be even more important in the nation's many one-newspaper towns, where journalistic complacency often goes unchallenged."[1]

The *Review* has often covered a wide range of subjects usefully, disclosing Mayor Daley's shortcomings, harassment of poverty workers, vote frauds, the blind spots of the establishment press in reporting riots and violent death, and newspaper boosterism in the handling of corporations' annual reports on business pages.[2]

The editors of the *Review* frequently run stories rejected by local newspapers, even though they were prepared by reporters on assignment. One was an article on the National Consumers' Union by Diane Monk of the Chicago *Daily News*. "The article did not run because the editors thought the NCU might be seeking publicity," wrote a *Review* editor. The story, which was strongly critical of supermarkets, supported other articles in the *Review*, including one entitled NEWSPAPERS SEE NO EVIL IN SUPERMARTS. Some of the "unfit" articles are only mildly controversial in tone, while others are heavily one-sided reports. The *Review* itself is intensely personal and publishes many first-person articles.

Most of the content focuses on Chicago journalism, print and broadcast, and local media executives are mentioned so frequently that they have become widely known among *Review* readers. In an interview with Chicago *Tribune* editor Clayton Kirkpatrick, reporter Lewis Z. Koch revealed some of the pressure that *Review* writers face:

> I wasn't being completely open in my remarks to Kirkpatrick. I had actually wanted to begin the series with the Chicago *Sun-Times* and [its editor] Jim Hoge, mainly because I had more access to information about the *Sun-Times* and Hoge than I had about the *Tribune* and Kirkpatrick. But Hoge was terribly reluctant and [*Sun-Times* publisher] Marshall Field V suggested that before an interview of their editors was allowed, I or the CJR people should "do" the people across the street. I rather resented the not-so-subtle hint that I or the CJR "did" anybody but since I didn't want to abandon the project, I decided to call Kirkpatrick. I had explained that I was going to write what I hoped would be a four-part series on the Chicago newspapers and their editors and that I would like to begin the series with the *Tribune*.[3]

The *Review* often chides Field. One issue carried his picture under the headline DOES THIS FACE LOOK FAMILIAR? The story reported: "Marshall Field, 29-year old publisher of the Chicago *Sun-Times* and *Daily News*, has had his picture in his papers 24 times this year. . . . There's a strong temptation to suggest that Field's frequent appearances in his own pages are part of a calculated plan to endow the young publisher with instant prestige."[4] Although the *Review* covers national trends in journalism, its local focus has enabled it to point up many flaws in Chicago journalism. In one instance, when a ring of prostitutes was arrested in a prominent hotel, conventional Chicago papers failed to name the hotel. The *Review* made this absurdity clear by naming the hotel and then publishing a satire in which the name was omitted from a society news story. The *Review* insists on ethical conduct for Chicago reporters no less than for editors: "In one article, *Sun-Times* reporter Ben Heineman, Jr., son of the president of Chicago's Northwest Industries, accepted part of the blame himself for the failure of the city's newspapers fully to pursue leads that pointed toward police responsibility for the death of four Negroes. . . . The *Review* pointed out that city hall reporters normally accept Christmas gifts from aldermen and get at least $200-300 and 25 to 30 bottles of booze each year."[5]

The *Review* is written and edited by several aggressive young reporters, among them former *Chicago Today* education reporter Ron Dorfman, *Daily News* education reporter Henry De Zutter, and *Sun-Times* feature writer Lillian Calhoun. By far the most celebrated contributor is nationally prominent cartoonist Bill Mauldin, who works for the *Sun-Times*. He lends his prestige with biting, memorable cartoons that are published on the front page of the *Review*.

The contributors received little pressure from their employers until they published a scathing piece about Bailey K. Howard, who then headed the *Daily News* and *Sun-Times* combination. *Daily News* executives issued an ultimatum to De Zutter, the *Review's* first editor. As the *Review* reported, "Either De Zutter's name would disappear from the masthead of CJR or he would be reassigned [at the *Daily News*] to a position less sensitive than the education/radicals beat, like maybe writing obituaries or reading race track copy (although racing news is likely too sensitive over there, too)."[6] Later the order was rescinded. The *Review* reported, "De Zutter's name could remain on the masthead if his title wasn't so impressive, and if persons currently employed at other newspapers could be found to join CJR's editorial board. Since it had previously been agreed by the editors of CJR that this was a desirable goal, De Zutter acquiesced."

The *Review* sometimes publishes memos from Chicago media executives which take issue with *Review* pieces. For instance, *Sun-Times* editor Hoge responded to a *Review* charge that a story about a real estate deal had been killed by saying that the story "relied so heavily on an anonymous letter that had been received by another newspaper and anonymous sources [that] the editors felt that without more specific documentation and attribution the story amounted to little more than unjustified character assassination."[7]

The *Review*'s possibly negative aspects were perhaps expressed in a memo that publisher Marshall Field wrote to his staff: "Many of us had high hopes that the *Chicago Journalism Review* would develop into a journal of ethical criticism of the media. But it is with increasing dismay that we perceive some of the editors and contributors to the *Review* in violation of copyright, in unauthorized use of company files and memoranda, and unable to distinguish between the confidences of 'on-time' communications and their desire to publish titillating innuendos about the process of journalism."[8] These are central problems, but whatever the judgments of them, it is clear that the *Chicago Journalism Review* has broken new ground in American journalism, trying to create more ethically sensitive news media for Chicago from inside.

The Unsatisfied Man

The *Unsatisfied Man*, published in Denver, Colorado, takes its name from a statement by the legendary Denver newspaperman F. G. Bonfils: "There is no hope for the satisfied man." The paper is similar to the *Chicago Journalism Review*, and in fact the founders, working newsmen in Colorado, prepared for their project by meeting with the Chicago group for "spiritual guidance." They then formed the Colorado Media Project, Inc., and issued this prospectus:

> For journalists—be they editors, publishers or reporters—public opinion and the opinion of their peers are among the few sanctions which exist. There is no accrediting body which dictates who may or may not practice, nor should there be. Instead, what is needed is a forum in which observers in and outside the media can engage in responsible public commentary on the deeds and misdeeds of the media.

"It should be obvious," wrote Denver newsman Charles Carter in the first issue in September 1970, "that this project has largely grown out of dissatisfaction with the performance of the state's news agencies, who for the most part are our employers." But the *Unsatisfied Man* also promised fairness and balance. As Carter wrote, "We are convinced . . . that in many cases the newspapers and broadcast news outlets of Denver and the rest of the state perform well. We intend to point out what we believe are the strengths of the media as well as their weaknesses." This attempt at balance brought praise from *Saturday Review*: "Denver's tabloid shows a fundamental integrity and intelligence, resourcefulness and creativity in exploring story sources, balance and the courage to praise as well as criticize."

An eight-page, tabloid-sized magazine with a large editorial cartoon on the front page (by Rob Pudim of the Denver *Post*), the *Unsatisfied Man*'s columns are open to "any intelligent documented criticism of the media, from whatever source," and while most are written by practicing newsmen, journalism professors, lawyers, and others have also contributed.

One article in *TUM* which asked disquieting questions about newspapers in Aspen, the ski capital, asserted: "Journalism in Aspen is as full of spirit and madness as the community itself, a movable feast and famine blending a lot of small town skepticism and a little big-city sophistication." The author, a former editor of the Aspen *Illustrated News,* said his article was "personal, prejudiced and rambling in the style of the Aspen newspapers themselves."

Other articles have reviewed the performance of the ethics committee at the Denver *Post,* equal time on Colorado radio and television stations, the press coverage of a free university encampment in Denver, *Cervi's Rocky Mountain Journal,* a suburban newspaper chain, rural journalism, advertising, and photojournalism practices. A column headed LAURELS AND HARDLIES briefly assesses press performance. For example:

> LAURELS to Richard Tucker for his tight, revealing precinct analysis of the Denver mayoral elections in the May 20 *Rocky Mountain News.* When compared with the far wordier Denver *Post* coverage (including a special section), Tucker's article demonstrated that length is seldom a substitute for getting to the heart of a matter.

> HARDLY had the Denver *Post* started "coordinating" the news of the 1976 Winter Olympics when it began turning its attention to another matter. This time it is an event of considerably less news value—a June 13-18 art auction to raise funds for a local university library. But the Voice of the Rocky Mountain Empire nevertheless vowed to pull out all the stops and give it the mighty Wurlitzer treatment.[9]

The *Unsatisfied Man* suggested that undue publicity given to former convicts returning to their communities inhibits rehabilitation. It quoted one convict: "I know a lotta guys down here [at Colorado State Prison] that could've made it—if it hadn't been for the press." In its "First Annual Deb Ball Quiz," *TUM* challenged its readers to determine whether "selected gush" from two Denver newspapers was from the white or black debutante ball.

More often than the other journalism reviews, *TUM* criticizes broadcasting. For instance, it published an attorney's critique of the shallowness of a Denver television station in meeting its public service obligations:

1. No locally originated programming in prime time (other than news shows).
2. Forty-seven old movies.

3. Public service programming concentrated on Saturday afternoon and Sunday morning (when station profits are least affected).
4. Network-provided programming filling almost the entire operating schedule from morning to night.
5. Eighty percent of the programming consisting of entertainment and sports.
6. An obvious lack of quality children's programming.
7. No programs dealing specifically with the Black community or Chicano community.

This analysis was disputed in the next issue by a television newsman who argued each of the charges and complained that the attorney "failed to offer a realistic and specific yardstick of performance in television public service."

The St. Louis Journalism Review

In 1970 two St. Louis *Post-Dispatch* reporters returned from a national meeting sponsored by the editors of *Chicago Journalism Review* and decided to start a St. Louis review. The rationale of the St. Louis group that was formed centered on the failure of media leaders to understand the changes in modern communications needs that were believed to require changes in many media traditions and operations.

In their first issue the editors announced that they hoped the *St. Louis Journalism Review* would become "to the regular newspapers and the radio and television stations what those media are to government and other institutions. The news media are counted on to report to the public on all institutions and evaluate their performance. However, no one reports on the media or evaluates their performance. In St. Louis we intend to take on that task."

Nine large headlines were splashed across page one of that issue:

PULITZER PRIZE WINNING REPORTER QUITS POST-DISPATCH IN PROTEST

ST. LOUIS MEDIA MAKE CERVANTES THEIR CAUSE

POST AND GLOBE SPLIT PROFITS

PRINTERS REJECT CONTROVERSIAL PAPER

BLACKS AND THE MEDIA

POWER FAILURES GO UNREPORTED

GOVERNMENT INVADES MEDIA FILES

KPLR FIRES 17 OF 20 NEWSMEN

PAPERS BUY BUSCH LINE

In subsequent issues, the *Review* charged the local press with lethargy. For instance, it strongly criticized the failure of the St. Louis papers to investigate a local Negro boycott of Anheuser-Busch products. And in a December 1971 story it attributed the success of the annual United Fund drive to the "free public relations services provided by the St. Louis media." "Public relations handouts," the *Review* said, "turned up on front pages and in featured broadcast news spots without any exploration by the media of the administration of the fund itself or of the agencies which benefit from the drive. This despite the fact that in November 1970 a professional management group hired by the United Fund itself substantiated criticisms made earlier by citizen groups."

Although the tone of the *St. Louis Journalism Review* is somewhat sensational, the paper has been widely praised. *Columbia Journalism Review* said the first issue seemed "even-handed, comprehensive, even a little heavy. But the tone throughout is that of determined journalists who know what they want."

There is some evidence that St. Louis media executives have not been overjoyed with the *Review's* caustic criticism. In fact, the *Review* staff seems to fear possible reprisals and thus gives its reporters the choice of whether or not they want a by-line. Although by-lines enhance credibility, Ted Gest, a member of the *Review* editorial board, was quoted as saying, "We are a relatively small city and people felt their employment would be in jeopardy."

The Hawaii Journalism Review

Like all journalism reviews, the Honolulu-based *Hawaii Journalism Review* has a strong local bias—although it is more evident here, even to the point of parochialism, because local issues in Hawaii rarely emerge as national issues on the mainland. The *Review* looks like the Chicago and Denver reviews—a newsletter-magazine format with a prominent editorial cartoon—and it, too, is edited and published by working journalists. Only articles from working journalists are published, but the editors welcome replies and rebuttals from anyone mentioned in an article. Subscriptions are free and no advertising is published. The six-page, letter-sized paper depends for its survival on donations from journalists. In 1973 the *Review* indicated a financial strain and sent distress signals in the form of a letter asking for contributions. The *Review* has a rotating editorial board and lists no editor.

From the first issue, in 1971, the *Hawaii Journalism Review* has been low-key but critical. In an article chiding the Honolulu *Advertiser* for its restaurant guide, termed little more than "trade handouts for the purchase of ads," the *Advertiser* restaurant columnist was accused of grinding out puffery to please the advertisers: "If the food is horrible, she raves about the decorations."

Advertising masquerading as news has been a frequent target, as in this July 1971 story, which ran under the head NEWS SPACE FOR SALE:

> OCCASIONALLY FOR SALE: News pages of the *Sunday Star-Bulletin* and *Advertiser*. PLEASE CONTACT: Ted Smiley, editor, Hawaii Living section; or Buck Buchwach, vice president and director, Hawaii Newspaper Agency.
>
> Section "E" of the Sunday newspaper is skillfully disguised as news of real estate, home improvements and furnishings, and a reporter's observations on property development. But if you have such news to bring to the paper's attention, do not look for reporter-editor Ted Smiley in the news offices. His desk is closer to the source of his paycheck—the groundfloor offices of the Hawaii Newspaper Agency. That is where the ads are sold.

The story carried a detailed accounting of advertising in the guise of news and held that an "advertisement should be clearly marked that. And reporters should work for a newspaper's editorial arm, not its advertising office."

Strongly newspaper oriented, the *Review* does occasionally cover the work of wire services and broadcasting stations. Perhaps because of the relatively small journalistic community in Hawaii, most of the criticism is more personal, less corporate in tone than that of the other reviews, which sometimes seem to speak of the "media" as a distant, dehumanized giant. One issue of the Hawaii review carried a good-natured column by the *Advertiser* city editor taking issue with one-sided reporting in the *Review* as well as poor writing and proofreading.

The Philadelphia Journalism Review

Founded in April 1971 on the theory that the power of the press could be used to improve the press, the *Philadelphia Journalism Review*'s first issue carried an article about how the *Le Monde* staff runs that elite French newspaper, blamed the "lazy press" for Pennsylvania's "no-right-to-know" law, reported a survey of the "heights and depths of editorial feeling" at the Philadelphia *Inquirer* after the newspaper was sold to the Knight group, and commented on "the grand manner of objectivity."

The *Review* began as an organ of the *Inquirer*'s City Room Committee, a group elected under the auspices of the American Newspaper Guild's Philadelphia local, but now includes on its editorial board representatives of the three major Philadelphia papers as well as radio and television stations. The review had a conspiratorial air at first, according to Donald Drake, a *Review* editor:

> Management greeted us with much suspicion. . . . In the beginning some editors didn't even want to be interviewed until McMullan [John McMullan, *Inquirer* executive editor] had three of us attend a conference of editors to explain our plans. Since then, especially with

the second issue, things have opened up. McMullan complimented us on our second issue, as did Greenberg [Robert Greenberg, the city editor]. We now have support from a variety of other media—the *Bulletin,* UPI, WHYY-TV. Writers and skeptical staffers who didn't want to be associated with it in the beginning are now volunteering ideas, writing stories and accepting assignments.[10]

The June 1971 issue carried THREE VIEWS FROM THE TOP, a thoughtful commentary by editors representing the city's three daily newspapers. One, George R. Packard of the Philadelphia *Bulletin,* wrote that a journalism review can accomplish much if it resolves these basic questions:

1. Is it going to be equally critical of all media here, or is it touchy for a group spawned in Knightville to mention such embarrassments as phony action lines . . . ?

2. Will it improve or destroy the sometimes fragile relationships between reporters and editors? Should all of us—editors and reporters—guard our every word lest we be quoted—possibly out of context and without right of reply—in the next issue of the *Review?* Shouldn't both editors and reporters have the right to be wrong once in awhile and to shout about it off the record? Should personalities become issues?

3. Aren't the best papers in this country, such as the Washington *Post,* really reporters' newspapers? How did they get that way? Didn't they give reporters maximum scope to develop their talents? Didn't this in turn attract the best reporters, who knew more about their subjects than the editors, and could express it better? Shouldn't editors' authority be sequential, not hierarchial? Isn't a paper thus dependent on the standards set by its top reporters? If this is true, will a review which sets up an arbitrary relationship between reporters and editors really lift our standards, or simply increase the potential of self-defeating bickering and misunderstandings?

4. I wonder if reporters should write, anonymously or otherwise, about the inner workings of their own papers. I note that the new review in New York will have "an ironclad policy never to commission or publish such articles" because of the possible conflict of interest.

5. Who will watch the watchdogs? Will reporters or editors stand as guilty before accusations of unprofessional or unethical conduct simply because they choose not to reply (or are not given a chance to reply)? Should they feel compelled to reply to an outsider who could not know under what pressures and difficulties they may have been laboring?

"A staff member's first obligation is to himself, then to his newspaper," wrote Rolfe Neill, editor of the Philadelphia *Daily News.* "His criticisms of his paper should be directed there." And *Inquirer* executive editor John

McMullan added: "The major pitfall I hope the *Review* editors will avoid is confining commentaries and criticism to after-the-fact publication. I would like to see more *Inquirer* staffers working in a constructive and timely vein to improve our newspaper, rather than lying in wait, so to speak, simply to enjoy the perverse satisfaction of public post mortems." All three editors supported the *Review*, if somewhat reluctantly.

The major shortcoming of the *Review*, staff member Donald Drake believes, "is not having enough in-depth, well-reported pieces, as opposed to opinion pieces."

Sharp criticism came from Norman Hill who called the *Review* "simply rotten." Writing in *Saturday Review*, Hill said: "Half its pages were devoted to a depressing spasm of sobbing over office economies instituted by the Knight management when it took over from the Annenbergs." Hill found such criticism shortsighted: "Many a derailed former newsman would advise that writer to pray that his management's economies keep the newspaper—and the writer's job—alive!"

The *Review* seems cluttered and produced with something less than professional quality printing. The writing cries out for heavy editing, a flaw made worse by deficient proofreading. The editors admitted that their first issues were erratic and that they looked to the time when the quality of reporting about reporting in the *Review* would improve.

(More)—A Journalism Review

The most impressive and ambitious review is *(More)*—named for the term journalists use at the bottom of pages of copy to mean "more to come"—which is published in New York City. The May 1971 pilot issue offered no "Ringing Declaration of Purpose," stating that "The trouble with such noble manifestos ... is that you have to live up to them." Editor Richard Pollak wrote that the editors' goal is "to cover the New York area press—by which we mean newspapers, magazines, radio and television—with the kind of tough mindedness we think the press should but seldom does apply to its coverage of the world. We hope to do this seriously, but not without wit, fairly but not objectively." The pilot issue was so successful and well-received that *(More)—A Journalism Review* began regular monthly publication in September 1971.

Written by journalists, *(More)* has sought to avoid disputes between reporters and management. Of his contributors Pollack has said: "We hope that their employers will have the common sense to recognize that a journalist ought to be free to write about his profession without feeling his job is in jeopardy. For our part we recognize the conflict of interest in asking a journalist to write about his own organization and consequently have established an ironclad policy never to commission or publish such articles."

(More) was the first journalism review with a full-time staff. William

Woodward III, 26, member of a well-to-do family and former Harvard *Crimson* editor, took a leave from the New York *Post*, where he had been a reporter, in order to be *(More)*'s publisher. Editor Pollak, ten years Woodward's senior, had worked for the Baltimore *Sun*; Worcester, Massachusetts, *Telegram* & *Gazette*; the Honolulu *Star-Bulletin*; and *Newsweek*. Widely known names abound on the publication's masthead: Paul Cowan, *Village Voice* reporter; Ernest Dunbar, former *Look* senior editor; Pamela Howard, New York *Post* reporter and daughter of Jack R. Howard of Scripps-Howard newspapers; Pulitzer Prize winner J. Anthony Lukas, formerly of the New York *Times*; A. Kent MacDougall, former reporter for the *Wall Street Journal*; Calvin Trillin of the *New Yorker*; and Mike Wallace of CBS News.

These editors and writers—and the highest editorial standards of any review—have produced valuable articles. One by former presidential press secretary George Reedy criticized Daniel P. Moynihan's much-talked-about *Commentary* article, "The Presidency and the Press," which had chided the press for not recognizing the excitement and stimulation of the Nixon administration. Another, written by Lukas, charged that *Reader's Digest* used its editorial space to help huge corporations hide their contributions to pollution, that the *Digest*'s "massive educational communications program is little more than a very expensive and elaborate advertising supplement."

One of the most notable articles was "An Adventure in 'the Big Cave' " by Charlotte Curtis of the New York *Times*, which described the behind-the-scenes intrigue at *Harper's* when Willie Morris was fired as editor. Disagreeing sharply with the many articles sympathetic to Morris and his colleagues, Miss Curtis wrote that what happened

> . . . is an unhappy tale of an almost willful failure to communicate and often astonishing inexperience—of a confused publisher who had never published a national magazine, of a head-strong editor who had never edited one and, not least, of a well-meaning owner, John Cowles, Jr., who had never owned one. And saddest of all, it is the story of a brilliant, young Southern writer [Morris] who felt driven to run with New York's literary pack and lost his way in an alien city he so aptly described as "the big cave."

(More) also slashed at Norman Mailer in a piece that *Life* originally assigned and later refused to print. The editors indicated that Mailer himself might have influenced *Life*'s scrapping of the project. Other subjects have included discrimination at the liberal New York *Post*, an examination of Washington columnists, the shaky start of Community News Service (which was designed to improve coverage of race relations in New York), all-news radio, life without television, and free-form ads.

(More) has, of course, excited controversy. One reader attacked it for "violation of reporting ethics so fundamental that it makes me wonder if the copy is being edited." A *Reader's Digest* editor, smarting from *(More)*'s

attack on his magazine's environmental series, said, "I have received a large amount of criticism from government and industry, yet my editors at the *Digest* have never once suggested I tone down my writing."

But the review has also been applauded. Former presidential aide and newspaper publisher Bill Moyers said: "Without something like *(More)*, the cries of 'Free Press! Free Press!' become little more than an excuse for mediocrity." Edward Barrett, former dean of the Columbia University Graduate School of Journalism, called the review "exciting, professional, generally constructive—and, more important, potentially a tremendous force on the side of the angels."

In May 1972, while the American Newspaper Publishers Association was holding its annual meeting, *(More)* sponsored its own two-day "A. J. Liebling Counter-Convention," named for the late *New Yorker* journalist who wrote caustic columns of media criticism. This provided a rare public forum for a discussion of the new journalism. Lively panels featuring Tom Wolfe, Pauline Kael, Tom Wicker, and Dan Rather gave *(More)* strong national visibility and made it the best-known journalism review in America. A second Counter-Convention was held in 1973.

Some Other Reviews

By 1973, several other reviews had begun publication—*Thorn: The Connecticut Valley Media Review* in Holyoke, Massachusetts; *Countermedia: The Alaska Journalism Review and Supplement* in Fairbanks; *The Twin Cities Journalism Review* in St. Paul, Minnesota; *Buncombe*, a review of Baltimore journalism; *San Francisco Bay Area Journalism Review; Houston Journalism Review;* and the *Pretentious Idea*, a review of Arizona journalism in Tucson. Both the Baltimore and Tucson reviews are published by college students and professors. Another paper, the Albuquerque, New Mexico, *Hard Times*, is not a journalism review, but it does offer a regular feature, "Those Other Media," which criticizes local newspapers and broadcast outlets.

An earlier publication, the *AP Review*, had died by 1972. Produced by Associated Press reporters in New York City, the review had offered a caustic analysis of the sprawling press association.

Another effort, somewhat less ambitious than most journalism reviews, was the *Nelson Society Newsletter*, published by the William Rockhill Nelson Society in Kansas City, Missouri. The society was named for the founder of the Kansas City *Star*, known for great investigative reporting, to try to move the paper back closer to the founder's principles. The *Newsletter* began, according to an unsigned article in the first issue, because of a "demand among staff members for an organization concerned with the issues of great journalism." The society died in 1972 during a Guild organizing election. In an early issue of the *Newsletter,* one divergent voice charged that the Nelson Society was a cop-out: "The journalism review movement here failed when members backed out in deference to management wishes."[11] Not so, said *Star* reporter Charles Hammer: "I was among a group of about ten staffers, not all of them Nelson Society members, who took part in talks with television newsmen and Charles Klotzer, publisher of the *St. Louis Journalism Review.* The aim was to create a *Kansas City Journalism Review.* After early enthusiasm we thought better of the idea."

A one-man journalism review, *Overset: A Review of Newspaper Journalism,* began publication in March 1972. Published in San Diego, California, by Robert Juran, who heads a newspaper consulting firm, *Overset* appears to be a muckraking alternative to the trade paper *Editor & Publisher. Overset* has a national orientation, praising press critics from A. J. Liebling to the *Chicago Journalism Review,* while roasting establishment journalism—especially chain ownership, which it opposes. Not a stickler for immediacy, Juran reprints long-forgotten press criticism. Produced in a magazine format, *Overset* makes ample use of line drawings, including, somewhat tastelessly, the brilliant work of the nineteenth-century etcher-caricaturist Gustave Doré as an editorial cartoon with a modern caption.

To help stimulate the journalism review movement, the *Columbia Journalism Review* produced an experimental "Atlanta Journalism Review" in its July/August 1971 issue, written from the viewpoint of working reporters by present and former Atlanta journalists. Articles included "Racial Coverage in Atlanta: Once Over Lightly," "Why Atlanta Needs a Media Review," "How Atlanta Magazine Lost Its Soul," and "Women in the Newsroom."

The journalism reviews are increasing at a remarkable rate in cities across the country, despite the struggle for their financial lives. But, as *(More)*'s publisher told *Newsweek,* "We're not in this thing just for money." Most of the reviews have been established with little more than private donations and occasional grants from such benefactors as the Stern Fund for Investigative Reporting, which has helped both the Chicago and New York reviews. Some income also comes from paid subscriptions to local reporters and to other persons and institutions around the country. Costs for reviews vary considerably—the Hawaii review costs $252 per issue to produce, the *Unsatisfied Man,* $400.

Appraisal

Uneven in quality, varied in appearance, nearly all of the reviews are nonetheless unified in their purpose: to improve press performance. The editors have means and methods as diverse as the media: some prefer genial chiding and constructive, low-key suggestions; others speak stridently, using the methods of the exposé and advocacy reporting. Still others set examples with thorough investigative reports, painstaking documentation.

The reviews are the most vivid outward manifestation of the desire of working reporters to share in the decisions affecting the operation of America's newspapers, wire services, and broadcast stations. They reflect a larger activist movement inside media organizations that has been characterized as a "rebellion." Produced by the men and women on the firing line, the reviews often strike out at middle and top management personnel, who are largely unknown to the public despite their power.

But the battle lines are not always distinct. Some reporters refuse to join in an activist effort, preferring instead to work quietly within their news organizations. Others worry about potential conflict of interest. Nor are the lines clearly drawn on the other side. Publicly, at least, many editors and publishers argue that they encourage efforts that will strengthen journalism. But some say, usually privately, that the reviews set up an adversary system between reporters and management. The news executives urge disaffected newsmen to work for improvement within their media organizations, not through adversary publications.

Bruce Brugmann, whose San Francisco *Bay Guardian* features a considerable amount of media criticism, is skeptical: "The editors of journalism reviews are not really activists. They haven't yet cut the umbilical cord." In Brugmann's opinion, journalism reviews are but a miniature reflection of the identity problem of the media: "They want to be part of the media and critics too. It is difficult, perhaps impossible to be both. These guys want to have their cake and eat it too."[12] But Al Delugach, a founding editor of the *St. Louis Journalism Review* who is now with the Los Angeles *Times*, may provide the perspective typical of those who work on reviews:

> It surprised me when it [the journalism review movement] began, because for years and years in my experience—and I guess years and years before my time on newspapers—reporters did all their grumbling to each other in the ranks—sort of like the enlisted men in the Army. There wasn't any recourse for gripes by newsmen except their mutual grumbling and consoling one another, for the sins of their editors . . . I think it is very helpful to have self criticism. And that's what a journalism review is doing.[13]

The Journalism Reviews: An Example

THE REPORTER AND HIS MASTER'S CHOICE
by Ron Dorfman

This article from the Chicago Journalism Review *is an excellent example, in style and content, of the passionate writing of the journalism review.*

Reprinted by permission from *Chicago Journalism Review*, May 1971.

It must be difficult for non-journalists who have lived through the past decade of escalating dissent, from Selma to sabotage, to understand why it is a political act of some significance, requiring courage, for a newspaperman to sign his name to a piece of paper endorsing a candidate for public office. And why even a relatively enlightened newspaper management might consider such an act a major transgression.

That very nearly all of the reporters and editors of the Chicago *Sun-Times* and Chicago *Daily News* supported the candidacy of Richard E. Friedman against Mayor Daley [in the 1970 mayoralty election] should come as a surprise to no sophisticated observer; working newsmen have historically been sympathetic to liberals while their bosses endorsed conservatives. (In 1936, the editorial page staff of the St. Louis *Post-Dispatch* refused to write the editorial Joseph Pulitzer Jr. had ordered endorsing Alf Landon, and Fitzpatrick refused to draw the cartoon. The publisher hired outsiders for the job.) But that they should publicly express their choice, and engage in a public controversy with management over their right to do so, signals an impending change in the ideology of American journalism, in the way newsmen think about their job and therefore in the way the public thinks about the news media, and the news. The event could have been more significant only if it had taken place at the New York *Times*, the standard-bearer of American journalism.

The event itself unfolded with the predictability of a play adapted from the morgue clippings of the Berkeley Free Speech Movement. It had been widely assumed that the two newspapers, both owned by Marshall Field V, would once more endorse Daley for re-election. In anticipation of that, groups of reporters at each paper circulated petitions, addressed to Field, stating that endorsing Daley would be "inconsistent" with the stands the papers had taken over the years on a wide range of urban issues, and asking Field to endorse Friedman. If Field could not bring himself to do that, the petitions said, he should endorse neither candidate. If he insisted on endorsing Daley, he should set aside space on the editorial page for dissenting staff opinion.

Most of the ringleaders doubted Field would accept any of these alternatives, and they began collecting money to buy an ad; indeed, Field's endorsements had already been written when the petitions were being signed and they ran in the *Daily News* March 17 ("We didn't expect them to do it on *St. Patrick's Day*, fer chrissakes," said one *News* staffer) and in the *Sun-Times* March 18. However, Field unexpectedly agreed to meet with staff representatives Monday, March 22, to discuss their petitions.

A strategy session was held Sunday afternoon in Mike Royko's office at the *Daily News*, and it was agreed that, in the separate meetings Field would hold with the two delegations, the staff representatives would take the same tack: ask first for free space on the editorial page, then, when that was refused, for an extended letter to the editor, then for permission to buy space.

That was the critical area. Illinois law requires that political advertising carry the names of at least two individuals. The staff people wanted to have their ads signed by two deskmen "on behalf of _____ members" of the newspaper staff. In the event Field would not accept that the plan was to use only the two names—since the publicity already accorded the controversy on radio and television, and indeed in the newspapers themselves, had already included the relevant numbers, and the appearance of an ad without those numbers would only occasion further publicity.

A nice strategy, but alas, it was not to be.

Daryle Feldmeir, editor of the *Daily News*, had been out of town the previous Friday, when Managing Editor Donald W. Gormley, after consultations in the front office, informally told staffers that the ad could not be signed "Concerned Daily Newsmen and Women" but would have to bear the signatures of everyone it purported to represent, and further, that anyone who signed such an ad would not be permitted to cover politics or be in a "sensitive position" on the newspaper, "for the foreseeable future." That policy had been established at a Friday meeting attended by editors of the two papers and their boss, Emmett Dedmon, editorial director of the *Sun-Times* and *Daily News*. But Gormley left town late Friday and "unfortunately," he told CJR [*Chicago Journalism Review*], "Feldmeir and I just never had a chance to communicate."

Feldmeir was back on Monday, and asked the staff representatives if they wished him to join them in the meeting with Field. "Are you going to represent our position?" one of the staff members asked. When Feldmeir said he couldn't do that, he was told to "wait for an invitation from Marshall."

Meanwhile, *Sun-Times* Editor James F. Hoge and a delegation from his staff were meeting with Field, and when the staff people asked if they could sign the ad with two names and a committee, Field opined that was agreeable with him and tossed the ball to Hoge.

"Absolutely not," Hoge said, and after some perfunctory argument, Field acquiesced. To permit that, Hoge said later, "would not be fair to the readers or to the political community." The staff committee was an ad-hoc affair that would be out of business as soon as the ad was paid for, "and I felt the only way to handle it would be with full attribution without any form of anonymity."

This, of course, placed the staff members in a bind. If they wouldn't sign their names, they couldn't place the ad, and if they did sign their names, they couldn't cover the news. ("Not every problem has a solution," Hoge told CJR.) The issue was left unresolved as the *Sun-Times* people left Field's office and the *Daily News* people trooped in.

The conversation proceeded in much the same way, except that when Field agreed to accept the two signatures-cum-committee formula and tossed the ball to Feldmeir, Feldmeir said, "I have no objection."

"You should know," Field told Feldmeir, "that the *Sun Times* has taken a different approach, that there has been a previous policy on this." Feldmeir said he would talk to Hoge about it, and later told CJR:

"Jim explained what his approach was and we worked out an understanding, and later met with Field and Dedmon. We agreed that in this instance, we would each pursue our individual policies, since I had already indicated to my people that they could use the committee approach. We then agreed that if the same ad were run in both papers my people would have to conform to the *Sun-Times* policy, and that in all future situations there would be a common policy."

(Feldmeir later told some of his staff people he felt they had "conducted themselves with real dignity and responsibility".)

¤   ¤   ¤

′ Conferring later Monday, the *Daily News* and *Sun-Times* staff committees agreed they would go their separate ways. The *News* star urban affairs reporter, Lois Wille, had been working on the text of an ad throughout the week. $1,501 had been collected from the editorial staff and $90 from other departments on the paper, and an additional $390 had come in from outside sources. The ad would be signed by assistant City Editor Rob Warden and Copy Editor Myron Beckenstein for "Concerned Daily Newsmen and Women"—a cloak for 88 members of the paper's news staff, ranging from a copyboy to an assistant managing editor, with service from one to 45 years. The group included 85 percent of the dayside city-room staff, the only ones approached. (That was the group conservative columnist James J. Kilpatrick referred to when he wrote March 26 of "fledgling pundits, wet with opinions . . . little inclined to cover the news." That was the group *Daily News* City Hall reporter Jay McMullen—who was not among them—referred to when he introduced a colleague to Police Department PR man Frank Sullivan as "the best-looking broad on the bomb-throwers' petition." That was the group derided by implication in another petition that appeared on the *Daily News* bulletin board favoring Mayor Daley and signed by "The Unconcerned Newsmen"—an apt title embracing six signatories.)

The ad as it finally appeared March 26 was an eloquent summary of the collective wisdom of the staff on such questions as housing, health, education, transportation, patronage and bossism. As more than one reader wrote the *Daily News*, it rang a lot truer than the "he kept the trains running on time" tone of the newspaper's own editorial. (Indeed, it is unlikely that many of the editors of the newspaper much believe in its editorial; Feldmeir told CJR that "I participated in the decision to endorse Daley and I support the editorial," and Hoge said it was "in the best interest of the newspaper for me to refrain from speaking about my own position." These statements have the ring of what is known in Stalinist bureaucracies as democratic centralism.)

The mood in the *Daily News* city room was jubilant. "It really improved morale," said one of the ringleaders. A former *Daily News* staffer, now a journalism professor, wrote that this was "the first time since I left that I wish I were there."

It was not quite so *freilach* down the hall at the *Sun-Times*. Folks were downright resentful, in fact.

"There was a lot of sparring back and forth in the next couple of days," said one of the *Sun-Times* organizers. "At one point, we told Hoge we would simply go in with the *Daily News* people and have the ad read 'on behalf of 174 *Sun-Times* and *Daily News* staffers.' But Hoge said we couldn't do that, that he had the power to block such an ad.

"We pointed out to him that the news story we had already carried said 86 staff members, without identifying them, and he said that was different from an ad, there wasn't space in a news story for all the names but they could require that sufficient space be set aside in an ad.

"It was all ridiculous and we were kind of demoralized but then somebody got the idea we could put the ad in the *Tribune*."

On Thursday, March 25, the *Tribune* gave tentative approval to the idea. But many staff members felt the ad should appear in the *Sun-Times*.

"We needed a united front against Hoge's intimidation," said another of the *Sun-Times* organizers. "It became a question of solidarity, of scabbing. We needed enough names to effectively deter any retaliation. You know, Hoge deserves a lot of the credit for this. If he hadn't been so heavy-handed about it, the whole thing probably would have fallen through."

Monday night, the 29th, a meeting was held at Riccardo's restaurant, the final go-ahead decision was made, and Tuesday Hoge accepted the ad with 61 names and an additional 30 names of reporters who signed a "chicken sheet," which let some waverers off the hook by allowing them to "support the right of newsmen and women to take such a public position" without taking it themselves.

The ad, using the Lois Wille text, was published in the *Sun-Times* April 1, and in the same day's editions, an editorial ran expressing "confidence in the professionalism of all members of our staff." But, the editorial added, "At the same time, we recognize our obligation to assign political coverage in a manner that raises no doubts about its impartiality."

Just what that meant was unclear at CJR press time. In the *Sun-Times* editions of April 5 and April 6—the day before the day of the election—some stories that appeared to require bylines were published without them, and City Editor James Peneff explained that signers of the ad (although not signers of the "chicken sheet") could not have their bylines on campaign stories to which they were assigned; Hoge later dissociated himself from this interpretation of the policy, saying he was not so much concerned with straight news or news features, as with interpretive reporting, and sensitive reporting in general. He implied in an interview that the reason one otherwise deserving reporter was denied a new and "sensitive" assignment was that he had signed the ad.

At *Chicago Today,* which had also endorsed Daley, the editors made space available the following day on the page opposite the editorial page for a rebuttal signed by 31 staff members, a reprise of last November's action in which the paper endorsed Sen. Ralph T. Smith and the staff was given space for an endorsement of Adlai Stevenson III. *Today,* since its inception in April of 1969, has provided space on the editorial page daily for the opinions of staff members, in a column called "Sound Off," and has stated to the public that reporters may use the space whether or not their opinion is the same as the editor's or the publisher's, and so the paper could not very easily have objected to the counter-endorsements.

Jim Hoge, the young editor of the *Sun-Times,* is a close friend of Richard Friedman; unless one is willing to impute to him the basest motivations of corporate politics, one must take him at his word that his Draconian reaction to the staff activity reflects a concern for "what is a proper way for a journalist to be heard, and what isn't."

"The challenge," he says, "is to keep from making ourselves easy targets, so that aggressive journalism can carry more weight." Conjuring the specter of Spiro Agnew, Hoge notes that it would be easy for Daley now to make an issue of the newspaper's coverage of social problems, political scandals, and the like. (The Mayor once accused militant black hecklers of being inspired by the Republicans.)

"Endorsements, which are precise political acts, are too easily misunderstood in the general public and in the political community if they are done by the same man who's covering politics. You can't ask people to accept things on faith," things like the integrity of a reporter who is known to favor one candidate over another.

Max McCrohon, managing editor of *Chicago Today,* reports that his staff got no adverse reaction from news sources when they pumped for Adlai Stevenson in November, "and frankly," he says of the editors' discussions of the subject, "we expected none." The editors placed no restrictions on who could sign the counterendorsement, "although we hoped the political editor wouldn't." (He didn't.)

McCrohon, whose Australian background may explain why he is less up-tight on this question than his opposite numbers at the Field papers, observes that when a newspaper endorses a candidate it says "this newspaper" and not "this newspaper's publisher."

"The average reader, given a moment's reflection," he says, "would understand that the newspaper staff embraces a variety of opinions."

Hoge objects on the ground that "A metropolitan newspaper is different from a journal of opinion, from other forms of communication. In a metropolitan newspaper you must have the appearance of impartiality as well as the reality. 'Objectivity'—and I don't like that word—is not a problem in this controversy. I'm trying to protect interpretive reporting as well as the straight recounting of events. It's the sensitive reporting that's most vulnerable if you don't protect it," if you leave open to question the motive of the reporter who's doing it.

How much can you really accomplish with an editorial endorsement anyway, Hoge wonders. "All you can really do with a newspaper is to change gradually the temper of the public dialogue. When I came to Chicago what I heard was that the public dialogue was structured and reinforced by the *Tribune*. One of the great services of the Field papers has been to widen the range of what can be discussed. It becomes part and parcel of all the little things you put together (to create the conditions for change).

"To do that we've attempted to build a public awareness that the *Sun-Times* is the paper you can turn to for good reporting, straight reporting, interpretive reporting. But you also have to watch for curve balls, and you have to avoid setting up situations in which you're vulnerable."

As Hoge says, not all problems have solutions. But all problems, sooner or later, in one way or another, are resolved.

The problem confronted here is one of the media's own making; Spiro Agnew, it may be said, represents a hoisting of the media on the petard of noninvolvement, part of the mythology created by the media to disguise the subservience of the press to the interests of the moneyed classes and, latterly, of the State. It is a mythology whose development was coincident with the monopolization of the press. (*Vide* Hoge's notion that "A metropolitan newspaper is different from a journal of opinion," which he explains by citing the obvious fact that most of the people who read such a publication share its general bias; but all that means is that the metropolitan press has been less than candid about what its bias is.)

In fact, the news media have been deeply committed, almost always on the side of the powers that be. Our "objective" reporting is like the "objective" scholarship of social scientists who study the powerless on behalf of the powerful, but never the powerful on behalf of the powerless; sharecroppers and barrio-and slum-dwellers do not distribute research grants like Carnegie and Rockefeller and Ford, do not employ newsmen like Pulitzer and Sulzberger and Field. And these same "scientists"—read that reporters and editors, if you will—convince themselves that their work will ameliorate the plight of the oppressed ("Comfort the afflicted and afflict the comfortable") when its only demonstrable effect is to feed the computers that produce new and more sophisticated instruments of social control.

Now Agnew, ignorant peasant lad that he is, has begun to say that the Emperor looks a silly ass going about naked. (Not that Agnew shares the sentiment of the previous paragraph. He has simply mistaken the media's superficial opposition to the war and its abhorrence of himself and his boss for the true ideological bias of the media.) But the Emperor has protested that, indeed, he *is* wearing regal robes, and his minister, Hoge, says the deception must be continued lest the citizens be misled into thinking Agnew is not himself going bareass.

Well, that won't wash, to punish the metaphor.

Some reporters have openly demonstrated their sympathy with the anti-war movement. Others have spoken out in favor of the war effort. Some women reporters have announced their commitment to the women's liberation movement. Others have said they are against it. Now some reporters have gone a step further and openly endorsed a political candidate.

None of this is especially revolutionary, except in the sense that more such acts are bound to follow (e.g., when Marshall Field decides next year to endorse Spiro Agnew's boss for re-election) and each makes it more difficult for the profession to perpetuate the nonsensical notion that a reporter is a non-human creature who understands everything and believes nothing. If the public had not been bamboozled in the first place by our own propaganda, there would be no problem and no need for a solution. The resolution of the problem will consist in the dis-enchantment of all concerned, and a more realistic public understanding of the role of the media.

Jean Schwoebel, diplomatic editor of *Le Monde*, has written that reporters must be "possessed not only of competence and professionalism, not only of talent which facilitates comprehension and carries conviction, but also of a spirit of responsibility, and even more of the courage to battle against myths, prejudices, ignorance . . . . "

Especially those we ourselves have engendered.

Notes

[1]"Self Criticism in Chicago," *Time*, March 21, 1969, p. 71.

[2]James Aronson, *The Press and the Cold War* (Indianapolis, Ind.: Bobbs-Merrill, 1970), p. 286.

[3]"Tribune's Kirkpatrick: There'll Be Some Changes Made," *Chicago Journalism Review*, June 1970, p. 3.

[4]"Does This Face Look Familiar?" *Chicago Journalism Review*, November 1970, p. 6.

[5]"Self Criticism in Chicago," *op. cit.*, p. 71.

[6]"A Letter from the New Editor," *Chicago Journalism Review*, January 1970, p. 5.

[7]"No Story About Charles Swibel Was Ever Killed," *Chicago Journalism Review*, January 1970, p. 6.

[8]"We Will Have to Act to Protect Our Publications," *Chicago Journalism Review*, January 1970, p. 8.

[9]"Laurels and Hardlies," *Unsatisfied Man*, June 1971, p. 15.

[10]Thomas J. Madden, "Journalism Reviews: Effects in Chicago and St. Louis; A Beginning in Philadelphia," *Philadelphia Journalism Review*, July 1971, p. 9.

[11]*Nelson Society Newsletter*, August 1971, p. 2.

[12]Interview with Bruce Brugmann, August 6, 1971, San Francisco, Calif.

[13]*St. Louis Journalism Review*, October/November 1970, p. 3.

The Advocates 5

If you mean by objectivity absence of convictions, willingness to let nature take its course, uncritical acceptance of things as they are (what Robert Frost calls the "isness of is"), the hell with it.

—Kenneth M. Stewart, *A Region's Press*

It was the most talked-about trial of the period, a *cause célèbre* long before the judge rapped his gavel: the Chicago Conspiracy Trial of 1969, growing out of the riots at the 1968 Democratic National Convention, the first and most colorful of a series of government prosecutions against radicals and dissidents during the late sixties and early seventies.

One courtroom observer was Nicholas von Hoffman of the Washington *Post*. Unlike the reporters who worked within the tightly disciplined and verbally economic style traditional in most court reporting, von Hoffman thought the trial a farce and covered it as though it were a theatrical event. *Newsweek* described him thus:

> Von Hoffman has come to the 23rd floor of the Federal building in Chicago to review a new play, produced by the theatre's richest backer—the United States Government, but manipulated by Abbie Hoffman, "street theatre social critic and public relations genius." Thus far the reviewer has not been very kind to the cast. Von Hoffman described Judge Julius Hoffman, the leading man, as "an aged hobbit who never stops talking . . . with the voice of a man reading horror stories to small children."
>
> The supporting cast has fared little better. David Dellinger is "the

old line pacifist-socialist who's only recently dared to grow sideburns"; Tom Hayden is "the loner, intellectual militant who doesn't fit into anybody's organization"; Jerry Rubin is a "free lance wild man" and the other defendants are "a couple of throw-ins nobody's ever heard of before." All meet in a "depressingly modern courtroom" to amuse the nation with their version of "The Great Conspiracy Trial."[1]

Leaving the courtroom one day, von Hoffman overheard Judge Hoffman in the elevator refer to one of the defense attorneys as "this wild man." When von Hoffman duly reported the remark in his *Post* column, it was followed by predictable explosions. The defense attorneys filed a motion for mistrial, which was firmly denied by the judge. Said von Hoffman, "I didn't write that because I thought it would change things. I wrote it to get the Establishment's goat."[2]

Von Hoffman is one in a growing corps of activist-advocacy journalists who usually write for the conventional press but who, he says, "cut through the crap and write about reality." Their work is opinionated and they admit it. Among them are writers like Pete Hamill of the New York *Post* and *New York* magazine, Jack Newfield and Nat Hentoff of the *Village Voice*, Gloria Steinem of *Ms.* and *New York*, and William Buckley of *National Review*. All are respected voices—some even leaders—in the advocacy movements they cover.

Other more singleminded advocacy journalists write for publications dedicated to a cause: women's liberation (*Off Our Backs*), ecology and new life styles (*Mother Earth News*), the Jesus movement (*Right On*). Of course there have been advocacy publications before, but never such an outpouring as appeared during the mid-sixties—new, cheaper printing processes have made it easier for struggling groups to spread their beliefs.

Advocacy in the Newsroom

Those who try to experiment with the journalistic form, arguing that their own biases should be injected into the news, have horrified those who regard "objective news," the attempt at separating fact and opinion, as the crowning achievement of American journalism.

Herbert Brucker, former editor of the Hartford (Connecticut) *Courant,* suggests how much the traditionalists value the conventional form: "... no one can argue away the fact that American journalism has now struggled for a century and a third to replace partisan propaganda with reporting that gets within hailing distance of the truth. And that kind of reporting is too valuable, not only to journalism, but to self government itself, to be discarded now in an emotional reaction fueled by the current political distemper."[3]

Many other traditionalists have become alarmed by the invasion of advocates. In 1970, Edward M. Miller, then the managing editor of the Portland *Oregonian*, issued a three-page memorandum giving the "official line on subjective (personal) versus objective (impersonal) writing":

> For as long as any of us can remember, the *Oregonian* has been an objective paper. The ideal has been to tell the story straight. This approach has been considered good journalism and good business. The policy will be continued in the foreseeable future.
>
> The goal of telling it straight in general news coverage has remained constant through the years, but techniques have changed somewhat. For example, in earlier years the *Oregonian* and the Associated Press leaned heavily on the "balanced" story which gave equal space to the arguments of quoted adversaries. Sometimes this resulted in misplaced emphasis.
>
> Today we are less rigid as regards sheer technique. In our day-to-day news coverage we do adhere to the idea of objective coverage. But this does not entail a conscious effort to balance the facts mechanically. It does imply that all the facts are presented and fairly on their merits, as nearly as we can see those merits. In controversial matters we do try to see that both sides have a proper treatment.
>
> Facts that the reporter and editors know to be true do not require slavish attribution but, where good authority is available, it should be utilized. Personal opinion is no substitute for digging to obtain material for a story.
>
> There is an argument of long standing, and popular today, that attainment of absolute truth is impossible, and therefore the search thereof should not concern journalists, and that personal appraisals of the reporter are sufficient unto this day.
>
> The *Oregonian* declines the argument because the argument is specious. We do not subscribe to the idea that because objectivity, complete objectivity, may be difficult it should not be attempted. Because every breath one draws may have some germs does not justify the idea of carelessly exposing oneself to contagion. . . . The ideal may be elusive but we should work towards it.
>
> In the past 10 years or so the *Oregonian* has gradually permitted increasing latitude to writers in explaining newsworthy situations and in interpreting the news. But the goal should be always: to inform; to clarify; to interpret; to simplify.
>
> We do draw a line. We must stop short of *advocacy* by the reporter. We cannot permit personal advocacy of a reporter's own viewpoint. The newspaper's opinion is reserved for the editorial page.[4]

At issue, Miller said, was the paper's reputation for "integrity of reporting. No single article, no matter how entertaining or persuasive, is worth tinkering with the reader's high esteem for this newspaper."

Significantly, when Miller's memorandum was read to a group of journalism students at the University of Oregon, they laughed. In a real sense, the objectivity question is a debate between generations. Students schooled in the scientific method know humans cannot be clinically objective. And they have been taught that the world is full of complex interrelationships. To them, the traditional arguments for objectivity sound simplistic and cannot be taken seriously. And at least superficially, the standard journalistic form *is* simplistic: information is presented in a *descending* order of importance, telling who, what, when, where, why, and how.

What critics protest is the traditionalists' assumption that the objective style prevents bias. Von Hoffman believes, for instance, that the astronauts were made the "who" in moon landing stories when the engineers should have been. Such writing, he says, is "as biased as any other." Slavish adherence to the objective form makes the journalist too malleable, says David Deitch of the Boston *Globe*: "A commitment to the notion of objectivity has in effect become a sign of manipulation, whether newspaper managements like it or not." Deitch's solution is "to admit that the editorial function is inherently biased, that reporters have opinions of their own and that newspapers, like other large institutions, are political entities."[5]

Brucker declares that critics of objectivity are really at war with superficiality:

> What they denounce as objectivity is not objectivity so much as incrustation of habits and rules of newswriting, inherited from the past, that confine the reporter within rigid limits. Within those limits the surface facts of an event may be reported objectively enough. But that part of the iceberg not immediately visible is ruled out, even though to include it might reveal what happened in a more accurate—indeed more objective—perspective.[6]

Brucker's argument fails to recognize the subtleties of socialization. Although he is not usually told what to write, the alert journalist soon learns that he ought not run counter to the publisher's biases and other newsroom taboos. As sociologist Warren Breed wrote in his now-classic paper, "Social Control in the Newsroom":

> . . . the publisher's policy, when established in a given subject area, is usually followed, and a description of the dynamic socio-cultural situation of the newsroom will suggest explanations for this conformity. The newsman's source of rewards is located not among the readers, who are manifestly his clients, but among his colleagues and superiors. Instead of adhering to societal and professional ideals, he redefines his values to the more pragmatic level of the newsroom

group. He thereby gains not only status rewards, but also acceptance in a solitary group engaged in interesting, varied, and sometimes important work.[7]

Even the journalist who is strongly committed to presenting truth may fine it difficult to determine what truth is. In 1970, communications researcher James Lemert reviewed the research literature on writers' biases and reported two studies which found that "subjects had more trouble writing when the material was presumably not consistent with their attitudes." Another study showed the opposite effect: "when the material ran against their attitudes, the writers bent over backwards in its direction, discarding more of the material they agreed with than we would have expected." In a fourth study, a researcher found that "when writers reported a talk they didn't agree with, they tended to quote it more and paraphrase it less than when they agreed with the talk."[8]

The Newsroom Revolution

For years journalists have believed that a reporter could not be a participant and maintain the detachment essential to the observer. So journalists generally have not been joiners of political organizations or other groups that might make their leanings visible. But if impartiality and detachment used to be marks of professionalism, this is now changing.

The new participant-observer style is exemplified by Norman Mailer, probably its most celebrated practitioner, Gloria Steinem, and Jack Newfield. But other, less famous journalists have also become involved in politics. A group of *Wall Street Journal* reporters marched in an antiwar parade in New York at the height of the peace movement, and Time Inc. employees used a company auditorium to protest the Vietnam war.

How do newsmen themselves feel about such involvement? A 1971 poll conducted by the South Carolina Press Association concluded as follows:

Promoting ecology and the United Fund is okay for the off-duty journalist, but he should stay away from controversial political activities. . . . The journalists were given a list of 12 activities, ranging from membership in civic clubs to participating in antiwar movements, and asked to specify which were improper for journalists. Thirty-three respondents nixed holding local political offices; 31 felt participating in antiwar activities or signing political advertisements was improper; 30 disapproved of holding state or national political office; 29 were against making speeches; and 28 disapproved of lobbying for nonjournalism legislation.[9]

Even von Hoffman holds that the reporter should avoid entan-

glements: "I make it a rule never to get close to the people I write about."
But this rule of thumb is difficult for an advocate to follow.

Nicholas von Hoffman, Maverick

Nicholas von Hoffman's books, articles, and frequent television appearances have made him one of the most visible advocacy journalists. His boss, Benjamin C. Bradlee, editor of the Washington *Post,* calls him "the truest American iconoclast since H. L. Mencken. He tilts at more cherished beliefs and more traditional institutions more effectively than anyone since the bad boy of Baltimore." Von Hoffman's dispatches are "personal, pertinent, articulate, vital glimpses of man trying to make it in a more and more complicated world," Bradlee says, but he adds, "if the truth be known, Nick von Hoffman can't write a news story to save his prematurely gray head." When von Hoffman was sent to Mississippi in 1966 to cover James Meredith's march across the state, his dispatches were a panorama of local sociology. As Bradlee wrote:

> But if Meredith's name appeared in the copy, it was purely an accident; there would be no normal time frame, and Nick always did feel that exact geography was barely relevant. An editor always had to write a lead to the story, explaining to the readers that this was a piece about James Meredith, that he was walking across the breadth of Mississippi, and that the events occurred yesterday. Only then were the rednecks allowed to relieve themselves.[10]

Von Hoffman found his way into establishment journalism circuitously. He worked for eleven years as an associate director of the late community organizer Saul Alinsky's Industrial Areas Foundation, which was engaged in community organization on Chicago's south side. Von Hoffman says that it was then that he learned to write; the blacks and Puerto Ricans taught him "how important it was to cut through the bull."

In 1963, von Hoffman was hired by the Chicago *Daily News.* He used and enlarged upon his contacts among blacks and other minorities, developed a youth beat, and covered the problems of students at a time when universities were near explosion. The next year the paper sent him to Mississippi to cover "Freedom Summer," a project to register black voters and to teach basic educational skills. Von Hoffman's understanding of community organization was useful to him as he covered the Council of Federated Organizations, which brought together several civil rights groups for unified action. He wrote primarily about people in the context of Mississippi; for instance:

> Some whites have come to recognize the rebellion welling up in the people they still refer to as "our nigras." They are galled by it, though, like the vindictive Hattiesburg housewife who said, "When I saw that

little colored girl of mine waiting in front of the courthouse with those common niggers I could hardly believe it. I would have let her go anyway. She was spending more time eavesdropping than cooking."[11]

After three years at the *Daily News*, von Hoffman was hired by the Washington *Post*. He writes the thrice-weekly "Poster" because as a *Post* editor put it, "We decided on turning von Hoffman loose in his own corner of the paper. He could not fit into our news columns and yet he is not a columnist really, either."

Here are two samples from "Poster," reprinted in von Hoffman's book, *Left at the Post*:

> When you've seen one, you've seen 'em all, these welfare ladies, fat from too much starch and too little protein, always out of breath, climbing the stairs by getting one foot up on the next step and then pushing down on the knee. That's how they get up to the second floor of the National Welfare Rights Office, just a few of them back in town to fulfill the scriptural injunction to be with us always, even unto and beyond National Togetherness week.

On Billy Graham:

> A piestical voice with mellow reverberations in the lower registers asked the people to drop their heads and close their eyes. That is how white occidentals indicate they are addressing their divinity. The TV cameras panned around the new Madison Square Garden, and the multitude—assembled to hear Billy Graham—looked like the Republican Party at prayer.

Gloria Steinem, Feminist

Best known as a promoter of women's liberation, Gloria Steinem has long been an advocacy journalist. One of the founders of *Ms.* magazine, a contributing editor and political columnist for *New York*, and a contributor to many other magazines, she has written personality profiles, entertainment features, and political pieces.

For a time in 1971 it seemed that she had all but given up writing, she spent so much time on the lecture circuit on behalf of the feminist movement. Pete Hamill, a longtime friend, said, "It's bothered me that Gloria has been so busy that she hasn't had time to do much writing. But I wonder if it bothers *her*—because I think she got into writing principally to express ideas, and for that reason she could quite happily move into some other mode of expressing her ideas—like politics."[12]

Steinem grew up in the slums of East Toledo, Ohio, later moved to Washington, D.C., and with high College Board scores and help from her mother, attended Smith College. After international travels and a stint with a student exchange organization, she began to write for *Esquire*, winning attention with a 1962 story about The Pill. She also posed as a *Playboy* bunny in order to write a 1963 article for *Show* magazine—a story which was a sensation, and made it easier for her to get writing assignments.

Her articles in various magazines gained considerable attention as *Time* and *Newsweek* both featured her in their media sections. She herself became a celebrity on the lecture circuit plugging political causes. In August 1971 she had become enough of a celebrity for *Newsweek* to devote a cover story to her. The large, wire-rimmed dark glasses she wore are so distinctive and identified with the women's movement that by 1973 a museum curator got a set of the glasses as an artifact of the women's movement.

She wrote profiles on James Baldwin, Jackie Kennedy, Julie Andrews, Mrs. John Lindsay, Michael Caine, Truman Capote, and other celebrities. From the outset, her articles were personal, always reflecting the Steinem point of view, which accentuates the role of the woman in the society. As she wrote in an August 1970 *Time* essay:

> Men assume that women want to imitate them, which is just what white people assumed about blacks. An assumption so strong that it may convince the second class group to the need to imitate, but for both women and blacks that stage has passed. Guilt produces the question: What if they could treat us as we have treated them?

Once established as a writer, she moved from personality profiles and pop culture pieces to politics. A 1968 article on the struggling beginnings of the women's liberation movement won her a Penney-Missouri Magazine Award, and later that year editor Clay Felker of *New York* invited her to be a contributing editor and produce a regular column called "The City Politic."

When John Lindsay made his first stirrings toward the Democratic nomination for President, Steinem blistered him in an article in the April 5, 1971, issue of *New York*, "Is Lindsay Deserting Us? Do We Care?"

> Once upon a time Big John Lindsay was the shining prince who cooled the streets, gave parks back to the people and made a lot of turned-off, numb New Yorkers feel mildly hopeful again. But it's worse in politics to have inspired hope and dashed it than never to have inspired hope at all—a fact that benefits the likes of Richard Nixon, from whom we expected almost nothing, and punishes a leader like Lindsay, who we once thought might change our urban lives. . . .
>
> Of those ordinary Democrats who have nothing to gain from Lindsay's possible ascent to the White House, the most cheerful, and least anti-Lindsay, seem to be more those who think Lindsay might make a better President than he has a mayor.
>
> "He's a rotten administrator, but in Washington, who would notice? He could look distinguished and not worry about his deficiencies," explained a Brooklyn precinct worker. "All he'd have to

do is sit there in the White House and create a nice moral atmosphere. It's *easier* to be President. Somebody else has to worry about the garbage."

Much of her writing is more notable for vehemence than for style. As a *Newsweek* article observed:

> All good political pamphleteers—from Payne to Shaw to Nicholas von Hoffman—cloak their sermons in style, but Steinem's prose is an after-thought. She manages to get up for the first sentence ("Once upon a time—say, ten or even five years ago—a Liberated Woman was somebody who had sex before marriage and a job afterward") but she is given to meandering and her endings sort of slump to the floor.[13]

Pete Hamill, Brooklynite

Advocacy journalists write about the things they care about, of course, but Pete Hamill seems to care about everything. In his mid-thirties, Hamill works for the New York *Post* and *New York* magazine. Like another Irish-American writer, Jimmy Breslin, whom he admires, Hamill writes passionately, his biases always close to the surface. For example, he wrote of Muhammad Ali:

> He is the biggest thing in this town right now, with men arguing about him until late hours, cabdrivers cursing him, patriots abusing him, and a hell of a lot of people loving him. He fights Oscar Bonavena next week, but the fight is almost incidental. Ali is here among us, back from the desert, and the town is better for his presence.[14]

Always the moralist, Hamill unleashes his impassioned style on urban problems as readily as on public personalities. Attacking high-ranking New York city officials who live outside the city, he wrote: "One measure of a man's commitment to a city is the fact that he lives in that city. If you love New York, you live in New York and by that simple choice you share the grief and hardship of the city, in exchange for its small wonders."

Hamill's first love is New York's largest borough, Brooklyn, where he lives. In a celebrated *New York* article, "Brooklyn: A Sane Alternative," Hamill urged uptight Manhattanites to savor the quality of life in Brooklyn. As a movement to make New York City the 51st state was debated in the early 1970s, Hamill urged that the city be broken into smaller administrative units—beginning with Brooklyn. As he wrote in June 1971:

> . . . it is one of the first afternoons of summer. A light breeze is blowing in the trees of Prospect Park across the way. Those trees were planted by the private citizens of Brooklyn, more than 70 years ago, before Progress and Good Intentions and Optimism to take the City of

Brooklyn away. The . . . trees . . . are still there. They were planted by people who believed in roots, believed in a sense of place, believed that human beings could do things for themselves. And I like to think, sitting here, that we could get that spirit back, that my kids could grow up on these streets and see grass planted and birds arrive in flocks, to roost again in the high places of the City of Brooklyn. It's time to plant trees again.[15]

Jack Newfield, New Leftist

Village Voice and *New York* writer Jack Newfield may be the prototype of the impassioned journalist whose chief passion sometimes seems to be to advance his own career. He describes himself as a New Left radical and writes about slum conditions, welfare mothers, populism, and favorite politicians. In a December 1970 *Harper's* article, writer John Corry called Newfield's style "mock outrage" and his articles "comic masterpieces," citing the following Newfield passage as an example: "And then, later that night, Kennedy would tell me and David Halberstam how much he loved people who worked hard with their hands, how much he preferred the white poor of West Virginia and Gary to the Manhattan intellectuals 'who spend their time worrying about why they haven't been invited to some party'."

What bothers Corry is Newfield's self-indulgence:

In a story in *New York* magazine [Corry says] in which he nominates Ramsey Clark for President, Newfield spends an intolerable amount of time saying he doesn't feel well, mentioning his friends, and then wondering aloud if he should take the assignment and write the story. As a way of building suspense this is not much, and it is hardly any surprise when Newfield decides on Page 3 that he will go ahead and do the story, anyway. Then, after comparing Clark to Gary Cooper, Will Rogers, Lincoln, and St. Francis, and giving him all the better of it, too, Newfield decides that he would make a hell of a President, but that the country may not deserve him.

Newfield is not always this way, and he often blends original insights and fine phrases. His 1969 book, *Robert Kennedy: A Memoir*, is regarded by many critics as the best of the books about Kennedy. Here is an example of Newfield's descriptive powers:

I was not fully prepared for the changes in Kennedy the first day I spent traveling with him as a reporter in November of 1966. Instead of the military crew cut, his graying ginger hair now lapped over his earlobes in the shaggy style of the alienated young. His blue eyes were now sad rather than cold, haunted rather than hostile. The freshly carved lines of sorrow in his brow, around his eyes, near his mouth, made him look ten, not five years older. The metamorphosis seemed to prove the wisdom of Albert Camus's comment that every man over forty is responsible for his own face. Robert Kennedy was two days past his thirty-eighth birthday when his brother was murdered.

James Ridgeway, Investigative Advocate

Of all the advocacy journalists, James Ridgeway may be the most determined and adept investigator. On the lecture platform, he does not act the part; he probes and cajoles, speaking quietly, slowly, deliberately. In his mid-thirties, Ridgeway is a modern populist who for a while attempted to publish, with radical journalist Andrew Kopkind, a "coherent radical analysis of society" in the form of a magazine entitled *Hard Times*. The Washington, D.C., radical magazine tried to do on the domestic scene what I. F. Stone was doing on international issues—namely, provide continuous coverage of institutional bumbling.

In his articles and books, Ridgeway is a tough investigator who always seems to wonder about his subject: "What's in it for him?" "Who's getting rich?" He is diligent; he often sifts through piles of charts and graphs, since he believes that the rape of the public interest will be found less from covering street demonstrations than from reading computer printouts. Most of Ridgeway's work is filled with numbers, charts, graphs, and references to obscure reports and technical publications. His writing is usually a rush of information and analysis, nearly always highly partisan. Noticing that considerable oil exploration was being done in Southeast Asia, Ridgeway combed oil industry publications and press releases; the result was an analysis in the February 1970 *Hard Times* showing ties between American oil profits and the continuance of the Vietnam war.

Ridgeway learned to be a reporter working on the *Wall Street Journal*, which he still respects. Its reputation, he says, is "based on the news coverage, which attempts to explain economic and cultural events briefly and clearly. Unlike so many other papers and magazines, the *Journal* reporters explain events to nonspecialist readers. Readers of the *Journal* take the paper seriously because, whatever their politics, they trust its judgment."

Ridgeway left the *Journal* to become associate editor of the *New Republic*. There he wrote and argued about auto safety (and even referred a publisher to the unknown Ralph Nader), environmental pollution, the emergence of the New Left, and provided early systematic criticisms and reports on the Vietnam war.[16]

Ridgeway is a strong conspiracy theorist. For instance, in a February 1971 *Ramparts* article attacking the U.S. mental health program, he wrote, "You don't have to be crazy to be against Mental Health. In its upper-case incarnations at least—a National Institute of Mental Health and hundreds of Community Centers—the Mental Health movement seeks a powerful estate in corporate America."

The article also enraged many mental health leaders with this accusation:

The backbone of the Mental Health movement is the drug industry. With Congress withholding funds for health care, and insurance companies still refusing to provide coverage against mental illness, the one alternative way for extending the Mental Health movement is in the development and widened use of psychotropic drugs, i.e., tranquilizers and stimulants. They are a major force in the "fight against mental illness," making possible the decline in hospitalized patients, and bringing thousands of people within the reach of the "movement."

Because he believes that "the energy crisis may be the great issue of our time," Ridgeway has forcefully probed the ecology movement. In his 1970 book *The Politics of Ecology* he charged that the principal environmental polluters—oil, gas, and coal companies—have taken over the ecology movement. The book explores "the underground war for control of the water-pollution programs, the key to control of other environmental policies, and the battle among the petroleum trusts for domination of the world energy markets." It is not surprising that many critics accuse Ridgeway of overkill and worse. In a review of the book in the October 20, 1970 New York *Times,* John Leonard wrote: "Mr. Ridgeway does some polluting of his own, of an ideological sort. It is true that most pollution is caused by technology and industry, not by overpopulation. But to leap from this fact to the conclusion that birth control programs are only a means of advancing American corporate interests is simple-minded. And to look the gift horse of Ralph Nader's consumer-interest study groups in the mouth, and to decide that what it's really all about is a power grab by a new 'elite' of lawyers, is preposterous."

Ridgeway certainly is quick to draw broad conclusions and slow to mention exceptions. For instance, in his book *The Closed Corporation: American Universities in Crisis,* he charges:

The idea that the university is a community of scholars is a myth. The professors are less interested in teaching students than in yanking the levers of their new combines so that these machines will grow bigger and faster. The university has in large part been reduced to serving as banker-broker for the professors' outside interest. The charming elitism of the professors has long since given way to the greed of the social and political scientists whose manipulative theories aim only at political power. Meanwhile undergraduate students lie in campus holding pens, while graduate apprentices read them stories. The stories are boring, and students turn to making their own "free universities" or spend their time hatching political revolutions on the outside.

Implications of Advocacy

Traditionally, advocacy journalism has made its greatest inroads in magazines. Long a staple of opinion journals such as the *Nation,* the *New Republic,* the *Progressive,* and the *National Review,* it began to invade the more widely circulated quality magazines such as *Harper's,* the *Atlantic,* the *New Yorker, New York,* and *Saturday Review.* Then women's magazines, men's magazines, and slicks like *Life* began to open their columns to the advocates.

In 1967, *Newsweek* broke its tradition of news reporting and analysis by producing a twenty-page section titled "What Must Be Done," a program to meet the rising demands of the black community. Editor Osborn Elliot declared, "the reason for this marked change of approach is that the editors have come to believe that at this particular time, on this particular subject, they could not fulfill their journalistic responsibility as citizens by simply reporting what X thinks of Y and why Z disagrees."

Slick advocacy magazines such as *Ramparts* and *Scanlan's* appeared during the 1960s. *Ramparts,* formerly a liberal Catholic literary magazine, began to espouse New Left rhetoric and to offer readers exposés (such as CIA links to universities) and other sensational stories. In the decade of the sixties, *Ramparts* was at the red-hot center of advocacy journalism. By using modern marketing techniques the magazine became central to the antiwar movement and other strains of dissent that swept the land. *Ramparts'* articles on "The Coming of the Hippies," ecology, and government corruption were widely discussed, and on several occasions exposés from the magazine were reported on the pages of the New York *Times.* Such writers as Robert Scheer on politics, Gene Marine on ecology, and Douglas Duncan on military affairs provided a lively flow of articles. Although the magazine was making money, the free-spending, free-wheeling style of former publisher Warren Hinckle III and others brought the magazine a $1.5 million debt by 1970. Since then, under new management, *Ramparts* has tried to regain its once vital position as an organ of political activism.

After being ousted from *Ramparts,* Hinckle, along with New York *Times* reporters Sidney Zion and John Leo, began *Scanlan's,* a short-lived radical monthly, which was published in New York City for several months during 1971. One issue of the magazine which was devoted to strategies for bombings had to be printed in Canada and was involved in a difficult tug of war with law-enforcement officials.

Carey McWilliams, editor of the *Nation,* saw all this as a return to "a continuing—but cyclical—tradition of reform journalism." In a quiet article in *Columbia Journalism Review* McWilliams pointed out that the advocacy journalists of the sixties and seventies were not much different from earlier muckrakers. Even a hasty perusal of nineteenth- and twentieth-century periodical indexes clearly indicates the role that advocacy has always played in magazine journalism. What is different today is its extraordinary breadth and force. The movement now cuts across a greater number and variety of publications, reaching larger audiences.

Radical Papers

Unlike the youth papers or the counterculture papers (discussed in the next chapter), the radical press is more political, advancing a strong leftist, revolutionary point of view.

The *National Guardian* of New York City was a strident voice of the radical Old Left since 1948. According to founding editor James Aronson, the publication "resisted internal dissension until the mid-1960s, when the stresses and strains of conflict within the radical movement became insurmountable."[17] Then the New Left, which was more freewheeling and less dogmatic, found it had fundamental differences with the Old Left. Out went the former editors and with them the old name; it became simply *Guardian*. In 1970, another staff split brought the birth of the *Liberated Guardian*, an anarchist publication.

This division between the Marxist-Leninist Old Left and the anarchist New Left was analyzed by veteran Communist leader Gil Green in *The New Radicalism: Anarchist or Marxist?*

> The youth consciousness produced by the upsurge of the Thirties was not counterposed to the growing class consciousness of the time, but tended to merge with it. Today's brand of youth consciousness is different. It tends to think of youth as a separate class, even an oppressed class, [or] if not a class, at least a caste. . . . Yet to one degree or another the vast majority of youth today feel a special kinship with each other, flowing from dissatisfaction with the world as it is and with the ways of their parents.

Published by a staff of nine people who rotate positions, the *Liberated Guardian* presents analyses of national and international events and liberation struggles, usually written by young people involved in them. The paper is attractive graphically, with photographs, line drawings, and imaginative horizontal layouts, and it has featured full spreads of revolutionary art. Most of the articles are long and packed with detailed information, and usually counter official or governmental views of events. For instance, the paper described the August 1969 bombing of the University of Wisconsin research center in terms sympathetic to the bomber. Women's liberation, rallies for

Chicanos and Black Panthers, Fidel Castro, the Soledad Brothers, and, of course, the war in Southeast Asia have been central concerns.

The style is strident, as in this September 8, 1970, description of the Oakland, California, police: "They take a man, bring him in. They go down in West Oakland, pick up everyone they can pick up. If the police stop you and you haven't been to jail, you go. No such thing. Every black person that you bring in here and put on the stand got some type of record, and you can prove anything on him. All you have got to do is accuse him, and then you say it is justice."

Another leftist publication is *Win*, a magazine published twice monthly and loosely tied to the War Resisters League. A mixture of radical and counterculture material (including "wire service" copy from the Underground Press Syndicate and Liberation News Service), the paper's past favorite subjects have been revolutionary politics, antiwar mobilization, radical history, war crimes, military deserters and resisters, the Black Panthers, women's liberation, and gay liberation.

Despite its coverage of all of the usual counterculture topics, the magazine was principally concerned with the Vietnam war and its impact on American life. But as the war began to wind down, *Win's* editors introduced a new phase, beginning in the August 1971 issue, when the publication had been moved to rural St. Remy, New York:

> When we began publishing *Win* six years ago our central concern was with ending the war in Vietnam. Since then we've changed in a lot of ways: we've grown from a mimeographed newsletter to a national pacifist magazine with a circulation of over 7,000; we've come to realize that the slaughter in Southeast Asia is not a thing apart from the ecology crisis, the roles that women are forced to play in this society, the kinds of schools we send our kids to, etc.; and perhaps most important we've learned that we can't change the world or stop the war by simply marching on enough picket lines, that to really grapple in a serious way with the problems that we face we have to begin to think and talk about some hard questions like what kind of society . . . we want to create, where the power in society really lies, and does organic gardening make a difference.

TO LOVE WE MUST FIGHT. This slogan appears beneath a picture of a fist clenching a rifle on the front page of a unique radical newspaper, *Rising Up Angry*. Unlike most such papers, which take up issues that appeal to a broad, though often poorly defined, audience, *Angry* is directed to poor residents of specific neighborhoods on Chicago's north side. It is the chief vehicle for a community organization also called Rising Up Angry, although, interestingly, the paper was founded first (in July 1969), the organization a year later.

The first issue was put together by a small group of revolutionaries who, one of them reported later (in *Seed*, November 1971),

... felt that the movement had been directed only towards students—that there was a youth culture thing going on but that it left out a lot of people and lots of these people didn't relate to the left or the revolution as it was. We wanted to bring our politics, politics of power for the people, in form that could reach everybody. So we put out a newspaper directed especially toward gangs, young people that didn't go to college, a lot of them that didn't finish high school, people out of the jails, people in the army.

The paper was first distributed free in the neighborhoods and at area high schools because the editors were trying to reach an audience that had never bought any kind of newspaper. Early issues were aimed at opposing racism, cooling fights among street gangs (by emphasizing the police were the common enemy), at idealizing the black struggle, and at promoting Black Panther programs.

Angry is a potpourri of information about self-defense methods, social services, radical politics, international movement news, and, most important, injustices and acts of repression in the neighborhoods the paper serves. A few articles have covered national and international issues—Angela Davis, Huey Newton, the Vietnam war—but most are neighborhood items. A February 1, 1971, editorial explains the paper's philosophy:

Rising Up Angry has put out a newspaper for a year and a half. People all over the city and all over the country have been digging the newspaper—the cartoons, community news, and the ideas. But there's still a lot of mystery about who we are, what we are and where we are going.

Rising Up Angry is a revolutionary organization made up of sisters and brothers from all over the city. Most of our people are from neighborhoods like Lincoln Park, Lakeview, Uptown, projects at Diversey and Damen, Armitage and Kedzie and from the Southwest side. None of us were born revolutionaries. We were into the same bullshit as everyone else—gang banging, racism and male chauvinism. The system had us fooled into fighting each other—gang against gang, men against women, race against race. Like fools, we hated each other, while lousy jobs, the army, jail, school and pigs in the street were making our lives miserable. So we made a decision about our lives . . . So we started by putting out a paper.

The paper strongly opposes drugs and drug dealers. In one article, "God Damn the Pusher Man" (August 3, 1971), a cartoon showed President Nixon looking on approvingly as a CIA agent and South Vietnam's Marshall Ky held a syringe. In Vietnam drugs are big business, the article said, and Nixon "ain't going to stop the situation. He can't. He's a pusher."

But *Angry* is not always so outraged; many articles are positive. And visually the paper often seems to be filled with pictures of smiling children (albeit with raised clenched fists). Visual appeal, in fact, is something *Angry*'s editors work very hard at, using spot color, overprints, and the like. More than most papers, *Rising Up Angry* is an active, indeed *activist*, force in its community. As one of the organization's posters proclaims: "Besides our newspaper that gives revolutionary news from around the city, the country, and the world, we have programs that help us deal with the problems that people have to face every day." These programs, as a standing *Angry* ad shows, include "free health care" and "welfare and legal counseling for women."

The "Jesus Papers"

At first glance, most religious papers or "Jesus papers" look like most underground newspapers: psychedelic art, counterculture cartoons, and radical rhetoric. On closer examination, they are something else—a religious revival in modern dress.

Jesus papers began appearing on the streets and campuses in 1969, about the same time a dramatic event occurred in Minneapolis, when a hippie was evicted from the Minneapolis Evangelism Conference but later readmitted because he looked more like Christ than any of the straight participants. This, says theologian Richard Lovelace, may have been "the overture to the present [religious] renewal among the street people."[18] Lovelace, a professor at Gordon-Conwell Theological Seminary, has analyzed the publications thus:

> . . . in some of the Jesus papers there is much aping of the youth culture which is plastic and unpersuasive (e.g., the self-conscious use of revolutionary language to sell religious answers) and this is likely to prove a passing fad once it is attacked. But there are in the counterculture vitamins that cannot be neutralized or contained by evangelical double-talk, and converts among the youth cultists are already infusing an irresistible dose of Consciousness III into their elders.[19]

The Jesus movement is not unified. Variously called Jesus People, Street Christians, Jesus Freaks, and Children of God (the most radical element), it is made up of factions and segments, of which the Jesus People are the largest and most moderate. University of Chicago theologian Martin Marty considers the movement part of the revival tradition in America, but other church leaders are uneasy about the Biblical literalism of the movement—indeed, in the words of Lovelace, some fear it may be "a conservative plot to swamp their hard-won social consciousness with a flood of indulgence selling." Dana Hawkes, a Baptist minister, considers the movement a paradox: "Today's young person is more educated and sophisticated than ever before, yet the Jesus movement, which resembles both a forest fire and a revolution, is reaching hundreds of thousands of young people with a message that is often rigidly fundamentalist, in an emotional style that has hitherto been reserved for the Pentecostals. And it is happening outside the Church, with an amazing lack of formal organization."[20]

The Hollywood (California) *Free Paper,* which has a circulation (unpaid) of 300,000, carries the message of the Jesus People and tries to explain the movement as "a loosely federated group of people who espouse a highly evangelistic, vocally and emotionally expressive brand of Christianity which is warmly sympathetic to long hair, beards, youthful dress styles and Jesus Rock music."[21] The paper blends news items, line drawings, and classified ads listing Jesus People Centers and urging runaways to return home. Countercultural exhortations are frequent—for instance, this undated (Volume 2, Issue 2) editorial:

> The Establishment has blown our minds. Are we going to allow this to continue? Or are we going to become true revolutionaries? Not just "re-acting" to issues forced down our throats by a corrupt Establishment. But by taking "action" and sieze the time!!!!
>
> Have we forgotten what history tells us about the greatest of all revolutionaries? How he was conspired against—found guilty of ridiculous crimes dreamed up by the Establishment just to have him locked up, shut up, and finally killed—dying wasn't enough—the mercenaries guarding his dead body had to plunge their shining daggers into his belly . . . just to make sure!!

Christ the Revolutionary is a frequent topic of the Jesus papers, and the editors are especially fond of a wanted poster bearing the likeness of Christ (though they seldom credit it to caricaturist Art Young, who drew it for *The Masses* in 1914).

Right On! was founded in 1969 in Berkeley, California, by Jesus people wanting "literature geared to the language and culture." As its editors wrote:

> So when we got some bread and some stories together, we put out a paper. It's been going like that ever since. We take each day and what comes down just as our Father gives it to us. Our paper hasn't been polished or perfect[ed]. We've made a lot of mistakes. But *Right On!* became a part of the scene, just like the other underground newspapers. Our only aim has been to run down the Father's plan to the people we know and love and hurt for. Lots of them have been drawn into his forever family through the paper. Some of them have written and now write for it.[22]

The mix of graphics, poetry, religious articles, and sermonettes makes *Right On!* look like a radical paper, but it is definitely conservative. As it says about Christian underground papers: "They show that something is happening among the youth of America that hadn't been expected. Right in the midst of a radical left movement and a heavy dope thing, lots of kids all over the country are finding that Jesus is the answer to their need and turning to Him as their Liberator and Leader."[23]

The Environment Press

Why did ecology become such a popular issue during the early spring of 1970? Because, writes James Ridgeway in *The Politics of Ecology,* "it momentarily offered the prospect of a new politics, a new set of symbols with which to rework the social order." One result was the new popular interest in farming, organic gardening, crafts, and other ways of clothing, feeding, and amusing oneself that did not rely on the technology of pollution. Responding to this movement, Stewart Brand "set out to evaluate, catalog and provide access to anything and everything that might be useful to an individual conducting a self-education or shaping environments." He began publishing *The Whole Earth Catalog.* As he states it:

> *The Whole Earth Catalog* got started in a plane over Nebraska in March 1968. I was returning to California from my father's long dying and funeral that morning in Illinois. The sun had set ahead of the plane while I was reading *Spaceship Earth* by Barbara Ward. Between chapters I gazed out the window into dark nothing and slid into a reverie about my friends who were starting their own civilization hither and yon in the sticks and how I could help. The L.L. Bean Catalog of outdoor stuff came to mind and I pondered upon Mr. Bean's service to humanity over the years. So many of the problems I could identify came down to a matter of access. Where to buy a windmill. Where to get good information on bee-keeping. Where to lay hands on a computer without forfeiting freedom.[24]

First published quarterly, at prices ranging from $3 to $5, the *Catalog* was a kind of ombudsman for counterculture how-to-do-it enthusiasts. Twice the size of most magazines and twice as bulky, it offered information on organic gardening, cooking, and making clothing; guided readers to the proper tools; reintroduced the seed catalog; and suggested a startling range of methods and items for those seeking the new civilization. "Access" was the byword—for everything from bottle cappers to spinning wheels.

The Whole Earth Catalog was so successful that its readers were shocked when Brand announced that the July 1971 issue, "Access to Tools," would be the final one. In it, *The Last Whole Earth Catalog,* Brand wrote:

> Fame
>   I/we've been subject to some, and you're partially responsible, so I thought you ought to know a little about it. Everything bad you've heard about fame is quite true. It can throw a personality into positive feedback, where audience demands drive his character past caricature and off the deep end. Its over-rewards can jade a palate permanently.

It wakes you up in the middle of the night with phone calls from whining strangers.

Worst of all is the classic bind of the successful do-gooder. If you do well, your opportunities to do more increase, as your stamina to do any decreases. You should relax, yes you should, relax, with guilt yammering in your ear. FUCK EM ALL! is no answer either.

The Last Whole Earth Catalog was even more successful: In 1972 it won the National Book Award in Contemporary Affairs.

Ohio-based *Mother Earth News*, a highly successful bi-monthly, appeals to the same readership. *Mother*, as it is called, is marketed like a paperback book, selling thousands of copies months after an issue is published. It has such a following, in fact, that it sometimes receives 5000 letters a month—about the same number as does the New York *Times*—and they are crammed into the columns by the hundreds.

"Want to learn how to milk a goat?" asked reporter Michael T. Malloy in the *National Observer*. "Or homestead in Canada? Or use an axe, build a tepee, grow herbs, or power your car engine with chicken manure? Then take a look at the *Mother Earth News*. You won't be alone. 'Mother' has discovered a world of frustrated pioneers out there, just dying to learn how to build a log cabin or heat a home with used crankcase oil."[25]

The editor is John Shuttleworth, who founded the publication in 1970 at age thirty-two. The purpose of *Mother*, he says, is to stir up a "gentle revolution because we are trying to help place bedrock, how-to information in the hands of people who are willing to work for a better life . . . rather than tear down."

Three common threads run through the articles in *Mother*, reporter Malloy says:

> They are relentlessly ecological, telling people how to live better without consuming, destroying, or otherwise using up their environment.
>
> They are committed to the old-fashioned virtues of self-help and independence, to making things instead of buying them, to producing instead of consuming.
>
> And they are, above all, positive. *Mother* is turned off by the consumer society, but she isn't angry at anyone. A Chicago policeman can read this magazine without being insulted.[26]

Published on newsprint with an attractive poster-style cover listing article titles, *Mother* covers such subjects as alternative life styles, build-it-yourself, communes, food co-ops, homesteading, living on less, recycling, shelter, and working for the fun of it. Readers are urged to move back to the land or to begin their own shoestring businesses. The articles are nearly always practical: "How to Get a Job on a Freighter," "Homestead Animal Care," "Organic Pest Controls," and the like.

"The Plowboy Interview," a regular feature, has probed the minds of various persons from Buffy St. Marie to Buckminister Fuller. In one interview a couple named Nearing were held up as "Mother heroes" because they had "been living today's counterculture for better than a generation":

Almost four decades ago [in 1932], the couple "dropped out" to a rockscrabble mountain farm in Vermont's Green Mountains where they spent the next 20 years rebuilding the soil, constructing solid homestead buildings from native stone, growing their own food, heating with wood they cut by hand and co-authoring numerous books and magazine articles. Tick off any of the present's most "in" passions—woman's lib, equal rights, organic gardening, vegetarianism, radicalism, homesteading, subsistence farming, ecology —and you'll find that the Nearings have been *doing* instead of talking for 40 years.[27]

A highbrow entry in the ecology field is *Environment,* published in St. Louis by the Committee for Environmental Information, distinguished scientists who make up the magazine's Science Advisory Board. Louis T. Kinnie, coordinator of educational resources for the magazine, writes that the committee and the magazine were founded because:

... despite their formidable technical content, the issues of modern public life remain matters which demand *value judgments* from the citizen and his political representatives: these issues therefore require a confrontation between ascertainable scientific facts, and ethical religious and political principles.
... in order to reach a responsible judgment on such public issues the citizen himself must have the relevant scientific facts, and understand them, otherwise he cannot play his rightful role in guiding his own destiny and in meeting the demands of his own conscience.
... scientists, as the custodians of the relevant technical knowledge, have an obligation to bring it before their fellow citizens in understandable terms: but with respect to the resultant value judgments, scientists have a greater or lesser competence than any other informed citizens, and ought not abrogate these decisions to themselves.

Articles in *Environment* have popular titles, but like a scholarly journal they are laced with charts and graphs and each article ends with a detailed bibliography. This mix of popular appeal and scholarship is suggested by these titles and article blurbs:

"Questions for an Old Friend"—DDT, long believed to be harmless to man except in massive doses, is now known to cause infertility, stunted growth, and a variety of chemical changes in concentrations to which all of us are exposed.

"Cloud on the Desert"—The Four Corners electric power complex in the Southwest will produce almost as much smoke as the entire New York metropolitan region.

"Last Year at Deuville"—A Belgian magazine reports that your chances of getting sick at many European beach resorts are doubled if you go into the water.

"The State of the Bomb"—A report from the Committee for Environmental Information on the status of the nuclear arms race.

"The Price of Beef"—A hormone used to hasten the growth of most beef cattle may remain in the meat in concentrations known to cause cancer in animals.

The Feminist Press

United principally by the desire to gain women full equality, the women's liberation movement is made up of many factions that sometimes seem to agree only that women get a bad deal. With so many viewpoints, it is not surprising that the movement has given birth to many newspapers, magazines, and newsletters. By 1972, according to *PM*, a movement newsletter, there were over 150 such publications.

Many have lively and challenging names: *Ms., Ain't I a Woman!, It Ain't Me Babe, Free and Proud, Off Our Backs, Pissed Off Pink, Underground Woman,* and *Velvet Fist.* The publications cover a wide range of sisterhood concerns: equal pay for equal work, day care centers for working women, an end to sexism in the media. Some, like *Off Our Backs,* are highly political and seek radical change. Others, like *Women: A Journal of Liberation,* resemble scholarly journals, with measured language and intellectual rationale for political and social positions.

When women's liberation began to attract attention in the late 1960s, the underground papers offered a sympathetic hearing, carrying columns and articles about the movement. But sympathetic articles were often negated by what the women termed sexist advertising. The inconsistency helped to transform some such papers, among them Chicago's *Seed,* which in 1969 stopped accepting classified sex ads and later stopped accepting Playboy Theatre ads. An unsigned article in the June 29, 1971, *Seed* expressed the difficulties of the transition:

> Sexism is something that we are struggling with constantly. . . . The anti-sexist movement in the country has a tremendous potential—both in terms of being able to show people how oppressed they are and to turn them on to new ways of living and relating to each other. Sexism affects everything from the anti-war leafleter who only hands leaflets

to the men walking down the street in couples, to the headings of letters. . . . All of us on the *Seed* staff want very much to break out of all that—but it is very hard, and much too easy to backslide. All too often male staffers find themselves laughing at sexist jokes, or going off on macho ego trips about strength or expertise. We need very desperately your aid and encouragement in helping to overcome this—and we especially need your criticism.

Soon the staff began to answer letters addressed in "sexist" fashion with a form letter: "We are no longer answering mail addressed, 'gentlemen,' 'dear Sirs,' or any other heading which denies the existence and/or importance of women on our staff. We do *not* hold that the important people in any organization or business are men. On the contrary. The eleven people running the paper are of equal editorial importance. 5 of them are women. The president of the corporation is a woman. The typist is a man. Raise your consciousness."

Parodying newspaper women's pages, *Seed* has carried its own "men's supplement." Indeed, although the paper presents articles on many counterculture issues, women's rights dominate, and the magazine-cover-like front page frequently celebrates the movement.

Rat, in the mid-sixties and based in New York, is recalled by one staff member as being considered "one of the best underground newspapers." This meant, he said, that "it had the flashiest reportage of movement happenings and the cultural revolution, combined with enough pornography to titillate both the straights and 'liberated' males." Like *Seed*, it too underwent a change; as a writer in the January 12-29, 1971, issue put it: "A few of the women who had been working on *Rat* had been trying to get across to the men that the pornography was an insult to us and how it wasn't "in the nature" of things for women to be doing most of the shitwork. Finally they told the editor they wanted to put out the next issue with women, and he agreed, thinking it would be a good way to get them off his back, then things could go back to normal."

The women at *Rat* were a mixture of Weatherwomen, feminists, Yippies, gay liberationists, movement heavies, but they seemed to enjoy working together. One wrote, "It took me awhile to realize why I felt so good and strong: there were no men around to either put down the work I was doing (or assume I couldn't do it in the first place . . . which meant I never tried) or to make me feel like a ball-breaker when I did assert myself."

Rat went on to become a women's movement newspaper—produced by "tough, fierce women," according to James Ridgeway. How tough was shown when the paper ran a picture of a plainclothes cop and the caption that he was "the pig responsible for helping bust six people last week. He now has a goatee and a mustache (add your own). He probably cannot be used around movement groups again, but we should still continue to find out about the way he worked, and raise each other's consciousness about who we should trust and work with."

Rat's layout and design are cluttered and sometimes obscured with heavy color overprints, too much bold type, and dark photographs. The writing is often weak and imprecise and the editing and proofreading sloppy. But the paper offers a strong voice for a segment of womanhood.

Everywoman is a feminist paper that has adopted the format popularized by music paper *Rolling Stone*: folded like a magazine but opening into a tabloid newspaper, and featuring offbeat covers and photographs ranging from a representation of a rape to a group of robots.

The paper was founded in May 1970 in Venice, California, and had a circulation of 3000 by 1972. It is published by a woman's collective which also operates a feminist bookstore, a speaker's bureau, and a publishing company, and which is linked to women's liberation radio and feminist theater. Written for educated readers, *Everywoman* presents short news items (many by Liberation News Service) and long essays such as "Equality Is Not Enough" or "Clothing and Sexuality." Photo essays, book reviews, and historical pieces (labeled "herstory") are regular features.

The *Everywoman* staff describes itself as "a complex of women from all backgrounds trying to work out a work and life style that will enable them to function as human beings in a country that tries to destroy creativity, autonomy, and spontaneity." Staff requirements, they say, are:

1) A willingness to work on trust, realizing growth comes best when emerging from within rather than [when] imposed from without.
2) Flexibility and interest in learning a variety of skills.
3) Indifference to status since we have no hierarchy.
4) Open-minded approach to feminism. If you have skills in some type of communication, fine. If not we'll teach you what we know.

A September 10, 1971, "herstory" told of ninth-century Pope Joan, a woman supposed to have been disguised as a man and elected pope:

The question, "Was she or wasn't she an historical figure?" is no longer easy to resolve. The core of historical truth, which must be there, is covered over with legendary accretions. As the story was commonly related, Joan struck up an amorous alliance with a monk and entered his monastery in male disguise—a deception not unheard of in those days. The pair eventually fled, and arrived in Athens, where Joan studied science and theology.

When her lover died, Joan continued her career in Rome, still disguised as a man, of course, and found there was plenty of room at the top. While she was pope, she became pregnant, and gave birth to a child right in the street during a papal procession, wouldn't you know it.

Off Our Backs, a sixteen-page tabloid begun in 1970 and offering a wide range of feminist material, takes advantage of its Washington, D.C., location to provide coverage of government actions affecting women. For instance, in April 15, 1971, an article on the politics of venereal disease argued: "In communities where people felt love, responsibility and commitment to each other, sex would not only be one expression of mutual respect and caring—health would be a collective concern and VD would be identified and treated. We should not need officials from a clinic or health department to investigate or track down our sexual contacts."

Off Our Backs sometimes runs profiles of leaders in the liberation movement, as in this one published June 1971:

> One day last week I pulled on my overalls and went to see Bella. A hike to the Hill, an elevator ride to the fifth floor of the Cannon Building. A short walk down a typically bleak government corridor. Congresswoman Bella S. Abzug. . . .
>
> Congress may kill Bella, and then again Bella might renew our faith in Congress. She might scare me into hoping, being as [a friend] put it ". . . a populist, a street person . . . ." But for my overalls and me it is a corrupt system that can't deliver, infected with the deadly etceteras and life-destroying habits. And I see her, Congresswoman Bella S. Abzug (D-NY), beating those angry feminist fists on the iron doors of an empty fortress. History may be listening.

Diverse in content, clearly written, and attractively designed, *Off Our Backs* is one of the most appealing feminist papers, and has achieved a circulation of 10,000. It publishes practical information about nutrition, health, abortion, and nursing infants; essays on social and political issues; and brief news items about the movement and its concerns. Even though it speaks to the converted, the paper takes little for granted. The rhetoric is calm—rational arguments in measured language.

Ain't I a Woman is more hostile and argumentative. Published tri-weekly since June 1970 in Iowa City, Iowa, by a collective of 450 women who describe themselves as a "wide conspiracy of radical lesbians," the twelve-page tabloid is as forthright as a bludgeon. For instance, it reprinted an editorial from *Struggle,* a Canadian feminist paper, which complained how distressed *Struggle* was at "some of the attitudes we have been picking up on from the women's papers we receive" such as "that middle class is being equated with reformist and that middle-class women must either deny their class background or resign themselves to being reformist." *Ain't I a Woman* responded:

> *Struggle* women are upset with being "caught up in accusations and confrontations when we should not be struggling with each other." What's the difference? Isn't it just that our middle-class "sensibilities" are offended by raised voices and anger. We've got to get

the pig shit out of our heads that equates confrontation with nonproductivity. Of course there's anger. Of course middle-class women will be confronted. But we can't just say "Sisters, let's join hands and discuss this rationally." The anger is real and justified and we've got to deal with it and listen to it and change. That's the rub. We're so fucking smug about this "revolution" that we're making that we can't stand the heat and the criticism. One thing is for sure—the revolution *can* go on without us.

The paper is frank in discussing female physiology; for instance, it once ran a two-page article on "Vaginal Politics, Menstruational Extraction," depicting with vivid language and photographs how women could deal with their unique physiological problems. There are also frequent discussions of lesbianism, as in this question-and-answer feature published November 19, 1971:

How do you feel about not having babies?

Answer 1. It's just not true that lesbians can't have or have given up having a family just because they don't relate to men. If I really wanted to have a baby naturally, I'd go get pregnant in some time-honored way. But there are plenty of children born already, and single-parent adoption is one clear solution to that problem.

Answer 2. Also there are many lesbians—married, divorced and single—who have children.

Answer 3. The myth of a woman's destiny and fulfillment being partially centered around having babies is pure bunk. A married woman with four children pointed out that child-bearing has been romanticized and mythologized all out of proportion.

Answer 4. I don't like kids, but that doesn't mean I have no family. All the women in the community are my family.

Answer 5. Several women explained that they live communally with people who do have children, and caring for and "raising" the children is done collectively.

Women: A Journal of Liberation is less timely than most feminist papers, but it offers detailed interpretive articles. A nicely illustrated quarterly that is published in Baltimore, its issues are built on themes: "Women and the Arts"; "How We Live, and with Whom"; "Women as Workers Under Capitalism"; "The Power and Scope of the Women's Liberation Movement." "Ladies in the Lab," published spring 1971, argued: "To many people, a career in the life sciences appears to be a glamorous one—full of exciting discoveries and high salaries. In the next few pages, I hope to show how great a misconception this is. I also hope to show how behind the 'men in white' stands a veritable army, most of whose members are women, who are underpaid, and who do not know, or will not admit, the magnitude of their oppression, and its roots."

This journal focuses largely on conditions. If its way of blending magazine journalism and scholarship may somewhat confuse its audience, it is nevertheless literate and interesting.

There are many other feminist publications, of course, as diverse as the movement itself: *Adam's Rib* is the publication of New York's Pussycat League, which promotes the "pride, pleasure, and responsibilities of being a woman"; *NOW News,* edited in Los Angeles by feminist Jean Stapleton, is associated with that city's chapter of the National Organization for Women; *Aphra,* a feminist literary magazine, is published in Springtown, Pennsylvania; and the *Spokeswoman* is a Chicago-based newsletter of tersely written items.

The most ambitious publication of the women's movement is *Ms.* magazine, which first appeared as a forty-page supplement to the December 20, 1971, *New York* magazine. As *New York* editor Clay Felker introduced it, *Ms.* would be "a national magazine edited totally by women" and would be devoted to women "not as role players, but as full human beings." The first complete issue of *Ms.* carried a feminist rating of the 1972 Presidential candidates and such articles as "Why Women Fear Success," "The Housewife's Moment of Truth," "How to Write Your Own Marriage Contract," and "My Mother the Dentist" (by Nicholas von Hoffman, the only male writer in the magazine). In the lead editorial, Gloria Steinem wrote about sisterhood: "I have met brave women who are exploring the outer edge of human possibility, with no history to guide them, and with a courage to make themselves vulnerable that I find moving beyond words."

Operating as a modified collective, *Ms.* began without an editor, then took on a highly professional one, Pat Carbine, formerly managing editor of *Look* and editor of *McCall's.* With Carbine and Steinem providing expertise, *Ms.* was off to the best beginning of any publication born of the women's movement.

Steinem and her collaborators understood the need for financial solvency, but still wanted to control their own magazine. Early in the planning they agreed to take in a minority stockholder, Warner Communications, Inc., which bought 25 percent of the magazine at a cost of $1 million.

The magazine's first issue in July 1972 sold 425,000 copies (250,000 had been hoped for) and the circulation continues to climb. The magazine was printing 530,000 copies per issue by 1973. The editors were gratified when more than 40 percent of persons filling out subscription cards sent money with the completed card. (The usual rate is 2 to 3 percent.) The magazine has such a loyal following that some readers even contribute money. Contributions, which have ranged from 75¢ to $200, according to Carbine, are used to send free subscriptions to "women college students, women in prison, and welfare mothers. We also send some free subscriptions to women whose husbands won't let them subscribe to the magazine."

Although major advertisers took a wait-and-see attitude at first, they came in droves after *Ms.*'s initial success. Advertisers from major auto firms to book clubs bought space. Such firms as International Telephone and Telegraph also bought space for recruitment of women into corporations.

Key staff members operate without titles and there is a tendency to share duties. "Everyone," says Carbine, "is equally involved in production. We ask every one within earshot for their opinion when a major decision is to be made. Everybody helps with everything. The woman who types the manuscripts also writes articles."

Carbine says *Ms.* is proving that "vitality exists in print and that when an idea is right and has an audience, it can be presented professionally and pay its own way." The magazine, she says, "is working at humanizing the roles of women and men. We are working for a society where human beings are free from birth with the freedom to be whatever he or she wants to be."

In the world of national magazines, where new entries often falter, *Ms.* seems to be assured of success.

Conclusion

By 1973 advocacy journalism had become a vital and vibrant force. In the late 1960s it split such newspapers as the Minneapolis *Tribune,* as staff reporters clamored for an infusion of advocacy in the news columns. And there is evidence of some change today. As one of the *Tribune*'s editors said in 1973, "There is no doubt that much of our reporting leans closer to advocacy than it did before, although we still reject the notion of pure advocacy." Other newspapers have had similar experiences, as those who demanded advocacy had a greater effect.

The single-minded journals of advocacy are also having a substantial impact. Their very existence is a powerful rebuttal to those who say that minority viewpoints lack access to media. Critics who assumed that the advocacy press would go away when the war in Vietnam ground to a halt were not in touch with the developments in the women's movement and other social and political movements. Content from John Shuttleworth's *Mother Earth News* began appearing as a syndicated column in a number of American newspapers. The new thrust of advocacy journals in the 1960s seemed destined to expand and accelerate during the 1970s. New movements and social interests would no doubt need organs for their point of view. For example, the amnesty issue aroused enough people for a successful amnesty magazine, *Amex* (short for "American Exile"), to begin in Toronto in 1972.

Time, resources, and personal interests of the authors have necessarily limited our view of advocacy journalism. We have not, for example, covered such black advocacy publications as the *Black Panther* and *Muhammad Speaks* because we believe they are best evaluated in the context of the black press generally. This is something that journalism educator Roland

Wolseley has done in his excellent, comprehensive survey *The Black Press, U.S.A.* Other ethnic papers, such as those published by American Indian and chicano groups, deserve thoughtful study. We felt that covering these publications as a part of the advocacy movement of the 1960s and 1970s would be highly misleading. They should have full and complete treatment in another book.

For similar reasons we have not included the rapidly expanding sex press, which ranges from such general periodicals as *Screw* and the *New York Review of Sex* to those that border on hardcore pornography (for example, *Horseshit* and *Ball & Chain*). Also within the realm of the advocacy press are such gay liberation papers as *Come Out* and *Gay Power*. While recognizing the importance of these publications, our research efforts have not included them in this study. We believe that these publications are best treated in the context of the sex press and the changes in sexual mores. That is not the focus of this book.

The Advocacy Press: An Example

FOR CESAR CHAVEZ

by Pete Hamill

In this 1970 column from the New York Post, *Pete Hamill demonstrates the passionate appeal he can make when he is of a mind to do it. The image of Chavez juxtaposed with a malevolent image of President Nixon provides the contrast that makes Hamill's writing so powerful.*

> *That winter of 1938 I had to walk to school barefoot through the mud, we were so poor. After school, we fished in the canal and cut wild mustard greens—otherwise we would have starved. Everyone else left the camp we were living in, but we had no money for transportation. When everyone else left, they shut off the lights, so we sat around in the dark. . . . —Cesar Chavez, quoted by John Gregory Dunne in "Delano."*

There were too many children sitting around in the dark and so Cesar Chavez came out of the fields and valleys of California, spreading the word to the chicanos, telling them that the time had come at last to organize. No more growers getting fat while Mexican kids ate mustard greens; no more walking barefoot to school on winter roads; no more bowing to Anglos for a job. It was time to form a union.

Chavez used non-violence as his best and almost single weapon; when Martin Luther King was being sneered at in Chicago and when New York radicals were talking up violence as the only solution to our problems,

Reprinted from the New York *Post*, December 7, 1970, p. 14.

Chavez remained non-violent. He knew that making true change was a long and complicated process, but he was in there to go the distance. Last summer [1970], five years after he started, Chavez and his people won their first major victory when the grape growers of California caved in and signed contracts with the union. They won it without cheap talk about revolution, without Weatherman lunacy, without killing anyone.

Chavez is in jail while the President of the United States turns shill for airplane companies. Nixon has placed the prestige of his office on the line for the SST, attacking the United States Senate for refusing to set up a private welfare program for the Boeing Company. Nixon always speaks out for those who purchased a piece of the Presidency with campaign contributions; when it comes to people like Chavez, when it comes to men who work with their hands and their backs in the lettuce fields of Texas and California, when it comes to the poor and the humiliated and the despised, Nixon is silent. He always is.

When Chavez was fighting the grape companies, Nixon tried to break the strike by having the Defense Dept. buy up millions of pounds of unsold produce. Now that Chavez has shifted his efforts to the lettuce workers, we can expect every GI in Vietnam to average seven or eight pounds of lettuce a day for a long time to come. The lettuce strike will not be a short one.

The lettuce companies seem to be insuring a long strike by their hard-headed opposition to Chavez, and the jailing of Chavez on Friday in Salinas, Calif. is not making a solution easier. The owners first tried to keep Chavez out by signing sweetheart contracts with those great friends of the Mexican-Americans, the Teamsters. The Teamsters operate like a business disguised as a union, and this was basically a pact between corporate managers. Chavez runs a union in the old style, and the owners wanted no part of him.

Three of the owners signed with Chavez after he called for a strike and nationwide boycott of non-union lettuce in August. The rest (representing 85% of the business) banded together to fight him, led by Bud Antle, Inc., part of the Dow Chemical Corp., those lovable folks who brought us napalm. (They also make Saran Wrap.)

The growers claimed in court that Chavez was really fighting a jurisdictional battle with the Teamsters, and on Sept. 14 the court agreed, declaring the Chavez strike illegal. But the strike continued, while union lawyers appealed the decision. Then in October, Bud Antle, Inc. got a friendly judge named Gordon Campbell to give them an injunction that barred a strike or boycott until the first case was settled. Campbell refused to stay the injunction during the appeal unless the union came up with $2,750,000 to protect the Antle company from any damages. The union doesn't have anything like that amount in its treasury, of course, and Chavez continued the strike. On Friday he was jailed for violating the injunction, with judgment and sentence coming from good old Judge Campbell.

The Judge gave Chavez 10 days, but then upped the ante by adding another indeterminate sentence. Chavez was sentenced for the duration of the strike and boycott, a form of legal strikebusting that should help to build faith in the system among his followers. Chavez has been in bad health for years and a long stretch in jail could kill him. But when they led him away, he shouted: "Boycott the hell out of them."

And that's precisely what should happen. No store that sells non-union lettuce should get any other kind of business. Saran Wrap can find some other customer. The restaurants using non-union lettuce can wait for orders. Giving up lettuce should be as easy a thing as giving up grapes was. It's a very small thing, but it's at least one way of registering one's disgust with a country whose jails are starting to fill with good men.

Notes

[1] "From-the-Hip Delivery," *Newsweek*, October 27, 1969, p. 112.

[2] *Ibid.*

[3] Herbert Brucker, "What's Wrong with Objectivity?", *Saturday Review*, October 11, 1969, p. 77.

[4] Internal memorandum to the *Oregonian* staff from Edward M. Miller, managing editor, October 14, 1970.

[5] David Deitch, "Case for Advocacy Journalism," *Nation*, November 17, 1969, p. 531.

[6] Brucker, *op. cit.*

[7] Warren Breed, "Social Control in the Newsroom," *Social Forces*, 33, p. 335.

[8] James B. Lemert, "Craft Attitudes, the Craft of Journalism and Spiro Agnew." Paper read at the Western Speech Association, Portland, Oregon, November 25, 1970. The studies to which Lemert refers are: Bradley S. Greenberg and Percy H. Tannenbaum, "Communicator Performance under Cognitive Stress," *Journalism Quarterly*, Spring 1962, pp. 169-178; Edwin P. Bettinghaus and Ivan L. Preston, "Dogmatism and Performance of the Communicator under Cognitive Stress," *Journalism Quarterly*, Summer 1964, pp. 399-402; Jean S. Kerrick, Thomas E. Anderson, and Luita B. Swales, "Balance and the Writer's Attitude in News Stories and Editorials," *Journalism Quarterly*, Spring 1964, pp. 207-215; L. Erwin Atwood, "Effects of Source and Message Credibility on Writing Style," *Journalism Quarterly*, Autumn 1966, pp. 464-468.

[9] "Limitation on Journalists' Off-Duty Activism Favored," *Editor & Publisher*, June 26, 1971.

[10] Benjamin C. Bradlee, in *Left at the Post*, by Nicholas von Hoffman (Chicago: Quadrangle, 1970), p. 9.

[11] Nicholas von Hoffman, *Mississippi Notebook* (New York: David White, 1964), p. 24.

[12] "Gloria Steinem, A Liberated Woman Despite Beauty, Chic and Success," *Newsweek*, August 16, 1970, p. 53.

[13] *Ibid.*, p. 55.

[14] Pete Hamill, New York *Post*, December 3, 1970.

[15] Pete Hamill, New York *Post, December 17, 1970*.

[16] James Ridgeway, "The New Journalism," *American Libraries*, June 1971, p. 586.

[17] James Aronson, *Packaging the News: A Critical Survey of Press, Radio, TV* (New York: International Publishers, 1971), p. 64.

[18] Richard Lovelace, "The Shape of the Coming Renewal," *Christian Century*, October 6, 1971, p. 1164.

[19] *Ibid.*, p. 1165.

[20] Dana Hawkes, "The Jesus People: Freaks or Friends?" *American Baptist*, September 1971, p. 8.

[21] *Ibid.*, p. 9.

[22]*The Street People: Selections from Right On! Berkeley's Christian Underground Student Paper* (Valley Forge, Pa.: Judson Press, 1971), p. 2.

[23]*Ibid.*

[24]Stewart Brand, *Last Whole Earth Catalog* (Menlo Park, Calif.: Portola Institute, 1971, distributed by Random House, New York), p. 439.

[25]Michael T. Malloy, " 'Mother' Taps Hippie Vein in Conventional Folk," *National Observer*, May 3, 1971, p. 9.

[26]*Ibid.*

[27]"The Plowboy Interview," *Mother Earth News*, September 1971, p. 6.

Covering
the Counterculture 6

The underground press is the loving product
of the best minds of my generation, running
screaming through the negro streets at dawn
looking for an angry printing press.
—Thomas King Forcade, in *Orpheus Magazine,*
1968

The counterculture. A culture "so radically disaffiliated from the mainstream assumptions of our society," says Theodore Roszak, "that it scarcely
looks to many as a culture at all, but takes on the alarming appearance of a
barbaric intrusion."[1] But a culture it is—or, as Roszak says, at least a mix of
two cultures:

> To one side, there is the mind-blown bohemianism of the beats and the
> hippies; to the other, the hard-headed political activism of the student
> New Left. . . . I think there exists . . . a theme that unites these varia-
> tions and which accounts for the fact that hippy and student activist
> continue to recognize each other as allies. Certainly there is the
> common enemy against whom they combine forces, but there is also a
> positive similarity of sensibility.[2]

If there is unity, there are also many differences in the counterculture—race, social class, religion, politics, and strategy for change. But the
members were together in a desire to be *different* from the mainstream of
American society. Those who talked of good vibes and those who talked of
bombing buildings both longed to overthrow the system. In many other
ways they were also much alike—in age (most were young), proximity (most
lived in urban low-rent or rural areas), common language (hip vernacular, of
course), art (psychedelic and pop-op), music (folk and rock), drugs (pot to

pills), and sexual freedom (the final rejection of Puritanism). By 1964 their unity found expression in media that have been called underground, alternative, and countercultural (we use the term "underground"). The new press provided a suitable psychological medium for the counterculture and, for some people, an economic base. As Richard Todd wrote in the *Atlantic,* it was "one of the few opportunities for a radical occupation, and for some the underground [was] a place of corporate drama."

The art was bold and psychedelic, and often done in full processed color. Stories were rambling and unstructured, with not even a nodding acquaintance with conventional reporting. There were no restrictions on language, even the earthiest, and no taboo subjects, whether free love and bisexual activities, drugs, or radical politics and attacks on the establishment. From the beginning, the underground press took an interest in social services, running columns to help their readers get access to public aid, free clinics, and government-surplus items. If the display advertising sometimes resembled that of the establishment media (such as in the record-company ads), the classified columns were highly unorthodox, offering dating and mating services for every imaginable experience.

Jesse Kornbluth, a Harvard senior, has called the underground press an example of "peer communication." While such papers may seem like "the blind leading the blind," he says, "there's a bit of self preservation in the refusal of adolescents to speak openly with anyone but their peers. And because only the young seem interested in rock music, youth culture reinforces itself, a process that explains the popularity of the underground press."[3]

Three underground editors, writing in *Fire: Reports from the Underground Press,* agree: "Amerikan boredom and destruction drove us out of our minds and we found each other. We are the future spreading faster than fire. We are the living connections within our generation." Jeff Shero of *Rat* likened the new papers to "a tidal wave of sperm rushing into a nunnery." Merilee Fenger wrote in *Montana Journalism Review* that undergrounds were "a primary source of fuel for the hippies' underground railway of revolt."

By 1967, radical journalist Andrew Kopkind could declare, "the loudest voice heard in America these days is the sound of insurgents chiseling away at establishments. Their vehicle is the underground press." Writing in the *New Republic,* David Sanford stated: "They are all the things their admirers think they are—exciting, informative, In, irreverent, refreshing, audacious, lively; they haven't sold out like everybody else. They are also recklessly undisciplined, often badly written, yellow and, taken in large doses, very, very boring."[4]

Writing in *Grassroots Editor,* San Francisco journalism professor Walter Gieber argued that "It is not a true or legitimate press of dissent; it indulges in grumbling and exaggeration without presenting a reasonable positive suggestion, let alone an alternative. Nor is it a muckraking press. A true muckraker is not a paranoid who indulges in vituperation and obscenity."[5]

A *Reader's Digest* editor attacked even more harshly: "Those underground newspapers in America who openly defend the use of propaganda to promote disruption are not journalistic oddities, but natural products of another editorial tradition based on the theory of V.I. Lenin, Soviet author and editor who helped lay the groundwork for international communism."[6]

But to Nicholas von Hoffman of the Washington *Post,* the undergrounds have passed "the most important test for American newspapers: After reading one, a reasonable man would want to burn his copy and hang the editor.... At their best, underground papers have been an alternative medium giving us information we couldn't get elsewhere. At their worst they have served as caricatures to show us how bad the straight press can be."[7]

First Stirrings

The underground press probably began in May 1964, when Art Kunkin, a thirty-six-year-old unemployed tool and die maker, spent fifteen dollars "to promote the concept of a new weekly tabloid," the Los Angeles *Free Press.* The image of a hip blue-collar worker sacrificing to bring out the first underground has romantic appeal, but Kunkin and the *"Freep"* are far more complex than the modern legend would have it. Kunkin had planned to be a geneticist, became a merchant seaman instead, then developed an interest in the social sciences. In 1961, he wrote a 500-page book on the American revolution, published later that year. Although he was unemployed and poor in 1964, he was prosperous by 1970. He now owns a small print shop, three bookstores, and a publishing house—a revealing commentary on the development of the underground.

Robert Glessing, author of *The Underground Press in America,* considers New York's *Village Voice* (established 1955) the pioneer underground paper. However, if the underground is defined as growing out of the psychedelic subculture of the 1960s, oriented to young people, and printed by offset lithography, the *Voice,* which has always been on the fringes of the establishment even as it promoted reform, hardly qualifies. As Paul Slater wrote in his master's thesis for the University of California, Berkeley, Graduate School of Journalism, although the *Village Voice* served as the model for Kunkin, "for eight years the *Voice* was in a class by itself. Kunkin, however, charted his own course and departed from the conventional format of the New York weekly, giving American journalism a new genre where even the once far-out *Voice* feared to tread."[8]

Like the *Village Voice,* Paul Krassner's *Realist,* founded in 1958, also helped create the atmosphere for the first undergrounds. Irreverent, often caustic, *Realist* was, Slater wrote, "lending its influence to the underground weeklies a decade later: a combination of wit and obscenity that is difficult to imitate but widely reprinted and quoted with Krassner's blessings."

Many widely known undergrounds were founded shortly after Kunkin began publication, most located in urban neighborhoods favored by hippies and students, such as Berkeley's Telegraph Avenue and New York's East Village. Often the undergrounds served as alternatives not only to the local community newspapers but to the student newspapers as well, most of which, though somewhat radicalized in the 1960s, were still tied to the university establishment and to a middle-class life style.

The size of the underground press is not known. Some who have studied their growth believe the high point was reached in the late 1960s with about 6000 papers—not including possibly 3000 high school undergrounds and about 100 GI undergrounds. But no one who has studied them believes that more than 400 or 500 were really stable, and even these figures seem high in light of the deaths of many that *seemed* stable. In 1972 the Underground Press Service, a sort of underground wire service, listed 400 papers as members, and Liberation News Service listed 800, but there is some overlap. Many of the discrepancies regarding the size and scope of the underground press may result from differing definitions. Robert Glessing, for example, includes in his book papers like *New Left Notes* and the *Chicago Journalism Review*. Richard Askin's survey, "Comparative Characteristics of the Alternative Press," lists the San Francisco *Bay Guardian*. These papers, however, are startlingly different from papers like the *Free Press*.

Changes in the Underground

Changes in the new media have paralleled changes in the counterculture itself. By 1973 the revolutionary posture was no longer so evident, in part because new staff members brought new ideas about how the papers should be operated, how they should look, and especially what they should cover. The changes seem to come in waves, and the undergrounds have been shaped by three:

1. During the *hippie period, 1964-1967,* the papers were primarily known for psychedelic art and essays on drug use, sexual freedom, and Eastern religion.

2. During the *radical period, 1967-1970,* the hippies were politicized and blended with the New Left and other radical political groups. The papers were heavy with articles about such political folk heroes as the Black Panthers and political organizers in a fairly simplistic stance of counterculture versus the straights.

3. During the *period of internal dissension and new complexity, since 1970,* the issues that once seemed clear-cut are more complicated, many

staff splits have occurred, and there have been debates about stance and tactics. Sexism in advertising is under attack, and the style of writing and appearance of the papers is moving closer to conventional standards.

Before the counterculture was politicized, the papers were alive with explosive, multi-colored psychedelics, and articles dug heavily into the drug scene, Eastern religion, music, the arts, and unorthodox life styles, reflecting the drop-out, cop-out attitudes of the time. Among the folk heroes then were Ken Kesey, Timothy Leary, Gary Snyder, and Allen Ginsberg. Near the end of this period some critics were declaring the new media completely predictable and dull.

Then on Memorial Day 1967 there was a massive "arrest-in" in New York's East Village. This and similar events over the country caused Paul Krassner to comment that "the flower children have developed thorns." The *East Village Other* declared the "death of the hippie and the birth of Free Men." As Paul Slater has pointed out, almost overnight the hippies and their communications media were politicized:

> The mentors of underground journalism now included the old, strictly political, Leftist press such as the *National Guardian* and publications of the Students for a Democratic Society. In California this meant the decline of such other-worldly papers as the San Francisco *Oracle* and the birth of other politically oriented papers like the San Francisco *Express Times,* responding to . . . the realities of the war, hostility from the straight world, repressions from police. The end of the groove. Good vibrations weren't enough.[9]

A stronger focus on writing, most of it political, reduced the attention to art, and articles glorifying drug trips gave way to those condemning repressive police actions. More articles were written on the war in Vietnam and its domestic reverberations. Soon, a number of celebrated conspiracy trials gave dramatic definition to the notion of a counterculture opposing traditional society. Old men like Judge Julius Hoffman of the Chicago Seven trial, J. Edgar Hoover, and Attorney General John Mitchell were portrayed as being locked in battle with youth. Black Panther leader Eldridge Cleaver, Angela Davis, and Abbey Hoffman became the heroes.

In February 1971, the Berkeley *Barb* reflected another change as the counterculture moved into a period of internal dissension. FREE TIM, AGAIN, the *Barb* cried in two-inch headlines. The story was the first of a number of incomplete and highly confusing reports that Timothy Leary was being held captive in Algeria by Eldridge Cleaver. Two of the *Barb's* favorite people had come into conflict. The strident editorials became ambivalent: "Why not write and let us know what you think?" This came when staffers were leading revolts on many papers, including the *Barb*. Strong editors fought staff members dedicated to a collectivist style of equal responsibility for management. The sharp issues which had served as a call to arms in the early days became cloudy. Vietnam was an issue only occasionally. When the women's liberation movement grew, it became apparent that few women had leading roles in the underground. Women's opposition to exploitation of the body came into conflict with the papers' policies on classified advertising.

Colliding With the Law

Considering how often the constituted authorities ignore libel, copyright, and pornography violations by underground papers, it may seem strange that underground editors complain so bitterly about repression. But it is true that skirmishes with the law are commonplace with the underground press. Indeed, the spectacle of multiple police actions and legal sanctions has few parallels in the history of American journalism. And although the conventional press has been a fierce champion of its own freedom, it has usually been silent when underground staffers are hauled into court and jailed.

The charges have been varied. Speaking for the drug culture has brought police raids, and creaky city ordinances against peddling without a license, rarely applied to the Fuller Brush man, are frequently dusted off and applied to the underground press. Special sanctions provided in school codes and military law have been invoked against the high school and GI undergrounds. At times the law has seemed unrelentingly resourceful. Consider what happened to *Kudzu,* published in Jackson, Mississippi, according to an account published in the *Nation*:

> Eight Jackson police officers, divided into two squads, appeared at the office. One group knocked at the front door and presented a search warrant. The other four kicked the lock off the back door without bothering to knock. All eight entered with guns drawn and proceeded to wreck the place under the pretext of searching for [Columbia University radical] Mark Rudd. After an hour's search, one of the officers announced that he had found some marijuana, in a crumpled paper sack which the *Kudzu* people avow none of them had ever seen before. The *Kudzu* account also accuses the police of ruining photographic materials, breaking parts of two shotguns and a rifle, and pouring liquid solder into the muzzles. They also made off with three personal address books which have never been returned. One of the *Kudzu* staff members was slugged during questioning.[10]

What appears to be a gross violation of due process in this account is echoed in dozens of similar stories by underground editors. Harassments of two undergrounds in San Diego, California, in 1970 led Professor Kingsley Widmer to write:

> A list of the "incidents" that have beset those putting out the *Street Journal* and *Duck Power* in the last three months would run to many

pages. Here are a few examples. A fund-raising party for *Street Journal* ... was disrupted by San Diego police officers, who searched residential as well as publishing premises without a warrant. On Christmas, the paper's offices were vandalized in a highly professional manner, publishing equipment being damaged to the extent of $4,000 to $5,000. The police, to put it generously, were not helpful. Nor were they more effective in discovering who bombed a staff member's car ... or who committed the other attacks on the paper's offices.... However, the police were quite able to convince a landlord not to rent to the group ... to maintain nuisance surveillance of the shop and staff ... and to arrest staff members on such charges as blocking the street (two people talking together), possessing a tattered driver's license (though on foot at the time), wearing improper dress (an army shoulder patch), and littering the streets (by dropping a cigarette butt).[11]

One of the most publicized confrontations ended in April 1971, when the Los Angeles *Free Press* carried a banner headline, NARCS 43,000—FREEP 0, and this notice:

> Memo to the 80 narcotics officers. On August 1, 1969, the Los Angeles *Free Press* published the names and addresses of certain California State Narcotics Agents as part of an editorial statement against the present methods of narcotics law enforcement. As part of a settlement agreement of the resulting civil law suit, the Los Angeles *Free Press* has agreed to publish an apology to the wives and children of those narcotics agents for the potential exposure to harassment they may have suffered as innocent parties to the listing.[12]

Signed by publisher Art Kunkin, the statement reported that the paper had agreed to an out-of-court settlement of $43,000 to avert further prosecution of a $15 million suit brought by the narcotics agents. Two years earlier the *Freep* had published the names and home addresses of several agents. "The roster had been obtained without authority—stolen, authorities put it, by a clerk in the attorney general's office who offered it to the *Free Press* for a price," Gene Blake wrote in the *ASNE Bulletin*. Because publishing the information was not illegal, the reporter and publisher were charged with the felony of receiving stolen property. They were convicted by a jury, fined, and placed on probation. Blake, who works for the Los Angeles *Times*, wrote: "Should this case stand and become a precedent, the impact on the investigative efforts of the press to disclose wrongdoing in government could be devastating."[13] But in April 1973 the California Supreme Court threw out the conviction on the narrow grounds that there was no evidence to prove the *Free Press* knew the list was stolen.

Art Kunkin agreed: "Although there are obvious parallels between the *Free Press* case and the present publication of stolen FBI files by every major newspaper in the country, no major newspaper or journalistic society has looked at the facts of the *Free Press* case and come to its support."[14]

In another widely known case, Tom Forcade, Washington correspondent for the Underground Press Syndicate, in 1971 was denied a press pass to cover the White House. The White House staff had called Forcade a "security threat"; Forcade held that the action was censorship against the radical press. *Editor & Publisher,* the newspaper trade weekly, seemed to find justification for the White House denial: "Forcade's predilection for sudden acts of violence is well known. He once threw a pie in the face of Otto Larsen, a member of the United States Commission on Obscenity and Pornography, and two years ago, during the Sigma Delta Chi convention in San Diego, he heaved an empty water glass at the press table, narrowly missing the *Editor & Publisher* reporter."[15]

Forcade found little support among members of the White House Correspondents Association. Association president Jack Sutherland, of *U.S. News & World Report,* reportedly "didn't want to involve himself in the situation." Forcade then requested membership in the correspondents' association, made up of those who cover the House and the Senate, and was approved by 60 percent of those voting.

Another test came when *Kaleidoscope,* an underground paper at the University of Wisconsin, published an anonymous letter in which the writer claimed responsibility for the August 1970 bombing of a mathematics research center that had killed a graduate student. Editor Mark Knops of *Kaleidoscope* refused to reveal to a grand jury where he got the letter. He was found guilty of contempt by a local court, a decision upheld by the Wisconsin State Supreme Court. Reported the *Freedom of Information Digest*:

> The state characterized *Kaleidoscope* as a newspaper "explaining and excusing murder and bombing," one that presented propaganda, not news. But defense witness and the *Chicago Journalism Review* editor Ron Dorfman testified that public interest requires "First Amendment Protection of *Kaleidoscope* in the same sense that the public interest requires protection of newspapers like the New York *Times,* which explains and excuses official and government violence—including bombing and murder."[16]

Another important point of collision for the undergrounds and the police is related to the common practice of having police departments issue official press credentials. This has been an explosive issue in only a few cases, notably in Los Angeles in 1970 when the courts held the *Free Press* did not qualify for a press pass. Few other counterculture papers have had this problem since they rarely seek police accreditation. Understandably, underground editors lash out at police intimidation and legal incursions on their freedom, but they seldom take collective action to prevent further harassment. Limited financial resources and the demands of regular production of the papers are among the reasons.

Three Papers and How They Grew

Of the thousands of undergrounds, only a few have become vigorous. Three of the most notable are the Los Angeles *Free Press*, the Berkeley *Barb*, and the Atlanta *Great Speckled Bird*. In preparing this impressionistic analysis, we took a hard look at 1971 and early 1972 issues of each, in some instances comparing them with earlier issues. Although the papers have changed, they still bear the marks of their beginnings, offering a litany of the counterculture with its favorite subjects and heroes. But the balance and the emphasis have changed.

The Los Angeles Free Press

Art Kunkin's troubles may have begun the day he installed a time clock—an establishment symbol to be sure—in the *Free Press* newsroom. Eight years after its founding, the *Freep* has gone through a metamorphosis. Psychedelic art is hard to find except in the ads. Now the top of page one is crowded with type and a banner headline, usually sensational, such as POISONS IN OUR FOOD! There are fewer stories now about Los Angeles, more about national issues. But unlike some undergrounds, the *Free Press* is largely staff written, infrequently relying on counterculture news services.

Especially striking in the once-tiny paper is the overwhelming display advertising—mainly from record companies and movie houses—and the hefty classified section, which sometimes runs ten to twelve pages in a forty-page issue.

In these more complex times, the *Freep* has had to deal with ambiguity. In December 31, 1971, for instance, it carried an article critical of counterculture folk hero Bob Dylan; beside it was the Rock Liberation Front's demand for an apology:

A.J. Weberman [a counterculture writer] began his personal campaign of slander against Dylan—in the true tradition of the sensationalistic press willing to print anything about someone famous—even organizing demonstrations at Dylan's home.... Weberman uses what he interprets from Dylan's music to try and kill Dylan and build his own fame. Now A.J. Weberman takes credit for Dylan's "George Jackson" song. More egocentric bullshit. Dylan wrote it in spite of Weberman and in spite of "the movement." Dylan wrote it because he felt it. A.J. Weberman's campaign—and the movement's complicity in it—is in the current fad of everyone in the revolution attacking each other and spreading false rumors about each other. It's time we defended and loved each other—and saved our anger for the true enemy, whose ignorance and greed destroys our planet.

The *Free Press* makes room for its critics, revealing the dissension in the counterculture. A November 1971 headline, for example, asked, IS FREE PRESS RELEVANT TO BLACKS? The response was carried in a staff-written interview with a black leader: "the paper gives no information about such things as the struggles of Black GIs, the liberation movements in Sudan, Southern Africa, or the Caribbean. He added that it makes no attempt to analyze in depth the various trends within the black movement in America today."

Critics point out that the straight press has assimilated some popular features of the underground papers (such as an unorthodox medical advice column, "Dr. Hippocrates," which began in the Berkeley *Barb*), but few have noticed how the undergrounds borrow from the commercial press. The *Free Press*, for instance, now carries Washington columnist Jack Anderson, who is certainly a muckraking adversary of government but hardly kin to the counterculture. Yet Anderson's 1971 and 1972 reports of secret White House documents caused the *Free Press* to praise him as "our columnist."

Favorite counterculture topics—drugs, sexual freedom, and the new life styles—are still featured, but now much more attention is given to lengthy interviews with rock stars—interviews often closely related to record advertising.

Politically, the *Free Press* supported the People's Party and its 1972 presidential nominee, Dr. Benjamin Spock. Other content includes how-to articles with a counterculture bent, such as consumer guide pieces on organic foods and in-depth features about natural childbirth. A column entitled "Hard Core Police News," features items from the police blotter that will cast the police in a negative light. In an attempt to mix media, the *Free Press* has a column called "Paper Radio," a transcription of radio interviews conducted by such sympathetic outlets as KDAY, Los Angeles.

Part of the paper's formula for success is the playing up of sensational angles of timely items (HUGHES: BIGOT BARON), and packaging them for maximum newsstand appeal. The paper is a little quieter than it once was, the writing is better polished, and the design is less amateurish. But it is still far from being the "great, grey lady" of the underground press. As Art Kunkin put it in the issue of September 10-16, 1971, after a split in which several staffers founded a weekly called *The Staff*: "All the public can do, then, when faced with two competing publications of similar nature, each putting the other down, is to see who really has the ability to survive the difficulties of publishing *in practice* and who performs according to the principles they profess *in practice*." If the real test is indeed survival, the *Free Press* seems to be durable indeed.

When the San Francisco *Examiner,* a Hearst paper, says "bearded leftists," "protest march," "riot," and "police officers reestablished order," the Berkeley *Barb* says "dissident elements," "pilgrimage," "confrontation," and "fuzz suppressed." The *Barb* is to the counterculture what the splashy New York *Daily News* is to conventional journalism. Colorful, brassy, strongly sensational, the *Barb* has been remarkably agile in keeping pace with counterculture developments. An early channel for the Haight-Ashbury flower people, the *Barb* was one of the first papers to reflect the "death of hip," turning to a more politically oriented content but retaining a smattering of psychedelic art and a heavy dose of sex ads.

Like the *Free Press,* the *Barb* is largely staff written, but it is much more devoted to its community—with the surprising exception that it devotes little space to the massive University of California campus, which is only a few steps away from the *Barb* office. The *Barb* captures the permissive style of the San Francisco Bay area, consistently carrying articles about gay liberation, activism at military bases, and conditions in California prisons. Stories often read like letters, and many letters to the *Barb* are presented much like news stories, with headlines and prominent placement.

Although the paper is a member of the Underground Press Syndicate, Liberation News Service, and the Alternative Features Service, local news commands priority. Some attention is given to international liberation movements—Latin America, Algeria, and Ireland, for example—or major counterculture-approved personalities such as Germaine Greer, Huey Newton, Shirley Chisholm, Daniel Ellsberg.

The *Barb* often covers the women's liberation movement, but it has been attacked for having sexist policies. Responding to a woman critic, a *Barb* writer insisted in the issue of November 26-December 2, 1971, that the paper was "blatantly sexual—not sexist," and that "prolonged reading of the paper will show that nudes rarely appear in the editorial content unless they are directly related to a news story (usually a public event at which nudity occurs)." He also went on to say: "The *Barb* censors ads minimally, on a basis which has never been clearly stated. I think the main point is to restrain certain advertisers from openly admitting they engage in illegal activities like prostitution. I have tried, in the past, to think up rules by which the *Barb* could rationally and consistently distinguish between ads which glorified sexuality and those which demeaned it. I was unable to do so."

Admitting that advertising for "personal body services . . . poses many dilemmas, and will be debated later," he then revealed the *real* reason the *Barb* accepted such ads by saying of the competing Berkeley *Tribe,* "the *Tribe* censors so severely that they perch precariously on the brink of bankruptcy." Indeed, the *Barb* might be hypocritical, the writer said, "but the hypocrisy is that of commercialism in an anti-capitalist paper—not of male supremacy." The same issue carried a story that began: " 'I started out as a call girl,' cheerfully admits Carol, who now thinks of herself as a sex therapist, engaged in helping men get over sexual hangups—in the most direct way possible."

There are many *Barb* articles about demonstrations and meetings. The Berkeley city council, with its radical members, has been covered carefully, but the *Barb* has not forgotten its adversary relationship to government. Attacking Berkeley's radical black mayor in the issue of December 17-23, 1971, a *Barb* reporter wrote: "In a backroom deal that would have made Richard Daley, [San Francisco mayor] Joe Alioto and Lyndon Johnson extremely proud, Mayor Warren Widener last Tuesday evening once again betrayed the student and radical communities that insured his election as mayor last April."

In appearance the *Barb* is a hodgepodge. Except for a large front-page picture—sometimes it consumes the entire page—the columns are crowded, packed with stories, headlines, and pictures that hardly leave space for the ads, which are banked along the sides and across the bottom. The back pages are devoted to the *Barb's* celebrated classifieds. Once consisting only of agate-type listing of sexual services and the like, the classified section is now alive with pictures. Human bodies are listed like used cars:

Black attractive chick will love to relax you, and make you feel better.

Handsome young weightlifter with an easy personality. Fantastically defined body. Eager to please. Professionally versatile. Heavy hung stud.

The back page is "Scenedrome," which presents "sounds, happenings, theatre, and flicks," and specifically points out events which are free. It is also a kind of counterculture social service directory, listing the phone numbers of abortion counselors, the Black Panthers, child health, various switchboards, gay liberation, and scores of other services.

The *Barb* runs counterculture comic strips, although not as extensively as other papers. In 1971 and 1972, the most frequently used strip was "The Continuing Adventures of Harold Hedd," a misunderstood freak. Once accused of being humorless, the paper now offers more features and editorial material designed to help its readers ridicule the establishment.

The *Barb* was the first of the counterculture papers to face competition from dissident staffers. In 1969, a group of staff members, angry over the profits of publisher Max Scherr, walked out after bringing out an issue with the headline BARB SOLD TO CIA. They founded the Berkeley *Tribe* which was published until 1972. The *Barb* has also experienced pressure from without. In 1968, for example, the nearby Richmond public library bowed to community pressure and banned the *Barb* from its shelves. There are periodic actions against the paper in neighboring cities.

But the *Barb*, like other durable undergrounds, has found a success formula, which often includes a sensational, humorous lead. Part of it is reflected in this lead on a story in the issue of January 14-20, 1972, about the inauguration of San Francisco mayor Joseph Alioto, then under indictment by the state of Washington in a fee-splitting case, for which he was later acquitted (JOE SWORN IN, BUT WHERE WILL HE SERVE?):

> Prominent San Francisco felony defendant, Joseph Lawrence Alioto promised free coffee and donuts last week to everyone who came to watch him take an oath of office as mayor of San Francisco.
>
> It is not every day that you can watch a felony defendant being sworn in as the mayor of the central city of the fourth largest metropolitan area in these United States, and get free coffee and donuts to boot. *Barb* hurried to arrive at city hall, San Francisco by 11:30 Saturday when festivities were to commence.

The Great Speckled Bird

In recent years, Atlanta has promoted itself as a progressive city with young ideas, the pivot of the New South. But the conspicuous absence of a counterculture community left the image somewhat incomplete. As late as 1968, one member of the Atlanta Chamber of Commerce was heard to say, "If psychedelic education is the trend, then goddamn it, let's have it here."[17]

He got his wish in March 1968, when the *Great Speckled Bird* was established as a bi-weekly counterculture tabloid. Its name came from an old Southern song sung by Roy Acuff of the Grand Old Opry. And, as one writer observed, "the song title came in turn from a Bible verse, Jeremiah 12:9, where the 'speckled bird' is used metaphorically to mean an outcast or ugly duckling."[18] In the first issue, a page one editorial promised "to bitch and badger, carp and cry, and perhaps give Atlanta (and environs, 'cause we're growing, baby) a bit of honest and, we trust, even readable journalism."

The *Bird*'s graphics are soft but striking. A full-page picture bathed in pastel colors usually dominates the front page. The gentle tone continues through the paper. It's no hodgepodge of type. Consistent headline styles give the paper a sense of unity. The writing, too, is more straightforward, less opinionated than that of other undergrounds.

Advertising content—mostly display ads about forthcoming concerts and films, contraceptives, and counterculture products—makes up a small part of the paper, considerably less than in the *Barb* or *Free Press*. The classifieds are unique: those for individuals are free; those for companies selling stereo equipment or other products are called "cashified ads." Unlike some of the ads in other undergrounds, these are no-nonsense listings of items for sale, personals, reform and revolution literature, and the like. Since 1971, sex ads have not been accepted.

Articles in the *Great Speckled Bird* about the Vietnam war, blacks, ecology, the military, local media, and alternative institutions have eased Atlanta into the counterculture. By 1972, the *Bird* was also talking about gay liberation, abortion, and slum lords. "From the beginning," writes Bob Goodman, a member of the *Bird* collective, "the *Bird* clearly differentiated itself from Southern liberalism and American imperialism, from straight society and linear thinking." Goodman goes on:

> The first issue bitched about the Atlanta Community Relations Commission, "a facade, an intended safety valve for urban disorders, and a sop to concerned liberals"; and badgered [the late] *Constitution* Publisher Ralph McGill, "manipulator and leading exponent of U.S. imperialism and deception; of pronounced self-righteousness and senility." It had coverage of draft resistance, a peace march, a GI pray-in and a police attack on black marchers in Social Circle, Ga. Reviews of a suburban production of *Lysistrata*, a speech by [Boston University radical] Howard Zinn, a dramatic portrayal of the life of W.E.B. DuBois, and a rap with jazzman Charles Lloyd. Head comix, the Awfully Sad Story of Negal the pure-bred Polish miniwolfhound who turns into a killer after joining the U.S. Army; and the first installment of a far-out Burroughsian stream-of-consciousness column. Echoes of Interzone. To Atlanta in early 1968, these were indeed alternatives.[19]

Among the few undergrounds to give much attention to country and western music, the *Bird* again reflects the tastes of many of its readers, but it also carries pieces on soul music, bootleg rock records, and similar subjects. Not all reviews are given to wide-eyed admiration, as in this article (July 5, 1971): "For some time now, Buck Owens has been wowing country music audiences with his red, white and blue patriotic guitar. Buck Owens is a first-rate entertainer, and doesn't need a red, white and blue guitar to be popular, so I assume that his motive for using it is not commercialism, but a real, if highly misguided personal belief."

The *Bird* follows the activities of former Georgia governor Lester Maddox with interest and occasional amusement and gives heavy coverage to such issues as housing conditions, land use, downtown development, freeway construction, and local taxes. It has treated Atlanta's mayor harshly, as in this story on November 29, 1971: "Atlanta's 'liberal' mayor Sam Massell has ordered his office staff to stop sending the *Bird* press releases. A member of the mayor's staff acknowledged that the releases are public information and said that *Bird* reporters can come to City Hall to pick them up. The Mayor, she said, simply feels that the *Bird* has been unfair in his coverage of him and doesn't see whey he should 'help' the newspaper."

Seven key *Bird* staffers get subsistence pay, about twenty dollars a week. Volunteers as well as paid staff make up a cooperative in which every member has a vote in determining policy. Like other undergrounds, the *Bird* started with very little formal staff structure and has slowly developed a division of responsibilities. Ideal arrangements don't always work, as Goodman explains:

> It is my personal opinion that, in the absence of formal and explicit structures, systems of informal (and usually cliquish and undemocratic) power relationships evolve. Informal power structures tend to be undemocratic because there is no way of calling the powerful to account, and because the absence of formal checks makes it easier for charismatic, strong-willed or skilled people to control by dint of those qualities.
>
> Such tendencies developed in the early *Bird*. Without anyone planning it that way, strong individuals—in most cases men—began to jell into positions of power in each area of the paper. There was some editorial collectivity, but it was an informal collectivity in which articles were passed from hand to hand within a (mostly male) in-group; final editorial decisions were made by the managing editor and there was no structural check on his decisions. The principle of one-person-one-vote which prevailed in weekly co-op meetings had limited effect on the day-to-day operations and specific decisions. Also, the process by which the co-op could replace people—and without this power, all checks are paper tigers—had never been defined.[20]

To correct these problems, editorial power was decentralized, and the managing editor became coordinator of the various editorships. During the Monday night meetings of the editorial board, co-op members help to shape each issue. In 1971, a women's caucus put an end to sexist ads and also waged a successful battle against male supremacy. A child-care co-op for women staffers was established, and women were given more than half the full-time positions and equal opportunity with men for leadership positions.

The *Bird* seems to have responded to change more smoothly and effectively than many of the other undergrounds. As one *Bird* staffer wrote, "Every underground newspaper has to get out front with its internal structure. Revolutionary papers must have a revolutionary structure."

The St. Louis Outlaw

In the spring of 1970, as the antiwar movement began to wind down, students, professors, labor leaders, and others in St. Louis began to itch to publish a paper that would express their other concerns. From this broad-based group came the nucleus of the St. Louis *Outlaw*. It is an interesting paper for many reasons, not the least of them successive confusions about purposes and many staff disagreements over goals that seem to epitomize the problems of many undergrounds.

One staff member recalls the early days: "The purpose of the paper was never clearly spelled out. In order to have a finished product, differences were papered over and a false tolerance was built up." Those who had participated in the early discussions "assumed they knew what the paper really should be and as a result resented anyone with a different idea."

The *Outlaw* sometimes seemed to be four different papers struggling for purpose and direction. A former *Outlaw* staffer wrote to Jules Asher, a graduate student at Kansas State University, to describe the four:

1. A paper which anyone in the city would read and which would deal with issues ignored by the *Post-Dispatch* and the *Globe-Democrat*. This approach emphasized muckraking and support for community groups.

2. A paper designed mainly as a vehicle for the Washington University Left. At the time the paper started there was an intense anti-ROTC movement on campus and many people assumed that as the leading struggle going on in St. Louis the Washington University scene was the most important. This paper was thought of as emphasizing anti-imperialism, ROTC, school repression and theories of education.

3. A paper to appeal across the board to all youth, particularly high school students. One member of the editorial board particularly wanted to organize a high school student union citywide and wanted the paper to deal with high school struggles mainly with some emphasis on clothes and music to which young people could relate.

4. A paper to appeal particularly to youth, but in tone and content to mainly "freaks" and youth culture. This paper was to emphasize dope, rock music, and fighting cops. Strongly behind this trend was a great "criminal" mystification—hence the name *Outlaw* which came from the song "We Can Be Together" by the Jefferson Airplane which says, "We are all outlaws in the eyes of America, to get what we want we lie, cheat, forge, fuck, hide and deal. We are obscene, lawless, hideous, dirty, dangerous, violent, and young and we are very proud of ourselves."

These intense differences were minimized at first, the virtues of compromise were accentuated, and the paper came out. It was a somewhat confused product which was not "really satisfying to anyone." Writes the former staffer:

Washington University kids thought it wasn't radical enough. High school kids thought it was too academic, people in communities thought it was too Washington University-oriented or too violence prone; freaks thought it was dull and adults thought it was freaky.... Many people throughout the city were impressed (though by different things) and even KSD radio called it "surprisingly cerebral and an important positive addition to St. Louis."

Topics covered in the first four issues reflected the differing outlooks and interests: antiwar issues, blacks, the draft, ecology, high schools, higher education, labor unions, letters to the editors, local political and governmental issues, media criticism, music, poetry, ROTC, and sports ripoffs, which charged professional athletics with disregarding the public interest.

In the April 24, 1970, issue, an *Outlaw* woman writer argued that the paper should not tolerate female exploitation, that it "should exemplify our political orientation and our new values and attitudes." Many underground papers, she wrote, were hypocritical in the case of women's liberation: "a cry is made for female liberation on page one, while ads for go-go dancers and sleazy nude films appear on the next. While there is a token female article in the paper, the remainder exudes male chauvinism and supremacy." Although two articles about women's rights had been published, the *Outlaw* was hardly a model for promoting women's liberation. Although the masthead in the first issue listed six women, a former staffer said that all important decisions were made by men: "The only woman who thought of herself as part of the editorial staff was living with one of the men and functioned as his secretary, making coffee, typing his articles, cooking his meals." Later, as criticism mounted, women were given more important roles.

Early *Outlaw* issues seemed geared to the belief that high school and college students, blacks, women, and workers could work together for massive social change. The paper described "the movement" in general terms and did not focus on a particular ideology, thus emphasizing the "common struggle." For instance, one writer stated that "black and white [high school] students, though not joined hand in hand, are rebelling and fighting to make changes in the establishment that their parents helped to create or at least sanction."

Some *Outlaw* editors seemed obsessed with the ROTC at Washington University in St. Louis; there were six articles about it in the first four issues alone. In a May 1970 article about a march, it was written: "Some of us [marchers] have begun building a radical movement at Washington University, whose first objective is to off ROTC. But that is only a beginning. Other people have been building movements to liberate black people."

The *Outlaw*'s coverage of working people was unusual. Even at the height of hard-hat animosity, in the summer of 1970, editor George Lipsitz was able to empathize with union members' support of the Vietnam war. Most workers, he said, do not oppose the U.S. economic system or "racism and imperialism," for, like most Americans, "they have been told all their lives that they are privileged and that their privilege is threatened by blacks and by people in the Third World." However, Lipsitz said, "lines of communication and support must be opened up so that working people realize that the repressive measures now being taken against blacks and students are ultimately designed for them, and so that students and blacks realize that they will remain forever isolated unless they make contact with working people and unite to fight the common enemy—the government and the system of corporate capitalism which sustains it."

The *Outlaw* analyzed the positions of the two St. Louis papers on such issues as bond measures, a bus strike, and anti-ROTC demonstrations. Lipsitz concluded: "To most of us, monopoly is the name of a game we played as children. To the St. Louis *Post-Dispatch* and the St. Louis *Globe-Democrat*, however, it is the name of a business practice which has enabled those two stern guardians of the public interest to rake in millions of dollars at the public's expense."

The diversified editorial content was supported (according to a content analysis) by a much less diverse group of advertisers, mainly clothing stores and head shops, but also record companies, restaurants, and book sellers.

Run by a collective with some strong personalities, the *Outlaw* encountered the problem of so many other counterculture papers: "Plenty of talk but no work," as one observer said. Because the *Outlaw* has no formal channels of review, articles appeared that offended some staff members; there were several charges of "ego tripping" and of "getting too ego involved in your own stuff." Differences became so heated that several members quit. The next three issues reflected the change; half the articles came from national sources, Liberation News Service, and other underground papers, and tended to feature national Movement personalities such as Huey Newton, Tom Hayden, and Angela Davis, and national issues such as the defense establishment and the Black Panthers. The paper still gave some attention to the working man, but there were fewer articles about Washington University and local high schools.

Reorganization brought new staff and collective decision making. All articles were cleared with the entire staff; even the layout was decided collectively. But new trouble came when those who had left the paper protested its new direction. That led to a meeting at which former staffers and others from the community aired grievances. The result was an editorial board "open to anybody who came along." It was not a popular decision. One member of the new editorial board wrote: "Because we wanted the paper to represent more people than it did, and because we believed that no one would want to do all the work involved in putting out a paper unless they were really sincere, we agreed. That screwed us."

The struggle between the old and existing staffs and their sympathizers was essentially between those who wanted a politically oriented paper and those who wanted a youth-culture paper. The two factions tried to coexist, but the division was too deep. "The eighth issue of the paper sucked," an old staffer said, "the ninth had good copy but the layout was terrible, and by the tenth we [the radicals] decided to quit and start another paper."

In the eleventh issue (January 22-February 11, 1971), a long letter explained the position of those who had left in the second split.

... we feel the *Outlaw* has limited its audience too greatly ... the *Outlaw* never came to any agreement about who their readers should be.... Writing style is often heavily academic and hard for people to read or understand. The articles in the *Outlaw* have also often reinforced false images other people have of youth culture by explaining how some people feel about certain things without explaining how they came to feel that way.... From the first issue the paper's goals have often been unclear.

The *Outlaw* has also had other problems. On two occasions, St. Louis printers objected so strongly to the anti-establishment content that the paper had to be printed elsewhere. The *Outlaw* has had trouble renting office space and, according to the *St. Louis Journalism Review,* its hawkers have been harassed "from downtown St. Louis to suburban Crestwood, [the police] usually citing the constitutionally questionable requirement of a permit to sell the paper."

But such difficulties have not prevented publication, and the quality of writing and design have improved. The *Outlaw's* initial sixteen pages have expanded to twenty pages and sometimes twenty-four. Published every three weeks, it now has a circulation of about 5000, and has focused on war, racism, youth culture, women's liberation, rock concerts, the Black Panthers, and the labor movement. Still, editor Fred Faust has worried that the paper is too narrow in its approach, that "maybe we're just talking to ourselves," and hopes for the day when it will appeal to a broader audience.

Counterculture News Services

In the mid-sixties, as more and more underground papers began to appear, their editors began to wonder how to go about getting news of the counterculture beyond their immediate communities. People in Berkeley were interested in Taos, Chicago, and the East Village. News of cultural and political interest to the underground traveled slowly in spite of the era of rapid communication. The underground needed its own service to spread news around the country more rapidly and efficiently than just a system of exchanging papers.

The first of several services, some now defunct, began in 1967 after Raymond Mungo and Marshall Bloom walked out of a Washington, D.C. convention of the United States National Student Press Association. USSPA was the sponsor of College Press Service, a news service for college newspapers and a youthful alternative to AP and UPI. It had a large clientele, but it was more concerned with the internal dynamics of higher education than were most underground editors. Thus, there was a ready market for Mungo and Bloom's new Liberation News Service.

Styling itself an alternative news service, LNS promised "to provide services which couldn't be obtained by any single paper but are increasingly

vital as more and more people come to depend on the free press."[21]
Reaching hundreds of underground papers by providing a weekly packet of
news and features, the LNS editors covered the 1967 Poor People's March
on Washington, police attacks on underground newspapers, the Black
Panthers, international liberation movements, student unrest, and many
other issues. In the spring of 1968, LNS moved from Washington to New
York. New staff members were hired, and a split developed. The Mungo-
Bloom faction favored "political news plus humor and light articles," said
Susan Johnson, a student who studied it. "The New York staff was in favor of
turning LNS into a service that printed hard political news designed to
radicalize its readers." The battle is described in Mungo's *Famous Long
Ago: My Life and Hard Times With Liberation News Service*. Mungo calls
his faction the "Virtuous Caucus" and the dissident group the "Vulgar
Marxists." According to Johnson:

> In the middle of August 1968, the Virtuous Caucus and the Vulgar
> Marxists parted ways. The scene of the final split could have been
> taken from a 1930s gangland movie. In the middle of the night
> Bloom's Band broke into the LNS office in New York, took all the files,
> the printing press, receipts, and mailing list. They also had a $6000
> check from the benefit showing of a Beatles movie. They took all of
> this to a farm in Montague, Massachusetts, and continued to publish
> the news service from there. The New York staff was not to be outdone
> in daring behavior. In the middle of the night they raided the farm,
> "liberated" the files, receipts, mailing list, and the $6000 check.
> Bloom pressed charges against the New York staff. The charges were
> later dropped.[22]

For a time, one LNS faction published in Montague, the other in New
York. Eventually, the Montague faction died. LNS-New York continues,
mailing packets of articles about counterculture activities, political events,
and other issues, as well as poetry, criticism, photographs, and comic strips.

LNS occasionally ridicules the commercial press. Here, for example,
in an undated 1968 release, New York *Daily News* coverage is compared
with that of *Rat*.

> In the *News*: A group of about 40 hippie types, bearded, beaded
> and foul-mouthed, invaded the studio of WNDT-TV, Channel 13, last
> night and, within sight and sound of thousands of viewers, tried to take
> over the station.
> In *Rat*: Somehow I had been asked by a decent fellow, Bob Fearo,
> to appear on WNDT-TV with Allan Katzman of the *East Village
> Other* and Marvin Fishman of the Newsreel to comment on un-
> derground media and the health of America. What can you say? I
> talked with several friends and could think of nothing profound
> enough to budge the type of people who watch educational TV.

By 1972 LNS was still shaky financially but claimed 800 subscribers.

Its staff, now predominantly female, offers "national and international news with an anticapitalist, antisexist, antiracist orientation." Packets are now mailed twice a week.

The Underground Press Syndicate, founded in 1966, is a nonprofit association of alternative papers and magazines. Operated by a women's collective in New York, it distributes weekly packets of news, graphics, and original articles as well as a digest of material from 250-odd papers. UPS also operates an advertising co-op, which handles ads from big corporations, and a legal service for underground journalists facing charges of pornography, obscenity, and the like.

Other news services include Amerikan Press Syndicate of Beverly Hills, California, which services the high school undergrounds; Rama Pipien World Press Collective, New Castle, California, a "loose syndicate of about 170 underground papers nationwide"; Reporters News Service of Washington, D.C., which specializes in domestic reporting, especially ecology; and Cooperative High School Independent Press Syndicate of Ann Arbor, Michigan, which promotes the high school underground.[23] Other specialized services promote the causes of blacks, Chicanos, and women, and there have been several antiwar news services.

High School Undergrounds

Colleges and universities proudly proclaim themselves centers of intellectual freedom, and most create an atmosphere that allows dissent. But because high schools have no such tradition, the advent of the high school underground in the late 1960s—a totally unexpected phenomenon—made huge waves.

In 1968, the National Association of Secondary School Principals reported that "59 percent of all high schools and 56 percent of all junior high schools experienced student protest; more than three-fourths of these protests involved conflicts over school rules."[24] To some school administrators, the "underground newspaper on the campus was as terrifying an image as a losing football team,"[25] says William Ward, a professor of journalism at Southern Illinois University at Edwardsville.

Education writer Diane Divoky believes the reaction of administrators encouraged the growth of high school undergrounds:

> It is no longer a secret that a growing minority of American high school students are in open revolt against their schools, their parents and their communities. . . . Because the schools provide no platform for the students' outrage, no vehicle for their voice, they have been forced to find their own medium: the underground—or independent—newspaper. Perhaps 500 have spring up over the past year [1969] or two.[26]

High school undergrounds are much less devoted to four-letter words than are their college counterparts, and few seem to have much interest in elaborate graphics. They are usually modest ventures, often only four pages, and their tone is personal, much like a letter to a friend. A few editors focus on external problems—ecology, voting, the draft, penal reform. But most are mainly concerned with school problems: dress codes, the content of courses, hair length, and student rights. Divoky believes that "two tenets underlie much of the writing and both are reactions to the most characteristic aspects of today's culture." One tenet, she says, is that, "in this depersonalized, technological society, what is needed is feeling. The emotional content of an idea, an experience, a commitment is what gives it value, what can be trusted." This passion goes hand in hand with another tenet—"a puritanical zeal for a rigorous ethic, an insistence on absolute honesty in public and private life. The students are uncompromising and see diplomacy as duplicity, ambivalence as weakness, and strategic maneuvering as a cop-out."[27]

Another observer of the evolution of high school undergrounds, Sam Feldman, believes "the concern expressed in many . . . is that they serve as an ombudsman for the students, providing feedback that is necessary to improve the system."[28]

Like the *New York High School Free Press,* some began in an atmosphere of turbulence during a teacher's strike; other papers were a response to the unwillingness of the conventional school paper to include news of interest to the dissidents. Spreading throughout the country during the late 1960s, the papers were, as Feldman puts it, "wildly funny, irreverent, biased, opinionated, and, occasionally, obscene."[29] Among them were the *Finger,* the *Neo-Dwarf, Pearl Before Swine,* the *Roach, Big Momma,* and the *South Dakota Seditionist Monthly.*

How many high school undergrounds have existed is not known. Divoky estimates 500, Robert Glessing, more than 3000. Many lasted only one issue, some for a school year. During a high school journalism day at UCLA in 1967, according to journalism teacher Gaye Smith, "about half of the participants stated that an 'underground,' i.e., unsanctioned, paper had been published on their campuses. Many implied that the staffs of the official school paper had been involved in the clandestine enterprise because they were repudiating what they thought was overly strict supervision of the official paper by school authorities."[30]

The high school underground has, of course, often been in roaring conflict with the establishment. In one celebrated case in Washington, D.C., a principal wrote in a memorandum to the faculty, "If you see any copies of the *Washington Free Press* in the possession of a student, confiscate it immediately. Any questions from the student regarding this confiscation should be referred to the administration. If you see a student selling or distributing this paper refer them [*sic*] to an administrator and they will be suspended."[31] The nearby Montgomery County, Maryland, school board chairman forbade distribution of the *Free Press* because "it advocates revolution and made disparaging remarks about the CIA and the police. Part of our job is to teach students to live within the law. After all, everyone has a little trouble with conformity sometimes."[32]

High school editors have even battled school officials in court. In a 1969 case in Illinois, students were suspended for violating school rules by distributing papers critical of the school administration. The court upheld the school, citing the "immaturity" of the students. In a Texas case later that year, however, the court ruled in favor of the underground editors because the school did not prove that the paper caused a disturbance sufficient to warrant denying students' First Amendment rights. The crucial test for the undergrounds in the courts seems to be whether they cause disruption. This is indicated by the U.S. Supreme Court ruling in *Tinker* v. *Des Moines Independent Community School District,* a case involving students who were suspended for wearing black arm bands. As one scholar analyzed it, "the Supreme Court overruled school officials on grounds that prohibiting expressions of opinions on public school campuses, unless it is shown that they will cause disruption, is violative of students' First Amendment rights."[33]

During its short life in 1970, *Issue,* an embattled underground at Stephen F. Austin High School in Bryan, Texas, crusaded for constitutional rights in an attempt to shame officials into complying with Supreme Court rulings on racial segregation, institutional prayer, and hair length. Several students who worked on the paper were suspended, but on August 24, 1970, the editors claimed credit for an administrator's leaving the school: "He left a losing football team, an award winning band, and an award winning choir. He also left a censored newspaper, closed student council meetings, an unworkable dress code, a segregated cafeteria staff, and what he thought was a conspiracy to take over the school."

Some idea of the appeal and effect of high school undergrounds is available in a study by Kathryn Wall, a high school teacher and former graduate student at Indiana University. Wall analyzed student attitudes toward the *New Amerikan Mercury,* which was established as an alternative to the official student newspaper, the *Optimist.* The *Mercury* was caustic and harshly critical of the regular paper and of the school administration, and its design was splashy. But its readership fell far short of that of the *Optimist.* Wall reported that 93 percent of the students in her sample reported reading the *Optimist,* compared to 39 percent who read the *Mercury.* Perhaps the fact that the official paper was free and students had to buy the *Mercury* accounted for the difference. Students involved in school activities were more likely to read the underground. But many students—38 percent—disapproved of the *Mercury,* labeling it "an extremist group-oriented student newspaper." Both in editorials and news content the school paper had greater credibility with its readers, even though 42 percent of the respondents agreed that the purpose of the underground was "to present students' rights, to discuss the other side of the school newspaper story, to act as a representative student newspaper or as competition to the school newspaper, and to serve as an outlet for extremist opinions."[34]

The high school underground now seems to be in decline. Principals no longer talk about it at their national meetings and many articles by high school journalism teachers suggest that the undergrounds hardly cause a ripple of controversy these days. Whether this is based on sound observation or wishful thinking is not known, but it does appear that some high school activists have found new challenges for their energies.

The more active days of the high school underground will be remembered, however. The papers were a channel for student discontent and were probably instrumental in bringing change at a time when students were demanding relevance in the classroom. Several collections of high school underground writing provide fascinating reading and a permanent record.

Rolling Stone

Borrowing generously from the underground press and traditional journalism is a bi-weekly newspaper-magazine that one writer calls "the best rock and youth culture publication in the country." With an audited, paid circulation of 225,000 and an estimated readership of 1,250,000 per issue, *Rolling Stone* is the largest and most widely quoted publication covering the counterculture. Although too much of it is traditional journalism for it to be called an underground paper, no one doubts its rapport with the young.

Like most of its underground cousins, *Rolling Stone* had its charismatic leader: Jan Wenner, a dropout journalism major from the University of California at Berkeley. A "totally freaked-out rock 'n roll fan," according to an associate at *Rolling Stone,* Wenner worked for CBS News in London and for *Ramparts* in San Francisco. As rock and roll editor for the brief venture of *Ramparts* into newspaper publishing, Wenner got the idea for a bi-weekly rock publication. With the help of the art director of *Ramparts,* San Francisco *Chronicle* columnist Ralph Gleason, and others, Wenner brought out the first issue in 1967.

The name for the paper does not come from the Rolling Stones rock group (although for a time in 1969 a London edition of *Rolling Stone* was published by a corporation owned by Stones musician Mick Jagger, who saw the magazine as a possible forum) but from the song "Muddy Waters." Charles Perry, an associate editor, said in an interview that the name was chosen to "indicate our interest in popular music and related things. The idea of gathering no moss seemed to give us elbow room. It didn't tie us down to any particular editorial tradition."

From the beginning, Perry pointed out, *Rolling Stone* offered its readers "a quiet page with clear, clean photographs and neat layout, in contrast to the underground press, most of which was devoted to heavy overprints and dark, cluttered art." The staff, which included an art director who was also a sculptor, experimented with graphics and design, producing a format that has been widely imitated. Although *Rolling Stone* appears to be a standard-size (8½-by-11-inch) fold-over news magazine, it opens into a tabloid newspaper. In a recent "Awards" issue (patterned after that of *Esquire*), the editors announced eight Like a Rolling Stone awards for publications that have adopted the style. Unlike the writing in most undergrounds, that in *Rolling Stone* is well written and edited. One disgruntled reader wrote, "Man, like your paper is so polished I would hardly care to wrap fish in it any more."

Technically a rock-music news magazine, *Rolling Stone* usually makes the rock scene central to its coverage of the counterculture. In the summer of 1969, most newspapers and magazines were covering the Woodstock, New York, rock festival. But *Rolling Stone* covered it in greater detail, and with acute reporting and analysis. A front-page headline read: WOODSTOCK: 450,000. Inside, another headline read: IT WAS LIKE BALLING FOR THE FIRST TIME. At the Altamont, California, rock festival later that year, at which a spectator was killed by a member of the Hell's Angels and at which there were many fights and injuries, *Rolling Stone* reported the event under a headline taken from the title of a popular record album: LET IT BLEED.

The magazine offers an imaginative blend of news, features, interviews, and reviews. It was the first publication to carry a story about groupies (February 16, 1969):

> . . . a groupie is a chick who hangs out with bands and becoming a good one is not entirely a simple matter. Says Henry, now a pregnant old-timer yenta of the San Francisco groupie circuit, "Being a groupie is a full-time gig. Sort of like being a musician. You have two or three girl friends you hang out with and you stay as high and as intellectually enlightened as a group of musicians. You've got to, if you're going to have anything to offer.[11]

Germaine Greer, the outspoken feminist and author of *The Female Eunuch*, came to the attention of American readers in *Rolling Stone*—some months before her famous battle with Norman Mailer. The magazine was one of the first to cover the "new nostalgia," with a special issue entitled "The Fifties." An interpretive article about the late "bad-mouth" comedian Lenny Bruce demonstrated *Rolling Stone*'s reportorial strength. While dozens of other magazines and newspapers were retelling the Bruce story, *Rolling Stone* was one of the few to offer detailed new information about the exploitation of Bruce by business interests. Hunter S. Thompson's brilliantly written political coverage of the 1972 Presidential campaign was gathered into a book, *Fear and Loathing on the Campaign Trail*.

The writing style in *Rolling Stone* is varied—about half the articles are bought from free-lancers, among them such notables as Tom Wolfe and novelist Herbert Gold. The writing is not only high in quality; it is also sometimes powerful: "A year ago on the Fourth of May—on a windswept sunny day exactly like this one—Dean Kahler, who wanted to be a cop when he was a kid, threw himself into the green grass on the downward slope of Blanket Hill and felt a 'bee-sting': a steel-jacketed National Guard bullet entered his lower back and blew apart his spinal cord."

Does *Rolling Stone* feed on fads to the exclusion of other issues and tastes? "No," says Charles Perry, "we are in the business of explaining and finding out things. We attempt to bring a wider sample of world culture to our readers than they would naturally pick up on. For example, from the beginning we have tried to maintain a high standard of modern contemporary poetry, books of foreign cultures, and many other things. *Rolling Stone* wrote about jazz when jazz was a naughty word and thought to be stodgy. We've also covered country and western music."

Not everyone is dazzled. In "*Rolling Stone* Gathers No Politix," which appeared in the March 1971 *Underground Press Digest*, Craig Pyes tells why he left *Rolling Stone*:

> The non-political state of mind—the form without content which existed/exists in *RS* is readily evident by a quick look around the magazine's new plush offices. Women at *RS* have the same status as women in any other large magazine, only under "hip" capitalism they are more lax about the dressing code, and they allow their employees to get stoned after every issue. But because the women are stoned and can tiptoe around with bare feet and bells on, portends no fundamental change in their condition . . . O Contradictions! Contradictions! The wallpaper along the corridor to Jann's office is a long line of silhouetted naked women, and above it some idealist has put a computer printout which reads: Fuck Capitalism!

About editor Wenner, Pyes said:

> Jann himself is not a villainous sort, not a robber baron or anything. Imagine being 24, having long hair, mod but sloppy clothes, paying yourself a little over 20,000 a year and being forced to sit in the outer offices of "enlightened capitalists," for whom you are dependent upon for advertising. . . . Unfortunately for Wenner, his only model of an editor was a bon vivant [*Ramparts'* Warren Hinckle III] who lives the journalistic myth—the machismo, drinking, carousing, extravagant, generous life-style.

Wenner's success has pushed him into other ventures, including an extremely successful book publishing operation called Straight Arrow Publishers. The company also published "Rolling Stone Books," written by *Rolling Stone* staff writers or free-lancers, often from the magazine articles. *Rolling Stone* has also gone international. A Mexico City publisher translates the magazine and circulates a Latin American edition. *Revolution*, an Australian youth magazine, provides its readers with an insert from *Rolling Stone*. And native-language international editions of *Rolling Stone* are on the newsstands in France, Germany, the Netherlands, and Scandinavia.

The Underground Press in the Military

As the war in Vietnam dragged on, the number of conscientious objectors multiplied, desertions increased, and soldiers spoke up, defying their commanders, demanding a greater measure of freedom, and fostering an antiwar movement within the military. Washington correspondent Robert Sherrill asked in an article in the *New York Times Magazine*, "Must the citizen give up his civil liberties when he joins the army?" And before long the young men in the military, like their peers in other institutions, had their own version of the underground press.

Andy Stapp, a young soldier who was court-martialed at Fort Sill, Oklahoma, in 1967 for refusing to obey an order, has written in his book *Up Against the Brass*: "I was surprised by the news coverage given my court-martial. It reached an international level and gave our movement the kind of publicity it needed to become widely known. The New York *Times* and New York *Post* carried factual accounts. Papers in Lawton (Okla.) and Oklahoma City bannered the story on page one and were generally hostile. America's underground press gave it prominent and sympathetic treatment."[35]

Stapp organized the American Serviceman's Union and created its official organ, the *Bond*, one of the earliest military undergrounds. The union's eight-point program was reflected prominently in the content of the *Bond*:

1. An End to the Saluting and Sir-ing of Officers.
2. Rank-and-File Control over Court-Martial Board.
3. An End to Racism in the Armed Forces.
4. Federal Minimum Wages for All Enlisted Men.
5. The Right of GIs to Collective Bargaining.
6. The Right of Free Political Association.
7. The Election of Officers by Enlisted Men.
8. The Right to Disobey Illegal and Immoral Orders.[36]

A version of the *Bond* had been published earlier, but the circulation had never exceeded 1000. The title referred to the bond between antiwar civilians and antiwar GIs. When the editor, Bill Callison, was arrested for draft resistance, he gave Stapp and an associate the name and mailing list. The first issue of the revitalized *Bond*, published in January 1968, carried items such as:

... The CO talked to us and, after giving his reasons for the extra work, threatened us with a charge of mutiny (which can bring a death sentence). But we stood firm and read the list of grievances.

There were seventy-five of us and mutiny charges against that many GIs would have made front pages. The CO continued to talk tough but the next day the extra duty we had been pulling ended.

Within a few months, the paper had more than 75,000 readers and led the way for an underground press movement on other military bases. In 1971, press critic James Aronson told a social science meeting, "There are 75—repeat, 75—newspapers being published by servicemen seeking to redress the grievances of America's foot soldiers, draftees and objectors the world over."[37]

The new undergrounds protested a range of issues including general conditions in the military, courts-martial at various bases, and racial problems, battling for new rights for servicemen. Most of the names reflected a defiant stance: *Marine Blues; Fun, Travel and Adventure; Gigline; Aboveground; Dull Brass; Eyes Left; Ultimate Weapon; Rough Draft; Shakedown; Fatigue Press;* and *All Ready on the Left.* Three of the most militant began publication in 1971: *Fragging Action,* published in Cookstown, New Jersey, for GIs stationed at Fort Dix; the *Arctic Arsenal,* Fort Greely, Alaska; and *Voice of the Lumpen,* a revolutionary paper published for black GIs in Germany by black exiles from the U.S.

Most of the military papers have been truly "underground." Few listed editorial staffers who have not been discharged, and there were few by-lines. Return addresses were changed frequently, and printing operations floated from place to place.

But so many of the papers have been effective that the brass has pursued them relentlessly. The editors who were discovered were often treated harshly. One editor whose record was spotless nonetheless was given a dishonorable discharge. Robert Sherrill reported that another was sentenced to prison for eight years for possessing marijuana, even though the amount was so small that it was destroyed while being tested.

The military response has not been entirely negative, although it is easy to wonder whether positive actions are self-protective. A "Guidance on Dissent" memo issued by the Department of the Army warned base commanders to guard against violations of GIs' First Amendment rights unless the undergrounds interfered with combat or morale. Robert Weis, a former serviceman, wrote: "If you publish an underground newspaper aimed at servicemen you will probably encounter considerable difficulty getting it into the hands of the average GI. But you'll likely have a high-level audience including your local commander and his staff, various colonels and generals at major command headquarters, a covey of high Pentagon officials, and if you're lucky, a congressman."[38]

The editors have said they wanted to "break the monopoly on the information input" in the military, just as the other undergrounds were doing outside. The high-level opposition to these organs of dissent may actually have helped some of them survive. With the end of the draft and the expected change in the composition of the military services, the more strident undergrounds diminished, although a number of papers concerned more with racial issues still exist.

There are few signs that the underground has had much impact on regular military newspapers, such as *Stars & Stripes* or base papers. One sign of some loosening up was the 1971 publication of an article entitled "GI Underground Newspapers: How the Army Red Tapes Its Knuckles to Strike Blows for Freedom of the Press" by Robert Ashby in *Family*, a supplement to the *Army Times*. The article was a critical account of the author's failure to persuade *First Army Voice* to publish a series of articles about the GI undergrounds. Ashby holds that official army newspapers were trying to replace the undergrounds. "If a soldier can write a letter to the editor or to an action line column in his post paper or read about controversial issues that interest him, the theory goes, he will be less likely to turn to an underground newspaper." But the underground editors doubt that the strategy will work. As one underground staff member told Ashby: "The Army can never allow more than token freedom, which will whet the appetite of the troops, and the Army will have to put on the lid. The underground press is here to stay."[39] The large numbers of minority group members who enter the military, even on a volunteer basis, may help fuel the military underground with demands for full equality. It could be that the military underground will be the vehicle by which the last vestiges of old military behavior will be aired.

The Employee Underground Press

Beginning in the 1960s, large industrial firms like Dow Chemical Company were frequently attacked by antiwar protesters on college campuses and elsewhere. Other industrial giants found it increasingly difficult to recruit new talent from among recent college graduates. Articles in *Business Week, Fortune,* and similar publications admitted that young people were less enamored of careers in business. Then the thrust of criticism of business accelerated.

Environmentalists went after the major industrial polluters. Ralph Nader and other consumer advocates leveled attacks on auto manufacturers, food processors, and others they said were lowering the quality of life in America. There were noisy assaults during annual stockholders' meetings of major firms, attempts by consumerism leaders and their supporters to take over the management of some companies.

The response of the business community was largely defensive. General Motors attacked Nader, even had him investigated and followed by private detectives. Presidents of oil companies gave speeches on the contributions their firms were making to beautifying America. Critics labeled such ads "eco-pornography" by those who used great quantities of natural resources while implying that they were actually misunderstood environmentalists. As one critic put it, "I fear that our children will grow up thinking that Georgia-Pacific and Weyerhauser are adjuncts of the National Park Service."

In sharp reaction, some employees of large corporations established underground papers. The audience was surprisingly large. Thousands of former students and war veterans who take counterculture media for granted were ready for such papers. "For the most part," says Joann Lublin, a reporter for the *Wall Street Journal,* "the underground papers have been started by college activists who entered the corporate work force with reservations and who view company publications as bland management mouthpieces. Many started as antiwar newsletters and then broadened into antimanagement papers."

Not surprisingly, the San Francisco Bay area probably publishes the largest number of employee underground papers. Three of the first were the *Met Lifer* at the Metropolitan Life Insurance Company, *Stranded Oiler* at Standard Oil Company of California, and *A T & T Express* at the Pacific Telephone and Telegraph Company. Others were published at automotive manufacturing plants in Michigan and at the Brookhaven National Laboratory on Long Island, New York. In the November 3, 1971, *Wall Street Journal,* Lublin also mentioned two other now-defunct papers in the Philadelphia area—the *Black Light* at INA Corporation, an insurance firm, and the *GE Resistor,* handed out for eight months in 1969-70 to 900 General Electric Company employees.

Most contributors and editors of company underground papers, Lublin reports, prefer to remain anonymous for fear of reprisals, in spite of the fact that signed articles might persuade management to give their complaints more serious consideration. But, says Lublin, "the paranoia of some staffers may be justified. Several editors of the monthly *A T & T Express* allegedly were identified and fired last year [1970], though the facts are in dispute. For a short time one *Met Lifer* editor lent his home address for mailed contributions to the *Stranded Oiler*—until, he says, he learned the local postal inspector had begun making inquiries as to who lived there."

Few employee undergrounds look very impressive. They are usually mimeographed or inexpensively printed, and the editors give more attention to content than to looks. The papers are often critical of both management and labor on issues—and the issues range from discrimination against females all the way to executive lunches. Most employee undergrounds seem mainly interested in correcting employee grievances and the dehumanizing aspects of organizational life. Some of the undergrounds died because of management harassment or because of lack of reader interest. However, they have had some influence on corporate communications; as one house-organ editor put it, his publication is now "more sensitive to the existence of the underground."

Here is a rundown on the more important employee undergrounds:

□ The *Met Lifer*. As former editor Dan Mood told the San Francisco *Chronicle*, "We were not advocating blowing up the building, but we wanted to make fun of the company mentality that smothers so many of the clerks and secretaries at Metropolitan." Another *Met Lifer* co-editor was Greggar Sletteland, who, according to *Newsweek* (November 8, 1971), led something of a double life:

> While he was running the paper, he served during working hours as assistant to Met Life vice president James Stretch, head of the San Francisco office. "The company never knew I was involved," he recalled, "although at times they must have guessed, since I wore long hair and work shirts. But they wanted to hire detectives to roust out the publishers. Ironically, they weren't so upset about the political stuff; they were more upset about the four-letter words."

The paper was known for its good-humored approach to company problems: content ranged from "anti-war stories to digs at irritating office supervisors who didn't bathe often enough. Sprinkled in were poetry, doodlings, and recipes ranging from guacamole to granola."[40] The *Met Lifer* folded in the spring of 1971 after publishing twenty-two issues. An average of 500 copies of each issue were distributed.

□ *Stranded Oiler*. Sixteen issues were published between July 1970 and January 1972, and usually 700 to 800 copies were distributed per issue. Rarely missing a chance to make fun of the Standard Oil Company of California, the paper ran a mock antiecology column called "Ask Dr. Ortho," which ridiculed Standard Oil's Ortho pesticide.

□ *You Can Dig It*. Written for workers at the National Can Company plant in San Leandro, California, this employee paper has a radical tinge. Part of it is written in Spanish for chicano workers. Among the subjects covered have been a poorly ventilated packing room, the Nixon administration, wage-price freeze, and racism. "I don't think the union or the management sleep well at night with this paper on their minds," a young black worker told the San Francisco *Chronicle*.[41]

□ *Brookhaven Free Press*. Published monthly since mid-1970, this paper at first required that writers' names be published with all articles. Then the editors began to allow anonymity when the author had a reasonable excuse. The paper has covered many topics, including the New York abortion law, the Vietnam war, pollution, the California farmworkers' strike, women's lib, and student unrest.

□ The *Rainbow Sign*. This Washington, D.C., paper is frequently praised for the quality of writing and editing. It circulates 6000 copies to employees of the National Institutes of Health and the National Institute of Mental Health in Washington and the Maryland suburbs. Published originally by the Vietnam Moratorium Committee at NIH and NIMH, the *Rainbow Sign* made ending the war its first concern, but later issues were concerned with federal health policies.

"It Will Never Last"

In 1964, when underground newspapers first appeared, critics said they wouldn't last. But ironically, by March 1969 even the underground editors were inclined to agree, though for different reasons. In the *Underground Press Digest*, Thomas DeBaggio wrote: "Whispering took a decided paranoid turn at the recent Washington meeting of underground newspaper editors . . . Walter Bowart, boss at the [New York] *East Village Other*, turned to me, pondered his finger a moment and said: 'I give us all about another year.' " Bowart and many of his colleagues believed then that the government, which had never looked kindly upon the newspapers, was ready for the kill. (*EVO* did, in fact, succumb in 1972, but the forces were economic pressures.)

But some of the papers are by now nearly a decade old, secure in spite of national economic crises. The old mainstays, such as the Berkeley *Barb* and the Los Angeles *Free Press,* are still thriving, with large circulations and presumably healthy profits. Some papers have died, but many new ones have emerged. The underground press and the atmosphere it helped to create were largely responsible for a new counterculture magazine, *Rolling Stone,* with a large national circulation. Many underground editors and staffs have now turned their energies from the broad-based and free-flowing content of the undergrounds to more specific targets: ecology, women's liberation, and the Jesus revival.

Although Jerry Rubin once suggested that "you can't trust anyone over thirty," it may be that the over-thirties will constitute a large part of the counterculture press audience of the future. Many of the papers that have survived rely on an older readership than they had imagined in the days when they peddled themselves as "youth papers."

Some of the energies of underground editors and their supporters have been diverted into the special-interest organs of political, social, and religious movements. The women's press and various religious papers have drained off some of the former undergrounders. What has been reported as a quieter trend on college campuses may also influence change.

Perhaps the true importance of the underground is the pattern for diversity it provided to persons wanting to express ideas. There is no doubt that that trait and the desire for expression are keeping many of the alternative papers alive in the 1970s. Whether the expansion of cable television options will reduce their numbers is difficult to determine. One thing is clear, though. The numbers of counterculture papers and their progeny is substantial and they show no sign of extinction.

The Underground Press: An Example

DISENFRANCHISED: NEWSPEOPLE AS NIGGERS
by David Deitch

Once the counterculture press talked only about drugs, new life-styles, and radical politics. But by the 1970s the papers, though still anti-establishment, had found new subjects. In August 1972, the Boston Globe *dismissed activist reporter David Deitch for violating a provision of his contract that prohibited outside work without management approval. But prior to being fired, Deitch had written the following article for the* Realpaper, *a small Boston weekly put out by former staffers of the* Phoenix, *an early and popular underground paper. The title borrows from Jerry Farber's well-known essay, "The Student as Nigger," widely reprinted in the underground press in the late sixties.*

Newspeople may not like it, snobs that they sometimes choose to be, but it just happens that the American Newspaper Guild, which endorsed McGovern for President the other day, is affiliated with the AFL-CIO. Now one can conceive of more desirable alliances in light of the labor bureaucracy's reactionary politics, or even argue with the limited vision of the trade union itself as an instrument of social change, but the organized newsperson's link to America's biggest league of workers historically made a lot of sense and is an important context in which to judge the Guild's decision to publicly back a political candidate and risk the approbation of some of its members.

For openers, I support the Guild's partisan act for its ultimate effect on journalists, and I believe that columnists such as Nicholas Von Hoffman who claim that it would "compromise every editor and reporter in America" are mouthing insidious poppycock.

Von Hoffman is disturbed that Charles Perlik, the Guild president, endorsed McGovern and that George Meany, the AFL-CIO president, didn't. The fact that he sees no contradiction here means that he believes newspeople to be substantively different than other workers. As a nationally-known, syndicated, journalistic "star," it's understandable that Von Hoffman should take such a position.

The obvious reason why the Guild hooked up with the trade union movement is that newspapers are a mass production industry, no different, say, than the automobile industry. This means that even though each writer knocks out a story at his own little desk, the newspaper product is manufactured by mass production techniques, guided by mass selling criteria, formed, molded and packaged by a profit-minded management

Reprinted by permission of David Deitch fron the *Realpaper,* August 8, 1972.

that relates to other managements and institutions with similar values. Somehow over the years a mystique has developed that the newspaper business is none of these things but something different and special, and in some ways it is. Hollywood had a few things to do with playing up that romantic notion. So did the Constitution, whose First Amendment uniquely protects this private business in America from government interference while it ignores similar protection for its workers.

The newspaper business, like the automobile business, requires workers who do as they are told so that a finished product may be turned out at a certain level of efficiency. The average newsperson gets about as much sense of the final product in its formative stage as the autoworker who screws on a door. Both industries utilize a management hierarchy to pump out orders and assignments. The newspaper worker and the auto worker have nothing to say about the final product that comes off the assembly line. The writer may contribute ideas and may be consulted, but he may also be ignored at management's discretion and in fact regularly suffers from management censorship in various forms when it suits their needs. He also suffers from the pre-censorship effects of meaningless assignments and from an internalized form of censorship in "knowing what is expected of him." Similarly, the auto worker has no decision power in the essential features of the car he produces, how long it will last, how economically it will operate, or its polluting and safety characteristics.

The men and women on the auto assembly line have no trouble thinking of themselves as "workers." To believe that you're a worker is to accept the reality that control over what you produce rests with someone else. Newspeople as a group, find it hard to swallow this reality. It doesn't fit in with their notion of being a "writer," which has that elite quality of professionalism. To think of yourself as a "professional" is to believe that you operate under some kind of openly declared technical and ethical standards. To date, no newsperson's Hippocratic Oath exists and it's easy to see why.

Professional standards, to the extent that they are made specific, must at some point conflict with the institutional requirements of the newspaper, which incorporates the profit-making ideology of the social system. Medical doctors are forever running into trouble on this score, it seems. If newspeople, for example, adopted as a standard the idea that they should function in "adversary" relationship, not only to the Federal Government and its "official sources" but to all forms of authority, then they must, if honest, reject the corporate ideology that manipulates them. A profession cannot be tied to anything but its own discipline, which means that newspeople cannot properly function unless they control their own material.

Given the conditions under which they presently must perform their tasks, newspeople are workers whether they like it or not, but they can become professionals if they choose. It seems to me, however, that managements have no wish for their employees to think of themselves as either workers or professionals, both of which may produce undesirable consequences for the business.

In reality, newspeople have almost no identity, which is exactly the way management wants it. Unable to conceive of their social role with any kind of precision, newspeople are incapable of determining and fighting for their rights. They reject being called workers, yet have formulated no professional standards. The best people leave the mass media in order to acquire for themselves an identity that is denied them by mass media managements. In all the major cities, reporters are putting out alternative newspapers in order to develop their own standards as professional workers. This is a serious indictment of the establishment press which, by its very nature, can only produce alienation for the bulk of its employees.

Instead of trying to particularize a set of professional standards for themselves, which would require an organized effort, too many newspeople are clinging to the vague notion of "objectivity" as the sole source of their diminishing prestige. It is this commitment to objectivity—whatever that may be—newspeople believe contains the core of their professionalism. But no attempt has been made to define objectivity in the context of a program of professional standards, which would amount to deriving a concept of objectivity as the behavioral *result* of standards created by worker-professionals.

In other words, the issue is not whether "objectivity" exists or is possible to achieve, but who decides these matters. The function of objectivity as an argument is to mystify the issue of controlling the product, which is why newspaper managements are only too eager to propagandize in favor of a tool they can use to manipulate their workers. It is the managers and the owners who decide what is objective and what is not, a rather ludicrous state of affairs given the obvious institutional biases of the newspaper business. Why do newspeople fall for that crap?

In endorsing McGovern, the Guild took a partisan, not a political, position. A political position would have been to state why the endorsement was made, why the choice of McGovern would make a fundamental difference to the country (I myself don't think it would) and to the way people live. This was not done. To have done so would have required an internal debate within the Guild, the precondition for which must be a minimum level of politicization of the members. The Guild can be criticized for making a bureaucratic, non-democratic commitment to McGovern in the same fashion as any other trade union run by non-responsive bureaucracy. But it shouldn't be condemned for confessing its bias.

To go along with that silly sham of objectivity is to say that newspeople ought to be disenfranchised of their political rights just because they happen to work for newspapers. Taking the argument to its logical conclusion, newspeople should be refused the right to vote! A major legal principle is involved here: you don't put a man in jail for what he might do. This means that performance is the criterion for judging his work. A General

Motors worker can believe that the Vega is a lousy car and nobody questions whether he ought to be on the line. If by making political endorsements newspeople are alleged not to be objective, then they must be shown where in their work. But don't say that newspeople can't be citizens of the country. This is the propaganda put out by newspaper managements and their collaborators to sustain their moral authority.

Notes

[1] Theodore Roszak, *The Making of a Counter Culture* (Garden City, N.Y.: Doubleday, 1969), p. 42.

[2] *Ibid.*, p. 56.

[3] Jesse Kornbluth, *Notes from the New Underground* (New York: Ace, 1968), p. 13.

[4] David Sanford, "The Seedier Media," *New Republic,* December 2, 1967, pp. 7-8.

[5] Walter Gieber, "Viewed with Disenchantment: The Underground Press," *Grassroots Editor,* March-April 1970, p. 5.

[6] News Release from American Bar Association regarding ABA booklet, "Lenin v. Franklin: Warring Revolutionary Traditions in Contemporary American Journalism," April 1971.

[7] "Underground Press," *Sixty Minutes,* CBS Television Network, January 19, 1971; transcript p. 5.

[8] Paul Alan Slater, "The Fifth Estate: Underground Newspapers as an Alternative Press in California," unpublished master's thesis, University of California, Berkeley, 1969, p. 15.

[9] *Ibid.,* p. 166.

[10] Freedom of the Press, 1970, *Nation,* January 4, 1971, p. 3.

[11] Kingsley Widmer, "Censorship by Harassment," *Nation,* March 30, 1970, p. 367.

[12] "Narcs 43,000—Freep 0," Los Angeles *Free Press,* April 23-29, 1971, pp. 1, 2.

[13] Gene Blake, "The Purloined List," *Bulletin of the American Society of Newspaper Editors,* November-December 1970.

[14] Los Angeles *Free Press, op. cit.,* p. 2.

[15] "White House Bars Forcade, Reporter for Radical Press," *Editor & Publisher,* November 20, 1971, p. 30.

[16] "Legal Struggles of Underground Press Will Test Press Freedoms," *Freedom of Information Digest,* September-October 1970, p. 4.

[17] William W. MacDonald, "Life and Death of the Hippies," *America,* September 7, 1968, p. 150.

[18] Bob Goodman, "The Great Speckled Bird," *Motive,* April-May 1971, p. 36.

[19] *Ibid.*

[20] *Ibid.,* p. 37.

[21] "What Is Liberation News Service?" The New Media Project, 3 Thomas Circle, N.W., Washington, D.C. (undated, but believed to be written in early 1968).

[22] Susan Johnson, "Bundles, Packets and How the News Gets Around Underground," in Everette Dennis, ed., *Magic Writing Machine,* University of Oregon, School of Journalism, Eugene, Oregon, 1971.

[23] Information about other counterculture news services in *Source Catalog, No. 1, Communications* (Chicago: Swallow Press, 1971).

[24] Mark J. Green, "Too Young to Be Free," *Progressive,* January 1971, p. 26.

[25] Bill Ward, "Reading Between the Lines," *SE Graphics/Communications,* December 1970-January 1971, p. 6.

[26] *How Old Will You Be in 1984? Expressions of Student Outrage from the High School Underground Press,* ed. Diane Divoky (New York: Discus/Avon, 1969).

[27] *Ibid.,* p. 10.

[28] Sam Feldman, "Going Underground," *Communication: Journalism Education Today*, Fall 1970, p. 12.

[29] *Ibid.*, p. 203.

[30] David L. Lange, Robert K. Baker, and Sandra J. Ball, *Mass Media and Violence, Vol. XI. A Report to the National Commission on Causes and Prevention of Violence* (Washington, D.C.: U.S. Government Printing Office, 1969), p. 203.

[31] Green, *op. cit.*, p. 27.

[32] Robert Trager, "High School, College Students' Rights Cases Could Indicate Liberal Trend in Codes, Press," *Communication: Journalism Education Today*, Fall 1970, p. 15.

[33] *Ibid.*

[34] Kathryn MacKinnon Wall, "An Indiana High School Newspaper and Its Underground Newspaper: An Attitude Study," unpublished master's thesis, Department of Journalism, Indiana University, Bloomington, 1971, p. 68.

[35] Andy Stapp, *Up Against the Brass* (New York: Simon & Schuster, 1970), p. 55.

[36] *Ibid.*, pp. 88-90.

[37] James Aronson, "The Great American Brainwash," Symposium on Role of Mass Media in Mental Health, American Orthopsychiatric Association, March 22, 1971, Washington, D.C.

[38] Robert Weis, "The Military Underground Press," *Magic Writing Machine, op. cit.*

[39] "Underground Newspapers: How the Army Red Tapes Its Knuckles to Strike Blows for Freedom of the Press," by Robert C. Ashby, *Family*, a supplement to *Army Times*, May 19, 1971, p. 12.

[40] Marshall Kilduff, "The Underground Papers: Getting Back at a Boss," San Francisco *Chronicle*, December 27, 1971, p. 6.

[41] *Ibid.*

7 Alternative Broadcasting

> *The media must be liberated, must be removed from private ownership and commercial sponsorship, must be placed in the service of all humanity.*
>
> —Gene Youngblood, in the *Videosphere*

The new journalism of the electronic media is still a bit formless, still groping for a distinct role, but it is providing an alternative. That could not have been said a few years ago. Then, the structure of broadcasting seemed almost impenetrable except to the wealthy. Now, however, the growth of cable television allows a diversity in broadcasting that was once unimaginable.

It is doubtful that the seeds of revolution have ever been sown by men of less revolutionary intent. Cable was devised by television servicemen in small towns and rural areas where TV reception was weak or nonexistent. They simply wanted to provide better reception and a larger selection of channels than the home-owner could get from the air. And for about twenty years, cable television was little more than a crude antenna system linking small-town America with the big-city channels and the networks. Now, however, cable is moving to the cities. The 1971 Sloan Commission on Cable Communications reported, in *On the Cable: The Television of Abundance,* that cable, together with allied technologies, seems to promise a communication revolution perhaps as powerful as the inventions of movable type and the telephone. The promise is twofold: First, cable can bring the viewer as many as eighty channels, including distant and local signals, and, second, cable makes possible home information centers, information storage and retrieval systems (hooked to libraries and data banks), and two-way communications systems.

Members of the counterculture often deplore the tools of advanced technology—especially computers and electronic gadgets—but they are embracing cable technology. As the editors of the underground periodical *Radical Software* have written:

> Our species will survive neither by totally rejecting nor unconditionally embracing technology—but by humanizing it; by allowing people access to the informational tools they need to shape and reassert control over their lives. There is no reason to expect technology to be disproportionately bad or good. . . . Only by treating technology as ecology can we cure the split between ourselves and our extensions. We need to get good tools into good hands—not reject all tools because they have been misused to benefit only the few.[1]

Some of those who hope to humanize the new technology believe that strong action is necessary. Gene Youngblood, of the activist publication *Videosphere,* argues: "We must make the media believable. We must assume conscious control over the videosphere. We must wrench the intermedia network free from the archaic and corrupt intelligence that now dominates it."

"Cybernetic guerrilla warfare" has become a favorite phrase of the radical activists who want to apply the methods of guerrilla warfare to the communications revolution. The war should be "small-scale and irregular, much like bombings, snipings, and kidnappings," Paul Ryan wrote in *Radical Software.* It should use the traditional tricks of guerrilla warfare for "cybernetic action in an information environment," as follows:

☐ Mixing "straight" moves with "freak" moves. Using straight moves to engage the enemy, freak moves to beat him and not letting the enemy know which is which.

☐ Running away when it's just too heavy. Leave the enemy's strong places and seek the weak. Go where you can make a difference.

☐ Shaping the enemy's forces and keeping our own unshaped, thereby beating the many with the few.

☐ Faking the enemy out. Surprise attacks.[2]

Ryan does not make clear *exactly* what is to be done. Like many of his fellow guerrillas, he sometimes makes plans that are cryptic, indeed even incoherent.

A more practical formula was sketched by Michael Shamberg in *Guerrilla Television,* a book that is a kind of *Whole Earth Catalog* compendium of information about tools, networking, economic support systems, cybernetic strategies and services, media buses—even video festivals. Although he speculates in the book about "how to bankrupt broadcast television," Shamberg differs with Paul Ryan and the others who want to apply the methods of guerrilla warfare:

. . . I do not call it "Guerrilla Warfare Television" because it is not a form of physical warfare or violence, any more than evolution is.

Guerrilla Television is by definition nonviolent because violence is a mode of social change which substitutes seizure and destruction of property for a genuine understanding of the difference between Media-America and a product-based culture. . . .

Guerrilla Television is grass-roots television. It works with people, not from up above them. On a simple level, this is no more than do-it-yourself-TV. But the context for that notion is that survival in an information environment demands information tools.[3]

Guerrilla Television strikes at the structure of network television by showing how low-cost portable videotape cameras, video cassettes, and cable television can be used to create alternate television networks that favor portability and decentralization.

It has, in fact, been the recent availability of electronic equipment that has spurred alternative broadcasting. As Neil Hickey put it in the December 9, 1972, *TV Guide,* "Two recent technological innovations make possible the entire alternative media movement: the portable, inexpensive TV camera; and the video synthesizer. In 1968, the Sony company introduced its Portapak TV camera and playback equipment: a lightweight (about 22 pounds), inexpensive ($1500) fully portable, battery-operated television system utilizing half-inch reusable video tape (as opposed to the 2-inch tape used by studio cameras) with instant replay and live viewing capacities."

As a member of the Raindance Corporation, a video collective, Shamberg helped publish the quarterly *Radical Software,* sort of an underground engineering manual on cable TV video-cassette film-making. Articles ranged from heavy opinion pieces ("Expanded Education for the Paperless Society") to the latest technique and equipment of videotape film production. The editors call for communication among guerrillas of the electronic revolution—those "committed to the process of expanding television."[4] But some of the communications in *Radical Software,* such as the article by Paul Ryan quoted earlier, confuse more than they clarify. The publication is probably most important as a directory and information exchange for a variety of video clubs, collectives, and firms.

Raindance Corporation is itself one of the leading organizations. Like most of the others, it makes videotapes: "Canal Street General Store," "A Nude Beach," "Yolo County Fair." Global Village, based in New York, specializes in videotape interviews ("Street Interviews and the Generation Gap"), music ("Live Rock Feedback"), and theatre ("Club Orgy—the Sexual Act on Stage"). Ant Farm, based in Sausalito, California, designs and constructs inflatables. Videofreex, based in New York, makes videotapes, using experimental techniques, and publishes an occasional tabloid, the *Maple Tree Farm Report.*[5]

The 1971 *Communications Source Catalog* lists twenty groups like these, all eager to use television to express themselves and to reach others. The catalog also lists several action organizations, including Action for Children's Television, a Massachusetts group that works to upgrade children's programming and advertising; the Woman's Rights Committee, a women's caucus at WRC-TV, Washington, D.C.; and Ecumedia, a quasi-religious organization that attempts "to make the media more responsible in a social, economic, and religious way."

Ecumedia illustrates the wide range of alternative television. Based in Baltimore, its operating expenses are paid by the Roman Catholic Archdiocese. The Baltimore *Sun* describes its programming:

> Ecumedia advocates programs that deal with moral and social issues—narcotics, racism, poverty, the generation gap. The format might involve discussion, drama, the dance, folk music, film, still photography or any combination of these, but the approach is the same: Present the issue, clarify the various points of view and involve the viewer or listener—but don't try to make up his mind for him.[6]

Ecumedia workers have charted four areas of responsibility: (1) creating and producing religious programs which they try to place on local radio and TV stations; (2) distributing religious programs produced by other groups; (3) acting as consultants for local groups that need help in producing religious programs; and (4) publicizing their programs and others, local or network, they feel are worthwhile. They also work with citizens' groups concerned with improving radio and television.

Open Channel—Public-Access TV

If the underground press is do-it-yourself journalism, then Open Channel of New York City surely is do-it-yourself television. In its issue of February 7, 1972, *New York* magazine included Open Channel in a list of "101 Signs That the City Isn't Dying":

> You, too, on the tube—In July 1971, the two cable television companies in New York City began to make available, free to all comers, "public access" television channels on their cable TV lines. Anyone can get free time, and Open Channel (49 E. 68th St.), a foundation-funded group, will help you produce your program. About 25 hours per week of public-access programming is now available on each of the two cable systems.

Newsweek has called free access "the most significant issue facing the burgeoning cable-television industry." The idea is simple: free air time is provided for groups or individuals who want to broadcast their messages. Open Channel is "the first, and still the largest, free-access experiment in the country," *Newsweek* has reported. Open Channel has given free air time to groups ranging from the Boy Scouts to supporters of black radical Angela Davis.[7]

In a proposal for additional funding, Open Channel reported that it had worked with more than 150 groups, producing fifty hours of television programming between June and December 1971. A staff assistant, Lowell Robertson, explained that "we have somewhat arbitrarily directed our efforts in assisting community organizations to produce their productions . . . as opposed to assisting individuals." Those who want to appear on the air can apply directly to the cable operator for space and time. In a prospectus, Open Channel proposed this ambitious program for 1972:

> Over the next six months Open Channel seeks to: assist a minimum of one hundred fifty different groups to produce original programs; originate approximately one hundred hours of real time programming featuring community events normally not covered by network television; generate widespread public understanding of and support for public access; provide production equipment and facilities for ongoing community training in video production; formulate and implement programs that assure the future of public access legally, technically and financially; reactivate unused studio facilities throughout [New York City] for the production of public access programs; develop the concept of neighborhood viewing centers in order to ensure that public access cable television is readily available to the entire community without economic limitation.

Open Channel is headed by a dynamic thirty-four-year-old woman, Thea Sklover, who in making public access a reality is offering a model for the nation. Two other New York City efforts in alternative broadcasting are New York University's Alternative Media Center and Global Village. The NYU program is directed by media activists Mrs. Red Burns and Prof. George Stoney, who focus their efforts on promoting the public access concept. They also act as a clearinghouse for information about cable TV alternative applications.

Global Village has been called "a kind of high-energy think tank, video theater, workshop and instructional center for anybody with a yen to make or display video tapes," says TV critic Neil Hickey. The organization describes itself in *Communications Source Catalog* as people "into televised, multi-sensory, multi-media video. We are videotaping relevant political events and people and kinetic compositions and presenting them in a visual counterpoint of nine TV monitors." Global Village was founded in 1969 by John Reilly and Ridi Stern, a documentarian and artist, respectively. Located in a warehouse and trucking district, they put together a television system and set up a small viewing theatre. They also teach a course at the New School for Social Research and help civic groups get their homemade programs on the cable.

Another attempt to promote individual involvement is Viewer Sponsored Television in Los Angeles. It aims to make up for the failure of commercial television, to "cover events in this community in depth," says Clayton L. Stouffer, a media and public health researcher at UCLA, who is president of the Viewer Sponsored Television Foundation. VSTV is an ombudsman for the community and is designed to have "maximum public involvement, including having people participate in production." VSTV, Stouffer says, hopes "to place a new breed of professional journalists in the saddle, answerable only to viewers. It is a radical departure from either commercial broadcasting or elitist educational or 'public' broadcasting."

Since 1967, VSTV has tried to obtain a television channel in Los Angeles as an outlet for user-supported or "voluntary pay" television. Lack of a tradition for this kind of television makes that difficult, but VSTV spokesmen have broader aims: to "develop into a production and procurement center that will distribute nationally."

The VSTV board of directors includes media experts, academicians, actors, community organizers, ethnic leaders, lawyers and psychiatrists. If the organization is granted a license for a channel, the board would be elected and controlled by the "viewer sponsors" whose contributions would support the station. They would pay twenty-five dollars a year, with lower rates for senior citizens, students, and residents of low-income areas.

Among the programs proposed by VSTV are the following:

Issue in Depth. An entire evening devoted to varying treatments of a single, often controversial issue. Subjects will include the economic basis of political power; military-political power; problems of minorities, the poor, the elderly, the unemployed; medical care. Audience participation in studio and by telephone.

Press Spectrum. Top journalists (including the underground press) analyze issues in confrontation format. Viewers participate by phone.

An Eye on the World. Programs of social importance produced by and for other nations. Includes documentaries, TV films, major event coverage.

News Satire. Biting satire on local and other news events.

Consumer Protection. Regular brief, factual reports of vital interest to consumer well-being, e.g., government findings on dangerous products, from autos to drugs and appliances; research on health, nutrition, etc.

Children's Magazine. Entertaining and nonviolent. Built around multi-ethnic personalities. Programs will tap abundant resources of Los Angeles and the rest of the world.

Stouffer admonishes citizens of Los Angeles to claim their stake in television. The failure of television, he says, "can no longer be treated merely as a failure to 'entertain.' Because stimulating, informational programming is tragically lacking, enlightened choice and participation in the democratic process suffer."[8]

Johnny Videotape

In Santa Cruz, California, Allan Fredericksen, who sometimes calls himself "Johnny Videotape," dreams of a time when:

> You as a member of the Santa Cruz community have some information you would like to share with the rest of the people. You go over to the Santa Cruz media center and borrow a Sony 21 lb. battery-operated TV recording system and videotape your message. After returning the recorder, you call Switchboard and schedule your videotape to be shown at 7 P.M. on Thursday night. Your program is listed in the Public TV Guide available at the local food market. On Thursday night, you go back to the Media Center and play the tape on the machine provided, which goes directly into 20,000 homes in the Santa Cruz area.

Fredericksen is a member of the Santa Cruz Community Service Television Project, a nonprofit organization that promotes "intracommunity communications." According to the *Communications Source Catalog*, "They want to make the community aware of its own potentials through the use of CATV ... to get video into the community where the action is, so that, rather than passively viewing, the community will be involved in production." *San Francisco Flyer*, a supplement to *Rolling Stone*, reported in 1971: "Johnny Videotape is whipping up a dream in sleepy Santa Cruz of telecommunications power to the people through a barrage of public information, legal maneuvering, city council challenges, a voter registration and petitioning drive, in order to create a free access cable television channel."

Fredericksen has been interested in television as a medium of social change since he bought a Porta-Pak in 1970. His work is acknowledged to have been a factor in changing the tide of an OEO Community Action Board election. A local newspaper even suggested that there was a radical takeover of the board.

With attorneys who are familiar with communications law, Fredericksen has devised a plan that would enable the city of Santa Cruz use of the cable television franchise tax paid by the Teleprompter Corporation to fund a public-access VHF channel for noncommercial and uncensored programming.

Fredericksen has written a 1972 how-to book, *Community Access Video*, which covers video hardware and methods of producing video software and tells how to free local cable television for alternate programming and how to form a tax-exempt, nonprofit corporation for twenty dollars. The book also includes notes on economic survival with video and on video experiences in Santa Cruz.

Top Value Television (TVTV)

Some of the individuals and groups we have mentioned have piqued the interest of a small portion of the general public. Video Free America, a San Francisco group headed by Arthur Ginsberg, became widely known through its productions "AC/DC," "Kaddish," and finally "The Continuing Story of Carol and Ferd," which shows the love story of a junkie and an actress in pornographic movies. Such productions marry video and theatre, with production by videotape and showings in theatres like the Mercer Arts complex in New York. But not until the Top Value Television (TVTV) group produced documentaries of the 1972 Democratic and Republican national conventions did it become apparent how inexpensive videotape production could be joined to cable television in a way that enables alternative television to become a strong force.

The TVTV documentary on the Democratic Convention was applauded by Richard Reeves, the astute political reporter for *New York* magazine; John O'Connor of the New York *Times*; and Renata Adler of the *New Yorker*. Some authorities considered "Four More Years," the Republican Convention documentary, even better. John Burkes wrote in the September 27, 1972, San Francisco *Examiner*:

> Top Value TV, a youthful alternative video group, produced "Four More Years" on less money than one network (NBC) spent on coffee in Miami Beach—$9000—and in an important way, scooped everybody.
>
> Because TVTV concentrated its efforts (all 17 staffers) on the unofficial side of the convention—on the people who came as delegates, as observers, as Nixonettes, as Young Voters for the President, as anti-Nixon street demonstrators, as media.
>
> The cameos of the big-time media figures are especially intriguing. You see John Chancellor describing the convention as "mainly an entertainment show put on by the Republicans." Walter Cronkite saying he thinks introspection is "not good" for journalists. . . .
>
> Young Voters for the President are seen complaining mightily that the media have got them all wrong—these Nixon kids are not being manipulated by party elders, they're doing what they feel like.
>
> In a subsequent shot we see a guy with a bullhorn telling a claque of Young Voters what to do about greeting a planeload of delegates. ("When they land, just stay still . . . We'll tell you when you move.")

We see the Nixon daughters, Trish and Julie, enmeshed in the most banal imaginable conversations at handshaking receptions. A TVTV reporter asks Julie if she doesn't get bored of all this handshaking. Her response:

"If you like meeting people, you can't be bored."

. . . This group, consisting of members of Ant Farm Video of San Francisco, Videofreex of New York, Raindance of New York, and others from Chicago, Texas and Ohio, uses half-inch videotape equipment.

It's a lot more portable than the big, heavy equipment the networks lug around, a lot less imposing—thereby less intimidating to interview subjects—and cheaper.

By network standards, this production was not viewed by a huge public. But it was shown on cable television in several major cities, making it clear that alternative television need not be limited to small theatre audiences. As networks of cable channels form, the prospect for wide showing of alternative productions seems assured.

Underground Radio

Although Federal Communications Commission licensing regulations prevent the development of an underground radio that would be an exact counterpart of the underground press, there are many efforts to transform radio. The Women's Center Media Workshop of San Francisco produces programs and spots that publicize examples of oppression of women. The Aquarian Research Foundation of Philadelphia promotes the development of block (lower power-limited range) stations. The World Peace Broadcasting Foundation of Des Moines distributes tapes of conferences and speeches on peace issues. Earth News Service of San Francisco tries to bridge the straight media and the underground press, using conventional techniques to promote radical ideas. Radio Free People of New York and Radio Free Chicago attempt to affect programming by distributing speeches, interviews, and other programs to stations, political organizers, and action groups.

Rick Beban, a San Francisco journalist, has called the new radio "an integral part of that vast swelling of underground consciousness apparent in the music and life styles of the young. Underground radio, from birth, has been a revolution, expressing, through music, words and attitude, concepts that no other form of radio would touch." Beban tells how Larry Miller, a musician, set out to change San Francisco radio. Hired by KMPX, Miller promoted his rock music show by distributing leaflets announcing that he would feature "folk rock." The program caught on. Beban has written:

Looking back, it seems odd that underground radio didn't start a lot sooner. The evolution away from Top 40 forms had begun much earlier, when Bob Dylan reintroduced folk music as a powerful medium for personal themes. Dylan symbolized the beginning of a new kind of consciousness among young people, as though they had begun to move to a different drummer, whose beat was not the same old 4/4. The consciousness began with the civil rights movement, spread onto the campuses, discovered drugs as a source of new energy, and spilled into the streets in a new kind of political body. Musicians took the older blues forms and adapted them to fit the new musical tastes.[9]

KMPX developed into a twenty-four-hour underground radio station. But then a labor dispute and battles over obscenity and drug songs slowed the pace of the underground at KMPX despite its success. Eventually, poor management and continued squabbling led to the death of KMPX as an underground station. Meanwhile, however, several other stations in the San Francisco area adopted the music and news format of underground radio in a search for the new audience. A similar trend followed in other markets around the country. Beban called it "a revolution in music and ideas, that *is* music and ideas. The concepts are the antithesis of what corporations must practice to survive, of what government can permit."

One of the most significant contributions to the underground is made by the Pacifica Foundation, a long-established listener-sponsored group of four stations (KPFA-Berkeley, KPFT-Houston, KPFK-Los Angeles, and WBAI-New York). Known for their open-microphone policy, the Pacifica stations have often skirmished with the FCC and various political groups. WBAI describes itself as "a community-sponsored broadcaster and offers its listeners such fare as gay news, women's liberation, consciousness-raising of women at home all day, black awareness, Young Lords, and other programs." Recent offerings of KPFK in Los Angeles have included "Alternative Radio—A Continuing Review of the Best of Pacifica"; "Crazy Love," a look at destructive ways of falling in love; "The Sour Apple Tree," part of an ecological awareness focus; and "The Love of Possession Is a Disease with Them," Tom Hayden reading from his book on Vietnam.

The underground radio movement has influenced college and university stations and others that try to serve counterculture communities. As Beban says, it is "not a sales concept, or a marketing idea, but a means of communication for a wide movement; a range of personalities and attitudes that a fearful government terms 'subversive.' As the Jefferson Airplane put it, 'We are all outlaws in the eyes of America.' "

Conclusion

Although alternative channels seem to hold more promise for an electronic new journalism, establishment television and radio are also involved. All-news radio stations like WBBM in Chicago have conducted many on-the-street interviews and have produced superb news documentaries. NET's "Great American Dream Machine" was an imaginative package of information, often in a new journalism format. It featured "Talking with Terkel," in which Chicago interviewer and author Studs Terkel conducted "rap" sessions with Breslin-like "little people" in a Chicago bar. The same program often provided expert investigative reporting and miniature documentaries that took strong positions on such issues as consumer problems.

In San Francisco, KQED-TV developed a full hour of local news that featured depth interviews, street coverage, analysis, advocacy, even an editorial cartoon. The program began during the 1968 San Francisco newspaper strike and continued under a grant from the Ford Foundation, which sponsored similar efforts in Washington, D.C., and Dallas.

On CBS News, Charles Kuralt's "On the Road" series was a creative example of visually descriptive reports on obscure places. Kuralt used many of the tools of the new nonfiction. Though he sometimes overwhelmed the viewer with classical metaphors and prose better suited to the print media, Heywood Hale Broun, also of CBS, often approached sports in much the same way. Conventional broadcasting is likely to take on more of this kind of color and flavor. But even if it does not, those who are shaping the alternatives are growing in number and influence.

Clearly, alternative broadcasting is a crazy-quilt of activity without cohesion. Most of the practitioners of this gadget-laden form of communication are still running several paces behind their technology. But the ranks of these young media pioneers will no doubt be infused with new energies and new vitality from even younger men and women who began using videotape equipment in grade school. The central question is not whether the technology will be available (it already is), but whether human beings will organize themselves to utilize it.

Alternative Broadcasting: An Example

THE WORLD'S LARGEST TELEVISION STUDIO
by Top Value Television

This is an excerpt from the transcript of the TVTV videotape documentary of the Democratic National Convention in 1972. All the conversations below appeared in the documentary.

Reprinted by permission of Top Value Television.

Conversation with Mrs. Alberta K. Johnson, a Wallace delegate.

MRS. JOHNSON: Oh, I'm *so* glad you ask me that, I think all of the media is slanted. They say, here we have an interview with thus and so; you know, everybody that has a title is supposed to be *so* important, and I'm not impressed. But, anyway, we interviewed, for instance, Senator so-and-so.

Now, Senator so-and-so said thus-and-so. Why don't they put the senator on and let him say what he said. I don't need an interpreter. Even if you don't know how to read and write, you don't need an interpreter when you're *listening*. . . .

CUT

MRS. JOHNSON (on playback, as she watches herself): . . . It's healthy to disagree, it's healthy to disagree. Here's a statement that takes a while to digest, at least it took me a while to digest. "Free men are not equal, equal men are not free." We all don't have the same faculties, we all don't have the same intelligence, I might be very good with my fingers to do some kind of pottery work, you might be very brainy and intelligent and then you could be a great scientist or something. So, as far as gray matter goes, I'm more intelligent with my fingers, you're more intelligent with your brain. Therefore, we're not equal in this thing; we're only equal in that we should be free, and the only way truly to be free is when you're liberated by believing in Jesus Christ. There is no other true freedom in the world.

CUT

MRS. JOHNSON: You want something?

TVTV: We already shot some tape, but we're going to shoot a little bit more, if you'd like to. . . .

MRS. JOHNSON: Well, whatever, I got time. . . .

TVTV: See, we shot a tape of you watching the tape of you, and then we'll show you the tape of you watching the tape of you, and then we'll make a tape of that.

MRS. JOHNSON (laughing): . . . So, when do I get out of here?

CUT

TVTV: You look nervous, like you want to get back to the floor or something. . . .

MRS. JOHNSON: No, but I think I better go, I think we talked enough. . . .

TVTV: I really appreciate it. . . .

MRS. JOHNSON: Thank you very much. I like you. I like you all.

TVTV: My name is Michael, by the way, and this is Andy.

MRS. JOHNSON: Hi-dy, Andy, and Michael, and all of you. . . .

TVTV: Joan. . . .

MRS. JOHNSON: Hi, Joan. . . .

TVTV: So we'll look for you tomorrow. . . .

MRS. JOHNSON: And what's his name?

TVTV: Chuck, I'm Chuck. . . .

MRS. JOHNSON: Hi, how are you. . . .

TVTV: Take it easy, Mrs. Johnson. . . .

MRS. JOHNSON (leaving): God love you. . . .

Notes

[1]"The Alternate Television Movement," *Radical Software*, No. 1, 1970, first page foldout.

[2]Paul Ryan, "Cybernetic Guerrilla Warfare," *Radical Software*, Spring 1971, No. 3, p. 1.

[3]Michael Shamberg and Raindance Corporation, *Guerrilla Television* (New York: Holt, Rinehart and Winston, 1971), Part II, p. 8.

[4]"The Alternate Television Movement," *op. cit.*

[5]*Communications Source Catalog* (Chicago: Swallow Press, 1971), pp. 51-56, and various issues of *Radical Software*.

[6]William Hyder, "Ecumedia Gets the Gospel on the Air," *TV Week*/Baltimore *Sun*, September 13, 1971, p. 1.

[7]"Do-It-Yourself TV," *Newsweek*, January 3, 1972, pp. 49-50.

[8]"You Have a Stake in Television—Claim It," pamphlet published by Viewer Sponsored Television Foundation, Los Angeles.

[9]Rick Beban, "Underground Radio," in *Focus Media*, Jess Ritter and Grover Lewis, eds. (San Francisco: Chandler, 1972), p. 48.

Precision Journalism 8

We may never see a medical writer who can tie an artery, but a social science writer who can draw a probability sample is not unheard of.
—Philip Meyer

A scientist listening to debates about the new journalism might wonder what all the fuss is about: the assaults on journalism may be new developments in style and content, but they leave the basic *methods* unchanged. To a scientist, practitioners of old and new journalism do not seem to be arguing about fundamentals but merely about different forms of the essay. A real change, one that would truly revolutionize journalism, would be taken when journalists learned to apply the scientific method in their reporting.

In essence, that is what the Special Commission on the Social Sciences (headed by Russell Sage Foundation president Orville Brim) said in *Knowledge into Action*, its 1969 report to the National Science Foundation:

> The social sciences can assist the mass media in reporting current social issues in depth and putting them in context. Nevertheless, with few notable exceptions, the relationship between journalism and the social sciences has never been close. Rarely do journalists, for instance, make more than spasmodic use of available social science knowledge when reporting unrest. A school controversy may be treated as an education story when it is in fact rooted in racial discrimination or the contest for jobs. Urban riots may be reported as a protest of unemployed black members of society when in fact the effective leadership has been supplied by the successful, upwardly mobile

members of the black community. Individuals with high visibility are accepted as spokesmen for a racial or religious group when they may represent only themselves or a very tiny minority—a fact which adequate sampling according to social science procedures would readily demonstrate.[1]

Both the Brim Commission and the Kerner Commission could find only one notable example of reporting "that made effective use of social science techniques and also used social scientists as advisers." That occurred in relation to the 1967 Detroit race riots.

Using social science research techniques, Philip Meyer of the Knight Newspapers' Washington bureau directed a study, "The People Beyond Twelfth Street," which surveyed the attitudes of Detroit blacks after the riots. Meyer urged that journalists try different methods of reporting: "My own answer is to turn to the vast body of methods for gathering and processing and analyzing information which social sciences have assembled, and, having turned to it, make it our own; or at least those aspects of it which we can use. . . . It used to be said that journalism is history in a hurry. I would argue that, to meet the needs of today, journalism must become social science in a hurry."[2]

Ben Wattenberg, a former aide to President Lyndon Johnson, and Richard Scammon, head of the Elections Research Center in Washington, also used the methods of survey research in researching *The Real Majority*, a 1970 book analyzing the American electorate. Wattenberg likes to think, he says, that *they* are the new new journalism. That is, they practice a journalism that is not subjective, but, in fact, he believes, is becoming more objective than ever before.

> We've got the tools now—census, polls, election results—that give us precision, that tell us so much about people. Yet at precisely the time when these tools have become so exact, the damn New Journalists [first-person advocacy journalists] have become so introspective that they're staring at their navel. The difficulty is that when you put tables in you bore people. Yet when I was in the White House, knowing what was going on, reading the New Journalists was like reading fairy tales. They wrote political impressionism.[3]

Although the techniques of social science research have never been used extensively in journalism, it is not true that journalists have always shunned science. University of Chicago sociologist Robert E. Park was a newspaper and magazine writer who became a sociologist—and a famous one—in his search for new tools of analysis. Walter Lippmann was trained as a political scientist, and in his early journalistic writing—and his famous book *Public Opinion*, published in 1922—made extensive use of the findings of social scientists. Publisher E.W. Scripps, whose career embraced both science and journalism, founded Science Service. Its director, William E.

Ritter, records that Scripps thought that "journalism might have in its foundation much of the attitude and method of science and might utilize to its own advantage much of the results of scientific research."[4] But the primary result of Scripp's interest was the reporting of science rather than the use of the scientific method in reporting. In fact, these and similar evidences of a link between science and journalism had so little impact on reporting methods that *Fortune* magazine was probably justified in announcing back in July 1935, "a new technique in journalism," which was simply the technique of the commercial survey, "a sampling of public opinion by methods long familiar to the industrialist in the sampling of ore and cotton."

If this survey was far less refined than those of today, *Fortune* did provide its readers with a roughly representative view. But as one student, Neil Felgenhauser, wrote: "In this first *Fortune* survey, the sample apparently was drawn by a quota method. In other words, the country was divided into five regions. Within each region, interviews were conducted on the basis of the regional populations compared to that of the United States at large, based on the 1930 census. In addition, interviews were allocated by community size and five economic classes based on home value or monthly rent."[5] The problem with quota sampling, as political scientist Bernard Hennessey points out, is that it has "inherent and obvious potentials for error. Interviewers cannot be expected to choose the 'right' respondents, even when given explicit instructions about the numbers of persons to interview from each of the categorical groups or strata."

By the fifties, reports on survey research had become commonplace in newspapers and magazines. Like the *Fortune* studies, however, most came from sources outside the publications and thus had little impact on day-to-day journalism. True, they were published alongside regular reporters' articles (some even summarized the findings), and this, at least, brought them to the journalists' attention. Even so, few journalists adopted survey research techniques.

Perhaps the most important reason for this lack of interest is that most news stories are researched and written in hours. Not many journalists are accustomed to devoting weeks to preparing, researching, and writing in the painstaking style of the social scientist, and few publishers and broadcasters will pay for such costly enterprises. The average reporter is likely to be too impatient for such methods, and few have the bent for science that the methods require.

Leo Bogart, a respected researcher who is also vice-president of the American Newspaper Publisher Association, has also pointed out that, to journalists surveys are identified with the hereditary enemy, the business office, and that surveys are thought of as being useful only in political reporting.[6] Newsmen are also hostile to survey research because many remember the disastrously inaccurate 1936 *Literary Digest* survey, which picked Alf Landon to win over Franklin Roosevelt for President. But this survey biased its sample by gathering names from telephone directories, magazine subscription lists, and automobile registrations—which during the Depression tended to list more Republicans than Democrats. Newsmen also remember the almost equally disastrous prognostications of pollsters prior to the Truman-Dewey Presidential election of 1948, although research methods have been greatly refined since then.

Press critic Ben Bagdikian sees two barriers to journalists' adopting the general insights and disciplines of behavioral science: "the vestige of anti-intellectualism . . . and the inherent and ultimately helpful prejudice within journalism in favor of the concrete and the immediate, which may mean that it will ignore even proven theories in order to report or detect a dramatic physical event, even at the risk of misconstruing it."[7] Bagdikian tells about a friend who became one of the whiz kids in Washington during the Kennedy administration, and after dealing with some of the best correspondents and columnists in the business came to see that—though some had first-class minds, a respectable body of knowledge, and knew what he was saying when he talked—somehow things never quite jibed, not only in their conclusions but in how they wrote. Then, as Bagdikian relates:

> One night we were having a drink, and he announced a discovery with excitement. He said, "You guys don't have any hypotheses!" And I think that's true. While the scientist is looking for regularity and universality, the journalist is often looking for just the opposite. He's looking for the different, he's looking for the concrete. I think almost every journalist has a strong built-in resistance to hypotheses. As viewed by the trade, the ideal reporter is the one who seems to reproduce fact, visible events, documented statements, in a succession which looks very innocent but of course is not, in which the reader finishes with his own hypothesis. This is the pervasive model, I think, of the good first-hand reporter. He does not present a hypothesis. He must appear not to have one.[8]

This is keenly observed, but as Bagdikian himself says, journalists *do* have hypotheses. Some that they disseminated after racial troubles in Detroit and Miami were tested by a Knight survey group:

1. The death of Martin Luther King caused a sudden gain for advocates of Negro violence and a corresponding loss of faith in nonviolent methods.

2. Negroes are turning away from the old goal of embracing a new ideology of black separatism.

3. The ideas involved in the expressions "black power," "black separatism," and "burn, baby, burn" are all different degrees of the same phenomenon: a growing, antiwhite militancy.

Although widely believed by newsmen and widely disseminated by them, each of these statements, Meyer found, "is demonstrably false in the cities where they were tested."[9]

The kind of precision journalism that results from using social science research methods is making a degree of headway because many journalists are aware that some of their methods result in misleading reports. It is making headway, too, because most schools and departments of journalism and communication are now exposing prospective journalists to the findings of social science research and training some in the methods, in part because the Russell Sage Foundation in New York works to link journalism and the social sciences by sponsoring conferences, publications, and training programs.

Philip Meyer, a Precision Reporter

Unlike many reporters, Philip Meyer did not become a specialist by accident. A soft-spoken native of Kansas, he had worked for newspapers in the Midwest before undertaking graduate work in political science at the University of North Carolina. It was there that he developed a taste for social science research methods. He joined the staff of the Miami *Herald* in 1958 to cover education and science. In 1962, he was assigned to the Washington bureau of Knight Newspapers, where his interest in social science was nourished by census data and other analyses handed out by the federal establishment. When he won a Nieman Fellowship for nine months of study at Harvard, he elected to take courses that would enable him to master social science research methods.

Like the rest of the media, the Knight Newspapers tried to report the racial troubles of the 1960s in the traditional way. Journalists are accustomed to covering chaos, but the riots caused them to wonder whether their traditions were good enough. An editor of the Detroit *Free Press* has written:

> . . . there were nagging questions that we believed should be answered without waiting for outside agencies to do the job. How do Negroes living in the riot areas feel about their human condition? What, exactly, are their grievances? How many of them took an active part in the rioting? Just how were the 43 riot victims slain and were their deaths necessary? What is the pathology of war in the cities? What is the role of Negro militants in the aftermath of the riot?[10]

To answer these and other questions, Meyer became project director of a survey sponsored by the Detroit Urban League and financed by Henry Ford II and two foundations. Meyer was assisted by two University of Michigan social scientists. They hired blacks to interview a random sample—one designed to ensure every black fifteen years old or older an equal chance of being interviewed—of 437 Negroes in the main riot areas of east and west Detroit. All the paraphernalia of social science, including an IBM 360 computer, went into the survey. But instead of presenting a heavy number-filled report, during the nine weeks after the riots the *Free Press* produced an in-depth series, "The People Beyond 12th Street," that was notable for its readability. On August 20, 1967, the front page of the features and editorials section was devoted entirely to an article in the series headed THE RIOTER—AND WHAT SETS HIM APART:

> Rioters are different. They stand in sharp contrast to the majority of Detroit Negroes who did not participate in last month's violence and who feel that violence can only hurt the civil rights movement.
>
> Though small in numbers, the admitted rioters in the Urban League survey represent a bitter reservoir of resentment and black racism.
>
> Their attitudes are typified by the 16-year old girl who told the interviewer: "I hate to see people looking different from me. I like my own kind."[12]

And on it went. Along with Meyer's strong prose and quotations were statistics about attitudes in the total Black community that put the riots in context.

A follow-up study made in 1968, "Return to 12th Street," included RIOT AREA SLOGAN—LET'S GET MOVING, BLACK POWER MEANS UNITY TO THE NEGROES, and NEGROES IN POLITICS WIN PRAISE OF BLACK COMMUNITY. The articles were displayed attractively with photographs and easy-to-read charts and graphs that pointed up significant survey findings.

The series was widely acclaimed, but Meyer himself was critical: "Useful as it was in telling the story behind the Detroit riot, the survey project was, in a sense, too late. Negroes should not have to riot before public attention is paid to their problems and grievances."

Meyer got the chance to use his method in a city of calm, Miami, where the Knight Newspapers organization owns the Miami *Herald*. The editors and Meyer hoped to measure the "moods and grievances of their still-peaceful Negro community." As their 1968 report, *Miami Negroes: A Study in Depth*, put it, the *Herald* survey was undertaken in less of a crisis atmosphere and thus was more thorough:

> A longer questionnaire was used, one that took nearly an hour to administer. The sample was larger—530 compared to 437 in Detroit. And the response rate was better, with interviews obtained from 83.5 percent of the homes in the sample, compared to 67 percent in Detroit. Landon Hayes, *Herald* market research director, who supervised the field operation, sent his interviewers to each address as many as nine times in order to find the right people at home.[13]

Interviewers worked every block that had 50 percent or more black families. As in Detroit, data provided population characteristics that reporters could use to write profiles with some assurance that the subjects were representative:

> Shirley Riou's problems are the kind few people outside the Negro ghetto can understand and few inside it can escape. "I'm the head of my house with four children to take care of and it's rough," she said.
>
> But things are getting better for Shirley Riou and she looks ahead with determined optimism. "The way I look at it, if you want to get ahead, you got to bear down."
>
> In her attitudes and her problems, 29-year-old Shirley Riou, of 750.1 N.W. 23rd Ave., has a great deal in common with most of the Negroes questioned in the Miami *Herald's* survey. If there is such a thing as a "typical" Miami Negro, Shirley Riou is one of those who comes close to matching the description.

The articles were supplemented by charts and graphs showing black attitudes toward integration, the annual income and the educational level of Miami blacks, and so on.

In a lecture at Indiana University, Meyer explained the value of precision reporting:

> As journalists we are in the business of creating oversimplifications. Without oversimplifying, we'd seldom communicate anything. But we have to be wary of going too far and we need to be choosy about the oversimplified stereotypes we create.
>
> The stereotype of the dashiki-wearing, separatist, bomb-throwing black power advocate serves only to confuse and alarm our uptight white readers. It does not illuminate. . . . Stereotyped thinking is a difficult habit to break, and the habits which we adopt as reporters quickly become the habits of our readers. It is therefore important to spot the important distinctions as early in the game as possible, and this requires some sophisticated, systematic techniques of gathering and processing information.[14]

In 1969, Meyer and his colleagues decided to study campus rebellions by surveying the attitudes of those who led the demonstration at Berkeley five years before in 1964. Meyer and Michael Maindenberg fashioned a report from computer analysis of 230 questionnaires and thirteen in-depth interviews, with former students identified through university and community sources.

On February 1, 1970, readers of the Miami *Herald* were greeted with a page one banner headline: BERKELEY REBELS OF '64: THEY'D DO IT AGAIN. The story, which also appeared in other Knight newspapers, began:

The young men and women who began the student rebellion five years ago in Berkeley, Calif., are older and wiser now.

Age has made them a little more settled and less visible but it has not made them feel less radical.

This finding, based on a six-month search for the rank-and-file Berkeley rebels of five years ago, contradicts a hope cherished by much of the older generation. The youth movement is not a passing fling by over-active children. Its effects linger when their childhood is gone.

The search turned up addresses of about two-thirds of the more-than 700 University of California students who were arrested in December 1964 for occupying Sproul Hall. . . .

In self-assessed radicalism, the group as a whole has changed hardly at all. But while radical thought has not diminished, radical activity has.

The overwhelming majority—90 percent—supports more recent campus disruptions which sprang from the Berkeley example, even though these involved tactics that were more violent and issues which were less clear.

Eighty-four percent, knowing the consequences of having been arrested and having accumulated the wisdom of five more years, would do it all again.

Their view about the trustworthiness and concern of the American government for its citizens differ radically from those of the nation as a whole. . . .

Thumbnail sketches were woven into the story: "Fred Miller is 24 today, married, and a father. He spent two years in the Peace Corps in South America. He is working, but he plans to go back to school for a doctorate in clinical psychology. He is against violence because 'you don't build a humanist society using inhuman tactics.' "

Meyer believes that one strong argument for precision journalism is that many cultural phenomena are diffused by the news media. "We should be conscious of our role as disseminators of mass culture and think twice about what we disseminate," he said in a February 1969 lecture at Indiana University. "Otherwise, we risk diffusing cultural friction and helping it to become cultural fact. If the world becomes what we say it is, we ought to be careful about what we say it is."

Precision in the News Magazines

Time and *Newsweek* now often use a blend of survey research and investigative reporting in national trend stories. *Time* employs Louis Harris Associates; *Newsweek* employs Richard Scammon, former director of the

U.S. Bureau of the Census, as a consultant on elections and polls and employs the Gallup organization for survey work.

"Has The Church Lost Its Soul?" asked *Newsweek* in an October 4, 1971, cover story. An editor's note outlined the reporting method: "To document the profound changes in American Catholicism, *Newsweek* commissioned a nationwide poll by the Gallup Organization that strikingly demonstrates how far many Catholics have moved from the formerly all-embracing mystique of "Holy Mother the Church." Other *Newsweek* correspondents across the country prepared mood pieces on Catholic clergy and laymen. A Washington reporter talked with key members of the church's national staff.

The story blended survey results and conventional interviews and documented research to produce a solid and readable report.

Three weeks later, in the issue of October 25, 1971, *Newsweek* again offered its readers extensive survey data in "How Will Youth Vote?" It combined a Gallup survey, a report by Richard Scammon, who is a *Newsweek* election consultant, and reporting by *Newsweek* correspondents.

Time uses fewer charts and graphs and more reporting from its correspondents, but survey research has provided the base for many valuable stories. "Suburbia: A Myth Challenged," in the issue of March 15, 1971, was based on polling by Louis Harris Associates in 100 towns and intensive reporting by staff correspondents in four representative communities. The editors and the Harris organization collaborated on preparing a nine-page questionnaire. Harris interviewers spent some 1,600 hours conducting in-depth interviews with 1,614 people. Back in New York the replies were coded, keypunched, and fed into an IBM 360 computer. From this process emerged not only statistical findings, such as income levels and the growth rate of communities, but some surprising attitudes on child rearing, sex, politics, drugs, crime and the virtues and problems of surburban life.

How the editors blend survey findings and the fruits of conventional reporting is illustrated by this paragraph:

> . . . In these spreading suburbs, in all their diverse forms, will come a further test of American democracy. The auguries are good: the Harris survey points to a high incidence of civic concern, and the example of Evanston indicates that the combination of civic concern with a manageable governmental unit can work very well indeed. Suburbia may never re-create the New England town meeting, but it could be the locus of a new localism that will succeed in allowing its citizens to reassert some control over their lives and their governments, to create a fresh sense of community and roots across the land.

Precision Journalism in Broadcasting

Anyone who gives much attention to election news on radio and television is aware that there precision journalism is firmly implanted.

Networks and stations may commission survey research during other periods, but on election night it is so dominant that it almost seems that the survey researchers and the computer programmers have taken over from the newscasters.

Although many broadcasters flirted with precision journalism during earlier elections, especially during the 1960 Kennedy-Nixon election, they began to refine their methods in the 1962 California gubernatorial election, when Richard Nixon ran unsuccessfully against incumbent governor Edmund G. (Pat) Brown.

Computers had been used before to project the results of key elections from fragmentary returns. In 1962, however, NBC worked out a refinement, which it dubbed "Dewline" (for Distant Early Warning line), of election results in key states. The system involved a method widely used by scholars in quantitative research: choosing a few election districts that mirror the entire voting population. By selecting districts that made up a statistically valid sample of the political, economic, ethnic, social, and geographic characteristics of the state as a whole, NBC hoped to be able to project results shortly after the polls closed—and hours before all the returns were in. NBC selected from among the more than 30,000 California precincts only 200 Dewline precincts, which represented less than 1 percent of the state's voting population. The voting in these precincts was expected to forecast the voting throughout California.

The last polls did not close until 8 P.M., some earlier, but the first faint signal from California's Dewline—662 votes from five widely scattered precincts—flashed trouble for Nixon at 7:45 P.M. Governor Brown had received 52 percent of the votes in these precincts. These were too few precincts on which to base a projection, of course, and the next three reports favored Nixon. Brown's percentage fell to 49, then to 48, then began moving up again to 49.

The next signals arrived in clusters, and Brown's advantage began to show firmly on the Dewline. At 8:30, only thirty minutes after the last California polls had closed, Dewline calculations were showing Brown with 51 percent of the vote. His percentage moved up to 53 (based on sixty precincts), wavered between 52 and 53 for nearly an hour, then went to 53 and stayed there.

The important point is that throughout this period the California Tabulating Center, which was set up in another part of the same huge NBC studio, was showing Nixon in the lead. That is, the Tabulating Center was gathering returns from all precincts, not just the Dewline sample, and it must have seemed to many viewers who were relying on these huge, slowly accumulating vote totals that Nixon was certain to win. NBC's political analysts, however, placed much more faith in the Dewline.

As the Brown Dewline percentage continued to hang on 53, the NBC analysts all but dismissed the huge voting totals; they were certain that Nixon would lose his lead and the totals would eventually begin to show that the Dewline projection was correct. This began to happen shortly after

10:30 P.M. During the next three hours, the Dewline held at 53 percent for Brown, and the vote totals began to move in that direction. First, Brown pulled up even with Nixon in the vote totals, then got 51 percent, then 52 percent. Brown's percentage of the total vote converged with the Dewline projection at 2 A.M. Both were then showing the governor with 53 percent.

Since then, of course, broadcasters have refined their techniques to the point where viewers and listeners can usually learn the results of Presidential elections an hour or two after the polls have closed, and long before even half the votes have been counted. It is an especially convincing kind of precision journalism.

Survey Research Problems

A Russell Sage researcher described what John Leo, former social science reporter for the New York *Times*, felt were the nagging problems of social science coverage:

> He noted that editors, in their effort to be up-to-date and intellectually fashionable, may espouse the importance of social-science coverage, but their visceral reactions when they see the copy are to discount its news value. Coverage of social science is not an area to which reporters are primarily attuned—"In sociology there are no 'events.'" Additionally, Leo noted that editors have trouble appreciating experimental methods using small, but statistically valid, samples. He told of once having an article dismissed because the sample size was "only 1,000."[15]

The Russell Sage Foundation report, from which this quotation was taken, revealed that in a one-week period, researchers found seventy-six articles of a behavior science nature in the New York *Times* and *Wall Street Journal*, but "only a handful drew in any significant way on behavioral science findings, methods or insights. Yet a clear majority of them could have done so effectively." Moreover, the report observed:

> In 29 percent of the articles, there was some approach, usually crude, to the survey technique. Often this amounted to a reporter interviewing individuals whom he chanced to come upon in one way or another, quoting a number of them and drawing conclusions. Rarely was there a clear effort to indicate what proportion felt one way and what proportion another. As in previous stories that were examined, such terms as "cross section" and "random sample" were used in a loose, nontechnical way that would make sociologists squirm.

The Russell Sage researchers discovered many journalists trying to report trends and changes, but that "almost never ... did they inject into the stories the precision and authenticity that even rudimentary social-science tools would have made possible."

Philip Meyer argues that "Any newspaper that can spare four reporters and one editor for two weeks can come close enough to duplicating Gallup's methods to compete with him in accuracy and to exceed him in color, anecdote and verbal description." He cited a 1968 Ohio election survey conducted by reporters for the Akron *Beacon Journal*:

> They used a stratified probability sample of geographic points and a modified quota sampling system—patterned after Gallup's—within those points and got an accurate picture of where the Ohio electorate stood in the few weeks before the election. Moreover, since the interviewers were reporters, they were able to shift their mental gears at predesignated points and conduct a traditional reporter's interview in depth on every *n*th call. This produced a random subsample of depth interviews with color, quotes, notes on the autumn leaves and county fairs and resulted in readable copy with flesh and blood to wrap around the numbers.[16]

If they are heavily laden with statistics and do little to show the reader what the story means to him, stories based on surveys are deadly dull. How they can be enlivened has been shown by Professors Alex S. Edelstein and William E. Ames of the University of Washington School of Communications, who have experimented with what they call "humanistic newswriting." They explain in an article in the *Quill*, "If the reader can identify with another person's experience, he feels less isolated as a human being. He develops a greater understanding of others and becomes more able to cope with events."[17] Conducted over a two-year period, the experiment brought newsmen to the campus for seminars, and faculty members visited Seattle newspapers as "humanists in residence."

Sue Hutchinson, environmental reporter for the Seattle *Post-Intelligencer* and a participant in the experiment, showed how humanistic newswriting can brighten and enhance a story by writing three leads for the same story:

> 1. The City Planning Commission yesterday recommended addition of an RM 1600 zoning classification to the Seattle Zoning Ordinance.
>
> 2. Additional land will be opened up for apartment house and townhouse development if the city adopts a recommendation made yesterday by its planning commission.
>
> 3. It may soon be possible for a poor family to slowly buy an apartment with enough room to seem like a home.[18]

Edelstein and Ames point out: "The first is a news report of what happened, stated in technically correct terms and all but meaningless to the reader.

The third lead would be written by a humanistically inclined reporter. It talks about what the event means to people. Humanistic reporting is not human interest reporting. The latter stresses unusual or unique qualities of individuals. The former tells how one person is like another, how he shared special human qualities with the reader."

Although the humanistic writing Edelstein and Ames promote can be used, of course, in many kinds of newswriting, it seems especially appropriate as a means of enlivening survey research reports.

A ready source of background material for precision journalists is census tract data. At Northwestern University, Professor George Heitz and his students in the problems of urban journalism have made the plunge into such data. Says Heitz, "the whole idea is to get incipient journalists used to digging for, handling, and interpreting data." Each student is given two contrasting census tracts in Chicago which are used to observe the quantitative differences between the two neighborhoods. Says Heitz: "Once they finish the data analysis, report on correlations or other significant indicators, they visit the tracts. That way, the data come alive and most students check their conclusions with local organizations, police, churches, and find that data background which they can supply elicits responses that are loaded with story possibilities. After the initial shock, most students find this an interesting, fun thing to do."

Students at other universities where science writing and behavioral science writing are stressed also get training in research methods, the tools of the precisionist.

With the exceptions already noted, precision journalism is at this point more a goal than a reality. Notable experiments have been conducted and a more imaginative use of survey research data is apparent. Yet, it is only a beginning of a cooperative liaison between the coolly detached methods of science and the inventively conceived prose of the writer. Together the two may move us closer to truth.

Precision Journalism: An Example

BLACK POWER MEANS UNITY TO THE NEGROES

by Philip Meyer

In the following story, Philip Meyer examines the attitudes of Detroit Negroes a year after the 1967 riot, using data from a special social science survey and adding impressions from interviews and other information sources.

The old Negro militancy is dead. A new, power-oriented, black militancy has taken its place in Detroit.

This change is not the alarming development that many whites might

Reprinted from *Return to Twelfth Street: A Followup Survey of Attitudes of Detroit Negroes,* October 1968, published by the Detroit (Michigan) *Free Press.*

think it is. Indeed, all it means is that blacks are beginning to become as aggressive and ambitious as whites.

The great majority of riot-area Negroes believe that their future depends on unified activity to vote together, organizing political and business groups together, and, at the same time, working on self-improvement through education and better family relationships.

Black power defined in this way has nothing to do with the extreme separatists who want their own black nation. It has nothing to do with rioting, past or future. It has nothing to do with hatred or rejection of whites.

Two University of Michigan political scientists, Joel Aberbach and Jack Walker, reached much the same conclusion when they reported last month on a survey which asked both blacks and whites in Detroit to define the term, "Black Power."

Negroes tended to define it in terms of black unity or getting a fair share for blacks. Whites, in contrast, were so frightened of these two words that they were "almost hysterical" in their response.

A [Detroit] *Free Press* survey, using a more elaborate statistical technique confirmed the finding that Black Power, defined as unified political and economic effort, is not related to extremism.

The name of the technique is factor analysis, which uses a computer to sift through a set of survey findings and determine the basic, underlying attitudes they represent.

The *Free Press* analysis showed that knowing a person's position on black political and economic power was no help at all in guessing his feeling toward black nationalism.

Thus, the analysis bore out the words of a black insurance man in the Twelfth St. area:

"Black Power is merely a means of black people coming together and being a united black people for building businesses, building pride, and what have you," he said. "That's all Black Power means. A lot of white people think that when you say 'Black Power,' it means rioting. Black Power does not mean that.

"Now if the final phase comes to fighting, well that could mean Black Power, too. But Black Power does not mean going up and down the road throwing bottles and bricks."

A resident of a large but run-down house on the East Side put it more succinctly: "White people got the money," he said. "We got to try to get it."

Black Power has become the dominant idea among the Detroit Negroes at the expense of the older kind of militancy which stressed integration and legal action instead of black unity.

In 1964, a landmark study by Gary Marx, now an assistant professor at Harvard, measured the old militancy with a series of questions dealing with open housing, public accommodations, dissatisfaction with the speed with which government was pushing integration, and a sense of being held down as indicated by disagreement with statements like "Negroes who want to work hard can get ahead just as easily as anyone else."

Four years ago, attitudes like these hung together statistically. A Negro who favored open housing, for example, was also likely to feel that Negroes could not get ahead just by working hard. Earlier this year, when the Miami *Herald* surveyed Negroes in its southern environment, the same index still worked.

In Detroit, it doesn't work. The items are no longer relevant to the existing mood or to each other. In the new spirit of pride and forward movement, a militant can now find himself agreeing with the statement, "Negroes who want to work hard can get ahead just as easily as anyone else."

Clearly, Detroit Negroes have found a new direction.

To define it and figure out who is following it, the *Free Press* gave each of the 452 blacks in the new survey a Black Power score of zero to six, depending on the number of items in the Black Power cluster he called "very important."

These Black Power items indicated agreement that Negroes should:

☐ Get more political power by voting together to get officials who will look out for the Negro people.

☐ Get more economic power by developing strong businesses and industries that are controlled by Negroes.

☐ Be active in political and civil rights organizations.

☐ Have better relationships within the family.

☐ Stop quarreling among themselves and unite efforts on issues that involve Negroes.

☐ Get more education.

Eighty-two percent of those surveyed said three or more of these actions were "very important." Two-thirds called at least five of the six "very important."

For the purpose of drawing a statistical profile of the new Black Power advocate, the *Free Press* interviewees were divided into two groups. Those who called five or more items "very important," were separated from the others for comparison.

The Black Power people tend to be tolerant, thoughtful Negroes who are opposed to violence and favor integration.

They are not the rioters.

Only 51 percent of those who admitted rioting in 1967 scored high on the Black Power scale, compared to 70 percent of the non-rioters.

People who prefer mixed neighborhoods are stronger Black Power advocates: 67 percent of those who want an integrated neighborhood are for Black Power, compared to 53 percent of those who do not.

A telling combination of political sophistication and frustration appears to move people toward Black Power. Both political knowledge and personal sense of political effectiveness were measured for each person interviewed.

The outcome:

Among people lowest in knowledge of political affairs, only 51 percent were strongly for Black Power. In the group with the highest political knowledge, 74 percent were for Black Power.

The political effectiveness test used questions asking for agreement or disagreement to questions such as, "I don't think public officials care much what people like me think." It produced the opposite result:

Among those who felt politically effective, 50 percent were strongly for Black Power, compared to 71 percent of those who felt they were ineffective politically.

Black Power, therefore, appears to be a rational approach to filling a genuine need.

The Black Power concept attracts people of strong religious conviction. The exact was true of the older Negro militancy in other surveys. The more religious people were, the less likely they were to become militant. Religion was an opiate.

But that old rule of thumb does not hold for the new militancy. Among those who call religion "extremely important" to them, 74 percent are strong Black Power supporters. Of those for whom religion is "quite important" or "fairly important," only 57 percent are strongly for Black Power.

Black Power is weakest as a philosophy among the well-to-do and the very poor. It is strongest among members of families with incomes between $2,500 and $7,500.

It is at this level, perhaps, that Detroit blacks can taste just enough of the good life to want more. "We're not poor," said a young bearded auto worker in the upper part of this income range. "But we're not very well off, either. Seems like every time you get an increase in pay, prices are going up."

Getting blacks their fair share of economic power is an appealing idea to him and persons like him.

Notes

[1] *Knowledge into Action: Improving the Nation's Use of the Social Sciences.* Report of the Special Commission on the Social Sciences of the National Science Board, National Science Foundation, Washington, D.C., 1969, p. 29.

[2] Phillip Meyer, "Reporters and Research Tools," Crosman Memorial Lecture, University of Colorado, April 14, 1970, pp. 5, 11 of Meyer's text.

[3] Cleveland Amory, "Trade Winds," *Saturday Review,* September 26, 1970, p. 8.

[4] William E. Ritter, *Science Service as One Expression of E.W. Scripps' Philosophy of Life* (Washington, D.C.: Science Service, 1926), p. 16.

[5]Neil Felgenhauer, "Precision Journalism," in *Magic Writing Machine*, Everette E. Dennis, ed., University of Oregon, School of Journalism, Eugene, Oregon, 1971.

[6]Leo Bogart, "Social Sciences in the Mass Media," in *Behavioral Sciences and the Mass Media* (New York: Russell Sage Foundation, 1968), p. 169.

[7]*Ibid.*, p. 47.

[8]*Ibid.*

[9]Philip Meyer, "The Risks of Interpretation," *Bulletin of the American Society of Newspaper Editors*, April 1969, p. 3.

[10]Editors of Detroit *Free Press, Reporting the Detroit Riot* (New York: American Newspaper Publishers Association, 1968).

[11]*Ibid.*, p. 44.

[12]Quotations in this section are from *Return to 12th Street: A Followup Survey of Attitudes of Detroit Negroes*, October 1968, published by the Detroit (Michigan) *Free Press.*

[13]Quotations in this section are from *Miami Negroes: A Study in Depth*, published by the Miami *Herald*, 1968.

[14]Meyer, "Risks of Interpretation," p. 4.

[15]Edward W. Barrett, *Surveys, Polls and Samples in the Media*, report to the Russell Sage Foundation, New York, 1971.

[16]Meyer, "Reporters and Research Tools," p. 6.

[17]Alex S. Edelstein and William E. Ames, "Humanistic Newswriting," *Quill*, June 1970, p. 28.

[18]*Ibid.*

9
The Future of the New Journalism

The status of the New Journalism is not secure by any means. In some quarters the contempt for it is boundless . . . even breathtaking.
—Tom Wolfe, in *Esquire,* December 1972

Although the new journalism is still an infant, many of its components are under siege, especially the new nonfiction. Dozens of articles have appeared in popular magazines and trade journals decreeing that it does not exist. At the end of a lengthy article in the *Village Voice,* Jack Newfield declared, "I think there is no such thing as New Journalism. It still comes down to good writing, and hard work and clear thinking. The rest is bullshit."[1] Agreeing, Jimmy Breslin wrote, "Believe me, there is no new journalism. It is a gimmick to say there is. . . . Story telling is older than the alphabet! And, that is what it is all about."[2] The seasoned voice of Lester Markel, retired Sunday editor of the New York *Times,* states these conclusions: "First, that the New Journalism is really not new; second, that only in the broadest sense is it journalism; and third, that many of the New-J's fail to recognize that the 'New' is not a substitute for the 'Old' journalism and that journalism generally has been in the process of change even if they have failed to notice it."[3] Michael J. Arlen wrote in the *Atlantic:*

> To begin with, of course, one can say that the New Journalism *isn't* new. That's a favorite put-down: the New Journalist prances down the street, grabbing innocent bystanders by the lapels, and breathlessly (or worse, earnestly) declaiming about his "new fictional techniques," or his "neo-Jamesian point of view," or his "seeing the world in novelistic

203

terms" and all the rest of it while the Old Literary Person gazes out his window and mutters: "New Journalism, indeed!"[4]

Such criticisms recall the complaint of the Chicago editor of the 1920s who declared, "What this paper needs is some new clichés." It is clear that many critics of the new journalism need to replace their clichés, especially the often-repeated statement (usually delivered with the smugness of one who possesses superior knowledge): "There is nothing new about the new journalism." About that there is no debate. Even Tom Wolfe has written resignedly: "Any movement, group, party, program, philosophy or theory that goes under a name with 'new' in it is just begging for trouble, of course. But it is the term that eventually caught on."[5]

It *is* the term that caught on, and that is why it is used in this book. As we pointed out in the first chapter, there are antecedents to all the forms that make up what is called the new journalism. The significance in the new journalism is not in newness, but in the coalescing of forms—some decades old, some that stretch back through the centuries—that amounts to a modern movement. The forms challenge the standard procedures and structures of journalism, and whether they are actually new is ultimately irrelevant.

Much of the criticism of the new nonfiction springs from adverse reactions to many who practice it. It has its unobtrusive personalities—Lillian Ross and Gay Talese, for example—but it has more than its share of practitioners who range from the irritating to the insufferable. Norman Mailer seems to ask to be disliked—in person and in print. Some of the young who model themselves on him—and think they model their writing on his—blend bad manners and bad prose. It was at least impolitic for Truman Capote to declare himself the inventor of a new art form. But it may be that Wolfe, who is personally engaging and who has done more than any other writer of the new nonfiction to promote that form, is responsible for more adverse reaction than any other new journalist.

By writing about the new nonfiction as though it were the be-all and end-all of new journalism, Wolfe has contributed much to the making of a new confusion. In this respect, Wolfe is a new nonfiction purist who is unwilling to include the entire continuum of related journalistic-literary developments into the definition of the new journalism. By mixing the serious and the jocular in an inextricable mass that wounds the literati, Wolfe has no peer. Did he really mean it when he wrote that in the literary world the new nonfiction was "causing panic, dethroning the novel as the number one literary genre, starting the first new direction in American literature in half a century"?[6] Or was this, like so much of his writing, hyperbole? In 1972, Wolfe explained at length in a controversial series on the new journalism that his published attack on the *New Yorker* was a mixture of fact and parody, and argued that not all of it should have been taken seriously. But the series itself carried a strong comedic theme. Satiric in some places, serious in others, it embodied Wolfe's mischievous spirit and his talent for irritating the critics. The series brought a new wave of criticism. Michael Arlen sneered at Wolfe's account of the birth of the new journalism as "Me and My Pals Forge History Together."

In the end, however, what matters is not the bickering over definitions and the clashing of personalities but the future of journalism. We are aware of the many personal factors involved in the torrent of criticism. Whatever the motivations of the critics, their effect has been positive because they have helped provide visibility for the new journalism during its formative period. But the central question is: will the new journalism continue? Again, we must remember that it is made up of several forms and media. Despite their coalescence, they spring from different needs, serve different functions—and meet different attacks from those dedicated to preserving conventional journalism. It would be incredible if all the components of the new journalism were to live or die together, although the future of four may turn on a single element.

♦

New Nonfiction

This is a demanding form, and it is nonsense to imagine that most journalists will be able to master it. But neither is it attainable by only a few. Harold Hayes, former editor of *Esquire*, wrote in 1972: "It must be hell these days for the poor news reporter in Topeka, sitting there punching out his one-sentence, monosyllabic news leads, wondering how many light years he must travel to get with it."[7]

Ironically, at about the time that issue of *Esquire* appeared on the newsstands, members of the Topeka Press Club spent an evening discussing the new journalism, and many of the Midwesterners indeed proved to be restless and ready for change. Of course, the straight news report will not disappear. It serves a valuable purpose, both in Topeka and in New York, for most events simply do not deserve the time and attention that the new nonfiction demands. Many are reported more appropriately in a terse, bare-bones form.

But touches of the new nonfiction are appearing in newspaper features, where it belongs, and the degree to which it becomes dominant in feature writing may depend largely on the amount of time the writers are given to develop their assignments. The new nonfiction has already won a secure place in magazines and books, and will win a larger one, for the simplest of reasons: for many journalistic reports, there is no better form. Moreover, the new nonfiction has been a financial success, making money for magazine and book publishers even during a bleak period in the national economy.

The Alternative Press, the Journalism Reviews, the Advocates, and the Counterculture Press

The future of all these may depend on the answer to a single question: Will the conventional press adapt itself to meet the challenges? So many elements of the conventional press *have* adapted themselves, at least to a degree, that the question might be narrowed: How *far* will the conventional press go in adapting? By analogy, when a minority political party begins to attract wide support, a major American party adapts part of that program to lure supporters of the minority party. The minority party usually continues to exist for a time, even to stand as an alternative, but its appeal is eroded.

It is unlikely that the conventional press will ever adapt to the point that all the modern muckrakers who operate the alternative press will have to give up, although the economic demands of publishing alternative papers restrict them to a shaky foundation. The desire of reporters on conventional papers to perform much as the muckrakers do is likely to make many of the conventional papers more challenging and useful, and thus hold most of the alternative press at the subsistence level.

Much of the future of the journalism reviews is tied directly to adaptation. Will the executives listen to their unhappy reporters and deskmen? Many executives are, though grudgingly, and it may be that relatively few reviews will continue. Still, it is possible that those who devote themselves to more than intramural complaining, taking up broader questions, will gain readers because of the widening public interest in the processes of mass communication.

Among the many kinds of advocates, columnists like Nicholas von Hoffman and Pete Hamill have shown that unorthodox views can be published in the conventional press and attract readers without cracking the temple walls. As a result, executives search for others like them. Conventional journalists are fighting advocacy in the news columns and in news broadcasts, however, and with a degree of success that suggests that the standard news structure will remain much as it is for some time. News analyses and interpretations are likely to become more flexible, with many verging on personal editorials. Some do now. Many advocacy publications face an uncertain future. As the conventional press slowly recognizes the rights of women, youth, and minorities, and gives them space and a voice, some of the fringe publications—especially those in continuing financial trouble—are likely to die.

Perhaps more than any other type, the counterculture press depends for its future on the adaptive mechanisms of the conventional press. Will conventional journals do more to cover the counterculture? The answer seems to be that they already are. The early period of startling success for the underground press taught them that they must broaden their appeal. But will the conventional journals also *speak for* the counterculture? Clearly they cannot, not in any convincing way, for they must continue to please an establishment that provides the advertising that sustains them, and they cannot displease the many readers who are repelled by or barely tolerate the counterculture. This leaves ample room for the counterculture press, which can cover its sphere better than can the conventional journals and speak for it persuasively.

Alternative Broadcasting

There is no doubt that the alternative broadcasters will multiply and that they face a rich future. The growth of cable television assures it. In fact, where once broadcasting offered so little opportunity for alternative voices that frustration was epidemic, cable may provide *too many* opportunities. The question is whether alternative broadcasting can fill the available time on the open-access channels of cable with quality broadcasting that will attract listeners and viewers. Whatever the quality, however, the growth of alternative broadcasting is certain.

Precision Journalism

This, too, has an assured future, but its rate of growth and dimensions are uncertain. Some publishing operations would welcome journalists like Phillip Meyer, who are equally at home with the art and the science of reporting, and at least a few publishers would give them occasional opportunities to use the full panoply of behavioral science research methods in reporting. But the overwhelming majority of young journalists are so lured by the art of reporting, perhaps especially the techniques of the new nonfiction, that they shun the science. Indeed, most of the prospective journalists who take courses designed to prepare them to use quantitative methods are openly contemptuous of the entire effort. A few of the others are so attracted by the methods that they abandon reporting and become researchers or teachers. Still, a few who believe that behavioral science methods are essential in some kinds of reporting are moving into newsrooms. Their effect will be gradual, but eventually it could have decisive impact.

Diversity: A Question

If there is anything genuinely new about the neo journalism it is probably its diversity. Never before has America experienced so many voices in the marketplace of ideas. The styles and media of the new journalism have opened avenues of expression to many who previously found no access to the mass media. For this reason it may be that the main contribution of the new journalism is in reducing the sense of powerlessness of those who speak through its conduits: writers who might have strangled on the rigidity of the old newswriting formula; others who simply wanted to speak their mind. In an age when the pressures of big government, multinational industries, and varying economic forces seem to have limited entry to major media, the liveliness and diversity of the new journalism are striking a blow for free expression. Other voices are being raised.

The central question, however, is not how many voices are raised but how many listeners care to hear them. It is one thing for journalists to glory in their wildly varied styles and media, quite another for them to continue to attract audiences after the edge of novelty has worn off. Diversity in journalism pivots on diversity in interest among the American people. Like the many journalists who are building careers on the new journalism, we believe the question "Who cares?" will be answered—many do.

Notes

[1] Jack Newfield, "Is There a New Journalism?" *Columbia Journalism Review*, reprinted from the *Village Voice*, July/August 1972, p. 47.

[2] "Making the Real More Real," *California Living Magazine*, San Francisco *Sunday Examiner & Chronicle*, November 14, 1971.

[3] Lester Markel, "So What's New?" *Bulletin of the American Society of Newspaper Editors*, January 1972, p. 8.

[4] Michael J. Arlen, "Notes on the New Journalism," *Atlantic Monthly*, May 1972, p. 43.

[5] Tom Wolfe, "The Birth of 'the New Journalism'; Eyewitness Report by Tom Wolfe," *New York*, February 14, 1972, p. 45.

[6] *Ibid.*, p. 1.

[7] Harold T.P. Hayes, "Editor's Notes," *Esquire*, January 1972, p. 12.

Annotated Bibliography

This is a bibliography *about* the new journalism. For specific examples *of* the new journalism, see the excerpts at the end of Chapters 2 through 8.

1. General Views of the New Journalism

Books

Dennis, Everette E., ed., *The Magic Writing Machine: Student Probes of the New Journalism.* School of Journalism, University of Oregon, Eugene, Oregon, 1971. An introductory essay defines and describes the new journalism.

Johnson, Michael L., *The New Journalism: The Underground Press, the Artists of Nonfiction, and Changes in the Established Media.* Lawrence, Kansas: University Press of Kansas, 1971. An early attempt to provide an overview of the new journalism, with a detailed analysis of three major stylists—Capote, Mailer, and Wolfe—as well as a sketch of the history of the underground press and media activists.

Wolfe, Tom, *The New Journalism.* New York: Harper & Row, 1973. An anthology of various writers of the new nonfiction, compiled and introduced by Wolfe and E.W. Johnson.

Articles

Arlen, Michael J., "Notes on the New Journalism," *Atlantic Monthly,* May 1972, pp. 43-47. Apparently inspired by Tom Wolfe's 1972 backgrounders (listed below) on the new journalism, Arlen says nothing is new about it, concluding that the new journalist "is less a journalist than an impresario."

Balz, Daniel J., "Bad Writing and the New Journalism," *Columbia Journalism Review,* September/October 1971, pp. 51-53. A personal view of the writing styles of new journalists and their effect on student writers.

Brown, Charles H., "New Art Journalism Revisited," *Quill,* March 1972, pp. 18-23. A university professor suggests the new journalism is in vogue because it is being practiced by great literary talents.

Buffum, Richard, "The New Journalism," Los Angeles *Times,* October 5, 1971, Sect. II, p. 1. The new journalism is "a risky business, but who is to say—once on balance—that it will not cut closer to the bone of truth about the human condition?"

Dennis, Everette E., "Brain Candy and Beyond: Seminars in New Journalism Kindle Student Enthusiasm," *Journalism Educator,* April 1973, pp. 3-5. Experiences with students studying the new journalism at Kansas State University and the University of Oregon.

Frady, Marshall, "Dispatches from the Dark Outback," *Bulletin of the American Society of Newspaper Editors,* March 1971, pp. 11-13. Written originally as a personal letter to Willie Morris, this account reflects Frady's view that "the celebrated new journalism is really the oldest literary form."

Hayes, Harold T.P., "Editor's Notes," *Esquire,* January 1972, p. 12. *Esquire*'s editor looks at some of the origins of the new journalism and grouchily calls new journalists "a gymnasium full of ill-assorted egos, ranging from the brilliant to the banal."

Markel, Lester, "So What's New?" *Bulletin of the American Society of Newspaper Editors,* January 1972, pp. 1, 7-9. Markel echos Hayes and urges old journalists to maintain perspective.

209

McHam, David, "Old Ain't Necessarily Good, Either," *Bulletin of the American Society of Newspaper Editors*, January 1972, pp. 3-6. An attempt to assess the internal conflict in journalism.

———, "The Authentic New Journalists," *Quill*, September 1971, pp. 9-14. A somewhat confused attempt to define new journalism. The author applies a personal standard—when well done (à la Wolfe, Talese) it is new journalism; when badly done it is activist reporting.

Newfield, Jack, "There's Nothing New About the New Journalism, Only Good Writers and Bad Writers," originally in *Village Voice*, May 1972; also *Columbia Journalism Review*, July-August 1972, pp. 45-46.

Ridgeway, James, "The New Journalism," *American Libraries*, June 1971, pp. 585-92. A look at new media, especially of an activist-advocacy stripe. Also an account of the life and death of *Hard Times*, the radical weekly founded by Ridgeway and Andrew Kopkind.

Rivers, William L., "Monitoring Media—The New Confusion," *Progressive*, December 1971, pp. 26-29. Attempts to define the new journalism in its various forms, suggests that the tools of the new nonfiction are worthy of further consideration and might be useful to the commercial media.

Robinson, L.W., and Hayes, Harold, and Wolfe, Tom, "The New Journalism," *Writer's Digest*, January 1970, pp. 32-35, 19. A spirited Columbia University symposium on subjective reality in journalism.

Tebbel, John, "The Old New Journalism," *Saturday Review*, March 13, 1971, pp. 96-97. A view of the trend toward subjective journalism in the context of journalism history.

Wolfe, Tom, "The New Journalism," *Bulletin of the American Society of Newspaper Editors*, September 1970, pp. 1, 18-23. A summary of Wolfe's popular speech in defense of the new journalism. Anecdotal view of its beginnings.

———, "The Birth of 'the New Journalism': Eyewitness Report by Tom Wolfe," *New York*, February 14, 1972, pp. 30-45, and "The New Journalism: à la Recherche des Wichy Thickets," *New York*, February 21, 1972, pp. 39-48. A two-part series, richly anecdotal history of the new journalism from Wolfe's viewpoint. Emphasis on the *Herald-Tribune*, *Esquire* and *New York* as springboards for the new form.

Wakefield, Dan, "The Personal Voice and the Impersonal Eye," *Atlantic Monthly*, June 1966, pp. 86-90.

Unpublished Materials

Howard, Philip M. Jr., "The New Journalism." Unpublished Master of Arts thesis, Department of Journalism, University of Utah, Salt Lake City, Utah, 1971. Offers three main conclusions: (1) fictional techniques are credible journalistic tools when every fact and detail can be traced to a real origin and situation; (2) the basic units of reporting for the new journalism go beyond the traditional who, what, when, where, why, and how to include whole scenes and stretches of dialogue; (3) nonfiction will find a place next to fiction as a medium to augment our understanding of ourselves or our place in time.

O'Connell, Mary Jean, "Some Historical Notes on the New Journalism." Paper presented at the History Division, Association for Education in Journalism, University of South Carolina, Columbia, South Carolina, August 1971. A historical overview of the coming of objectivity in American journalism, which is viewed "either as a norm to which journalism must be restored, or as an outgrown standard that is limiting the capacity of the press to convey to readers the larger truth of events and trends."

Newsom, Douglas, "The New Journalism." Paper presented at Theta Sigma Phi Regional Conference, Austin, Texas, March 18, 1972. A summary of various definitions of new journalism, with some historical background.

2. *The New Nonfiction*

Brady, John, "Gay Talese: An Exclusive Interview," *Writer's Digest*, January 1973, pp. 28-31. Talese comments on his working style, prose.

Brower, Brock, *The Late Great Creature*. New York: Atheneum, 1972. A novel about a journalist who approaches literature and in the process offers a rich discussion of the issues underlying the new nonfiction.

Howe, Quincy, "The New Age of the Journalist-Historian," *Saturday Review*, May 20, 1967, pp. 25-27, 69.

Kazin, Alfred, "Joan Didion: Portrait of a Professional," *Harper's*, December 1971, pp. 112-22. A beautifully written analysis of Joan Didion, which is instructive for students of the new nonfiction.

Krim, Seymour, "Won't You Come Home, Jim Breslin?" *New York Times Book Review*, March 1, 1970, p. 2. An appreciative view of the unique contributions of the new nonfiction writers and a lament that so many, like Jimmy Breslin, are forsaking journalism for indifferent novels.

Macdonald, Dwight, "Parajournalism, or Tom Wolfe and His Magic Writing Machine," *New York Review of Books*, August 26, 1965, p. 3. An early caustic view of the new nonfiction, by a distinguished critic. Tom Wolfe presents a response to these articles in his 1972 series (mentioned earlier).

Pinkerton, W. Stewart, Jr., "The New Journalism Is Something Less than Meets the Eye," *Wall Street Journal*, August 13, 1971, p. 1. A sketchy discussion of composite characters used by new journalists. Useful criticism of Gail Sheehy's "Redpants" and "Sugarman" articles in *New York*.

Wolfe, Tom, "Why They Aren't Writing the Great American Novel Anymore," *Esquire*, December 1972, pp. 152-58, 272-80. Wolfe's most scholarly and comprehensive musings about "the varieties of realistic experience." A useful insert in the article is "Appendixes to the Foregoing Work," in which Wolfe enlarges on his favorite themes about the status of the new journalism.

Three introductory statements by authors are particularly useful in understanding the new nonfiction. See introductions to Tom Wolfe's *The Kandy-Kolored Tangerine-Flake Streamline Baby*, Gay Talese's *Fame and Obscurity*, and Joan Didion's *Slouching Towards Bethlehem*.

3. Alternative Journalism

Brugmann, Bruce, Sletteland, Greggar, and San Francisco *Bay Guardian* staff, *The Ultimate Highrise*. San Francisco: Bay Guardian Co., 1971. The intricacies of the alternative journalism of this paper are shown in this well-researched attack on San Francisco highrises.

Ivins, Moll, "The Eyes of Texas Are Upon You: The Perils and Pitfalls of Reporting in the Lone Star State," *Houston Journalism Review*, January 1973.

McNamara, Stephen, "Underground for the Overclass," *Bulletin of the American Society of Newspaper Editors*, May/June 1972. Discusses development of the *Pacific Sun*, an alternative paper.

McWilliams, Carey, "Is Muckraking Coming Back?" *Columbia Journalism Review*, Fall 1970, pp. 8-15. The editor of the *Nation* says muckraking is a cyclical phenomenon in America.

4. The Journalism Reviews

Aronson, James, *Deadline for the Media: Today's Challenges to Press, TV and Radio*. Indianapolis, Ind.: Bobbs Merrill, 1972. A leading press critic's thoughtful analysis of the strife within the news media. An excellent treatment of journalism reviews, government and media clashes, other issues. Useful case study of the *National Guardian* as an alternative medium.

———, "Mediations," *Antioch Review*, Winter 1971-72. A laudatory view of Roldo Bartimole's *Point of View*.

Coren, Marty, "The Perils of Publishing Journalism Reviews," *Columbia Journalism Review*, December 1972, pp. 25-28, 41-43.

The New Press Critics. Supplement to *Columbia Journalism Review*, March/April 1972. One of several press review samplers run by *CJR*.

Parodies from the Chicago Journalism Review. Chicago: Association of Working Press, 1971. A lively collection first written by the editors of the now defunct *Chicago Magazine*.

The A.J. Liebling Counter-Convention attracted considerable attention in 1972. The convention, sponsored by *(More)*, the New York journalism review, is covered in the following articles:

Kroll, Erwin, "New Journalists, Old Journalism," *Progressive*, June 1972, pp. 38-39.

Long, Charles, "The A.J. Liebling Counter-Convention Colossus," *Quill*, June 1972, pp. 34-38. Capsule reports of important sessions at the counter-convention.

"The A.J. Liebling Counter-Convention," *Chicago Journalism Review*, May 1972, pp. 3-6, 24. Sympathetic account punctuated with frequent quotes capturing the flavor of the counter-convention.

5. Advocacy Journalism

Balk, Alfred, Kilpatrick, James, von Hoffman, Nicholas, Wicker, Tom, and Wills, Garry, "Personal Involvement: A Newsman's Dilemma," *Quill*, June 1972, pp. 24-32. A spirited symposium on reporter involvement, based on a session at the 1972 American Society of Newspaper Editors convention.

Deitch, David, "The Case for Advocacy Journalism," *Nation*, November 17, 1969, p. 531. A defense of advocacy reporting by a controversial Boston reporter.

Hvistendal, J.K., "The Reporter as Activist: A Fourth Revolution in Journalism," *Quill*, February 1970. A journalism educator explores the rationale usually offered for advocacy journalism.

Masterson, Mark, "The New Journalism . . . Can Truth Be Put in Concrete When a Reporter Is an Advocate?" *Quill*, February 1971, pp. 15-17. A young reporter discusses the subjectivity-objectivity debate in the context of new journalism and tells traditionalists not to be alarmed.

Porter, William E., "Radicalism and the Young Journalist," *Saturday Review*, December 11, 1971, pp. 65-66. In a perceptive article a journalism educator asserts that genuine radicals do not choose journalism as a field of study or a profession.

6. Counterculture Media

Books

Dennis, Everette E., ed., *The Magic Writing Machine: Student Probes of the New Journalism.* Schools of Journalism, University of Oregon, Eugene, Oregon, 1971. Includes three student essays on the underground press, including anti-intellectualism in the counterculture media, the military underground, and alternative news services.

Felton, David, *Shots: Photographs from the Underground Press.* New York: Douglas, 1972. Striking selection of photos from underground newspapers, mostly those distributed by Liberation News Service.

Glessing, Robert, *The Underground Press in America.* Bloomington, Ind.: Indiana University Press, 1970. A sympathetic treatment of the new media that swings a wide-angle lens at content, graphics, history, economic operation, and audience analysis. Includes a detailed study of about thirty underground papers.

Johnson, Michael I., *The New Journalism: The Underground Press, the Artists of Nonfiction, and Changes in the Established Media.* Lawrence, Kansas: University Press of Kansas, 1971. A sketch history of the underground press and a thoughtful commentary on its stylistic implications.

Katzman, Allen, *Our Time: An Anthology of Interviews from the East Village Other.* New York: Dial, 1972. Forty interviews with youth revolution leaders from a now defunct mainstay of the early underground.

Leamer, Lawrence, *The Paper Revolutionaries: The Rise of the Underground Press.* New York: Simon and Schuster, 1972. A historical treatment of the underground press, with examples and handsome illustrations. By far the broadest treatment to date.

Lewis, Roger, *Outlaws of America: The Underground Press and Its Context.* New York: Penguin Books, 1973. A useful contextual study by a British writer that links the underground press with sociopolitical trends. Strongest in its treatment of the radical bent in the underground in the late 1960s.

Madonia, Gail, *The Rise of the Underground Press.* New York: Praeger, 1970. An intriguing analysis and historical development of counterculture media and leaders.

Several excellent collections of writing from the underground press are also available:

Hopkins, Jerry, *The Hippie Papers.* New York: Signet, 1968. Mostly articles from the Los Angeles *Free Press.* Includes the popular essay "The Student as Nigger."

Kornbluth, Jesse, *Notes from the New Underground.* New York: Ace, 1968. A helpful volume that contains such widely known counterculture writing as Allen Katzman's "I Read the News Today, Oh Boy," and other items by early counterculture heroes such as Allen Ginsberg, Timothy Leary, Gary Snyder, and Alan Watts.

Paul, Jon and Charlotte, *Fire! Reports from the Underground Press.* New York: Dutton, 1970. A hodgepodge of graphic design and articles from underground and advocacy papers. Everything in the collection is strongly activist in tone.

Other volumes of interest include:

Forcade, Tom, *Underground Press Anthology.* New York: Ace, 1970.

Howard, Mel, *Countdown: A Digest of the Underground Press.* Published four times a year by Signet. A monthly publication since 1970, *Underground Press Digest* is a current and continuing source of informative articles.

Several collections of materials from the high school underground press are also available:

Birmingham, John, ed., *Our Time Is Now: Notes from the High School Underground.* New York: Praeger, 1970.

Divoky, Dianne, ed., *How Old Will You Be in 1984?* New York: Discus, 1969.

Libarle, Marc, and Seligson, Tom, eds., *The High School Revolutionaries.* New York: Random House, 1970.

Unpublished Studies

Askin, Richard H., "Comparative Characteristics of the Alternate Press, 1970." School of Journalism, University of Texas, 1970.

Preble, Lee A., "The GI Antiwar Press: What It Says and Why." M.A. thesis, School of Journalism and Mass Communications, University of Wisconsin, 1971.

Slater, Paul Alan, "The Fifth Estate: Underground Newspapers as an Alternative Press in California." M.J. thesis, Graduate School of Journalism, University of California at Berkeley, 1969.

Smith, Gaye Sandler, "The Underground Press in Los Angeles." M.A. thesis, Department of Journalism, University of California at Los Angeles, 1968.

Watts, Kathryn M., "An Indiana High School Newspaper and Its Underground Newspaper." M.A. thesis, Department of Journalism, Indiana University, 1971.

Guides, Directories

The Alternate Press Index, published quarterly by the Radical Research Center, Carlton College,

Northfield, Minn. A kind of Reader's Guide to the underground. Reviews and catalogs articles from about ninety underground newspapers.

Communications Source Catalog. Chicago: Swallow Press, 1971. By far the most comprehensive list of publications and organizations.

Radical Publications and Organizations Index, published by Liberation News Service, 160 Claremont Ave., New York, N.Y. 10027.

Spahn, Theodore and Janet, and Muller, Robert H., *From Radical Left to Extreme Right,* 2nd ed., Metuchen, N.J.: Scarecrow Press, 1972. Detailed annotations of a variety of journals of the counterculture, advocacy, and dissent compiled by experienced librarians and approved by the publications listed.

7. Alternative Broadcasting

Shamberg, Michael, *Guerrilla Television.* New York: Holt, Rinehart and Winston, 1971. The original how-to-do-it handbook on alternate television. Highly detailed on technology, somewhat spaced out on philosophy, which is arcane and difficult to follow.

Frederickson, Allan, *Community Access Video.* Berkeley, Calif.: Book People, 1972.

Radical Software, published monthly by Raindance Corp., New York City. No. 5 carries a lengthy directory of alternative outlets.

Communications Source Catalog. Chicago: Swallow Press, 1971. An indispensible directory of organizations and sources for material on alternate broadcasting.

8. Precision Journalism

Barrett, Edward W., *Surveys, Polls and Samples in the Media.* A report to the Russell Sage Foundation, New York, 1971. One of the most comprehensive analyses of social science coverage in the news media.

"A Computer Reporter," *Newsweek,* August 26, 1968, p. 78. Brief discussion of Philip Meyer's work in Detroit.

Dennis, Everette E., Rush, Ramona R., Jordan, David, and Stuart, Jeanne, *Reporting the Human Condition.* Report of the first four years of the Mental Health Mass Communications Program, Department of Journalism, Kansas State University, Manhattan, Kansas, 1972. A detailed review of the nation's only federally funded program for training journalists in mental health and behavioral science topics.

Edelstein, Alex S., and Ames, William E., "Humanistic Newswriting," *Quill,* June 1970, pp. 28-31. A report of a project of the University of Washington School of Communications aimed at more humanistic writing in the media.

Knowledge into Action: Improving the Nation's Use of the Social Sciences. Report of the Special Commission on the Social Sciences of the National Science Board, National Science Foundation, 1969. This is a much-discussed report by Orville Brim, president of the Russell Sage Foundation, on the status of the social sciences. Some especially apt comments about relationships of journalism and the social sciences.

Kristol, Irving, "The Underdeveloped Profession," *Public Interest,* Winter 1967, p. 36. Useful critique of journalism's primitivism.

Meyer, Philip, *Precision Journalism: A Reporter's Introduction to Social Science Methods.* Bloomington, Ind.: Indiana University Press, 1973. A comprehensive presentation of Meyer's philosophy and strategy for social science reporting, written in lucid prose.

———, "The Risks of Interpretation," *Bulletin of the American Society of Newspaper Editors,* April 1969, pp. 1-5.

———, "Reporters and Research Tools," Crossman Memorial Lecture, University of Colorado, Boulder, Colorado, April 14, 1970.

———, "Telling It Like It Is," *Seminar,* September 1968, pp. 15-18.

Yu, Frederick T.C., *Behavioral Sciences and the Mass Media.* Russell Sage Foundation, New York, 1968. An anthology of papers presented at an Arden House conference on the media and the social sciences. Views of leading educators, psychologists, and journalists.

Index